7

10a

Lionel Trilling and the Fate of Cultural Criticism

Lionel Trilling and the Fate of Cultural Criticism

By Mark Krupnick

Northwestern University Press
Evanston, IL

Earlier versions of chapters 2 and 7 were published previously in *Denver Quarterly* (1983) and *Humanities in Society* (1980). Portions of chapter 8 appeared previously in *TriQuarterly* (1985) and simultaneously in *Criticism in the University*, edited by Gerald Graff and Reginald Gibbons (Evanston: Northwestern University Press, 1985). Reprinted by permission of the publishers.

Cover photograph ©1985 by Jill Krementz. Reprinted with courtesy of the photographer.

Published by Northwestern University Press
Evanston Illinois 60201

Library of Congress Cataloging-in-Publication Data

Krupnick, Mark, 1939–
    Lionel Trilling and cultural criticism in America.

    Bibliography: p.
    Includes index.
    1. Trilling, Lionel, 1905–1975—Knowledge—Literature. 2. Trilling, Lionel, 1905–1975—Knowledge—United States. 3. American literature—History and criticism. 4. Criticism—United States. I. Title.
PS 3539.R56Z86   1985   818'.5209   85-21572
ISBN 0-8101-0712-0
ISBN 0-8101-0713-9 (pbk.)

For my mother and in memory of my father

Contents

Preface

I am grateful to the American Council of Learned Societies for a fellowship, supported by the National Endowment for the Humanities, that enabled me to launch this project; and I am grateful to the Newberry Library for another fellowship funded by the NEH that enabled me, some years later, to bring it to completion. I also thank the College of Letters and Sciences of the University of Wisconsin—Milwaukee and its dean, William F. Halloran, for support.

Of the individuals who helped me to sift the ideas that went into this book, Gerald Graff did the most. I am grateful to him for his initial interest in my project and for comments on successive revisions of the manuscript that helped me to clarify my ideas and improve the writing. I also thank Morris Dickstein for his helpful critique of the entire manuscript.

I have written a critical study of Lionel Trilling's intellectual development rather than a biography. But I have made use of information about Trilling's life whenever it seemed to shed light on his work. When I began thinking about this book, late in 1975, I had met Trilling only once, and then briefly, in 1970, at a party in his honor after the last of his Norton Lectures at Harvard. I thank Joel Porte for making that meeting possible and for his comments on portions of the manuscript that I have sent him.

Because I had become acquainted with the New York intellectuals at a late stage in their history, I tried to meet with a number of Lionel Trilling's contemporaries in order to expand my knowledge of his early milieu and to test my intuitions about the shape of his career. For answering my questions and commenting on drafts of individual chapters I particularly thank Clement Greenberg, Sidney Hook, George Novack, Meyer Schapiro, and the late F. W. Dupee.

For useful information and advice I also thank William Barrett, Jacques Barzun, Eric Bentley, the late Leslie H. Farber, Irving Howe, Alfred Kazin, William Phillips, the late Harriet Trilling Schwartz, and Sol Stein. I thank two of my own contemporaries for close readings of individual chapters: Mark Shechner (chapter 7) and Alan Wald (chapter 3). And I thank Charles Swann of the department of American Studies at the University of Keele in England. Our conversations in 1973–74, when I was a visiting lecturer at Keele, spurred me to this attempt to formulate better my ideas about self, society, and intellectuals in America.

I have worked at the present study, with long interruptions for other projects, over the course of ten years. During that time my view of Lionel Trilling has changed a good deal. But I have retained some parts of my earlier conception. An example is chapter 5, on the short stories and novel that Trilling wrote in the 1940s. On that subject my ideas have remained essentially the same since July 1976, when I formulated them in a letter to my former colleague Daniel Aaron. I thank Professor Aaron for his enthusiastic response to my ideas at that time and for his comments on another chapter that I sent him nine years later.

Finally, and most difficult to express adequately, I thank my wife, Jean Carney, for her steady encouragement and patience; and I thank her and our son, Joseph, for the pleasure of their company these past several years.

Chapter One

Introduction:
Lionel Trilling and His Tradition

merican literary criticism is going through its awkward age. Some recent titles point to its unhappy condition: *Literature Against Itself; Criticism in the Wilderness; The World, the Text, and the Critic.*[1] In these books we are shown criticism committed to its own self-marginalization, criticism wandering in exile, criticism cut off from the worldly world. There is, to be sure, a contradiction between the religious outlook that conceives of criticism wandering in the wilderness as it seeks the Promised Land, and the politicizing outlook that accuses contemporary criticism of being excessively unworldly. But our critics of criticism agree about the field's unhappy consciousness.

They agree also about the professionalization and specialization of criticism, and about the new guild mentality that has accompanied academicization. At present we have performance criticism, prophetic criticism, metaphysical criticism, creative criticism; we have reader-response criticism, phenomenological criticism, semiotic criticism, deconstructionist criticism; we have Lacanian criticism, Foucauldian criticism, Derridean criticism, and Derridean-Marxist-feminist criticism. What is in short supply is a kind of writing that once was the dominant tendency in American literary studies: cultural criticism.

In the 1950s it came to be understood that literature is in some respects a self-contained institution, with its own history and conventions. From this understanding it was a short step to conceiving of literary criticism as an institution, too, with the university as its home.

The results appear today even in criticism that presents itself as politically radical. Younger university-based critics who are zealous in remarking the shifting tendencies within academic literary studies have often shown little interest in the larger culture. Certainly it is hard to think of a well-known American critic of

1

the past two decades who has shown much sensitivity to the textures of American life. Nor have recent critics shown much interest in American literary criticism of the earlier part of this century, which was so preoccupied with American life and American culture as a whole. It would require a book by itself to explain how American graduate schools have produced a generation of students so knowledgeable about Georg Lukács, Antonio Gramsci, and Walter Benjamin and yet so ignorant of Van Wyck Brooks, Edmund Wilson, and Lionel Trilling.[2]

The story would have to focus on the academicization of criticism. The three American critics I have named were old-fashioned men of letters, American examples of a now-exhausted British tradition studied by John Gross in his useful book, *The Rise and Fall of the Man of Letters* (1969). Two of them, Brooks and Wilson, were not academics. The third, Trilling, established his reputation in the forties with essays in *Partisan Review*, a magazine of opinion as oriented to ideas of politics and culture as it was to literature. Brooks, Wilson, and Trilling were liberal critics who conceived of the critic's function in Arnoldian terms, and, like Arnold, they thought of themselves as "writers," not as philosophers of language. So much the worse for them, the new academic critic might say. What did they know about "theory"?

One main difference between the older generation of critics and the present generation of theorists is summed up in the fate of literary journalism. Fifty years ago almost all of the best critics in America made their living outside the university. The work of these critics was to be found in the *Nation* and the *New Republic* and the nonspecialist literary reviews. These critics were often immensely learned but not in the way of today's academic theorists. R. P. Blackmur and Allen Tate thought of themselves as poets. Even so densely theoretical a critic as Kenneth Burke thought of himself first as a writer. All these critics, as well as those, like Trilling and John Crowe Ransom and Robert Penn Warren, who had university jobs, started out trying to emulate the culture heroes of the twenties, modernist writer-critics like T. S. Eliot and Ezra Pound, Thomas Mann and André Gide. Only F. R. Leavis in England seems to have thought of himself as a full-time critic, and Leavis himself began as a cultural critic vaguely aligned with the radical movement of the thirties. The sense of

2

political urgency and the constraints of writing for magazines made for a lucidity in the older criticism that has since become unfashionable. The trenchancy of Tate and Philip Rahv owe a great deal to their connection with living history and to the fact that they were partisans, controversialists on behalf of their opposing worldviews. The pressures of history and the discipline of regular reviewing accounted for much of the strength, as of the weaknesses, in this culture of journalism.

Literary journalism nowadays just isn't as good as in the thirties, and it no longer commands the attention of serious students of literature. Something odd has happened. In the teens and twenties, critics like Van Wyck Brooks and H. L. Mencken regularly attacked the professoriat. They had good reason. Academic literary studies were boring, genteel, and provincial. Brooks and Mencken and later Edmund Wilson identified themselves with the new arts, and Brooks and Wilson also took up the cause of the new insurgent forces in society. They represented an avant-garde in literature and politics. Nowadays, the avant-garde has moved into the universities. By a strange turnabout, as the avant-garde abandoned bohemia for the English department, literary journalism became the refuge of humanistic orthodoxy, notably in the writings of neoconservative critics. That journalistic counterattack, conducted in the name of humanistic values, has frequently taken the form of middlebrow anti-intellectualism.

The result is a split in the culture of criticism: on the one hand, a highly professionalized academic criticism alert to the most advanced European thought, and, on the other, a rear-guard literary journalism. Both kinds of criticism have been deeply flawed in their different ways. Academic criticism has caught up with the most advanced Continental theory, but that sophistication has not protected it in many cases from a preening triviality. Instead of striving for a totalizing view, what Matthew Arnold called an "intellectual deliverance," advanced academic theory has disintegrated—without much sign of regret—into myriad "fields" and sects. Literary journalism, on the other hand, has been interested in the quotidian world, but at the expense of middlebrowism and a jeering disrespect for abstract thinking.

This split is not a new event in American intellectual history. In the late nineteenth century a vast chasm opened up,

3

separating the coarse facts of a commercial civilization from the genteel spirituality of the keepers of culture. The early poems of T. S. Eliot and the early essays of Van Wyck Brooks criticize this polarization. Nowadays the split persists in the mutual contempt of academic theorists and popular reviewers. Nothing could be wider than the gap between Harold Bloom and Geoffrey Hartman, say, and Gore Vidal and Alfred Kazin. Nor is the gap any narrower that separates academic quarterlies like *Critical Inquiry* from large-circulation periodicals like the *New York Review of Books*.

This polarization has had the effect of canceling the middle ground where literature and social thought might meet. We don't at the moment have the critic who can bridge the philosophical erudition of academic literary studies and the concern with manners and morals of the older type of cultural criticism. Paul de Man taught a generation of academic theorists that every kind of critical insight is purchased at the price of a corresponding blindness. Applying de Man's idea to his own kind of criticism, we see that academic literary theory has been blind to the near at hand, the concern with the way we live that marked American writing about literature from the time of Ralph Waldo Emerson through the 1950s. This older urgency about the quality of national life made American criticism a continuation in other form of the Puritan sermon and the Romantic spiritual autobiography. The new academic criticism regards such an interest as unliterary. As the French symbolists left their living to their valets, academic criticism now leaves American culture to the sociologists.

It has been a long time, indeed since Lionel Trilling in the 1950s, that a literary critic has come forward to explain America to its people. It is true that in the mid-sixties a literary man, Marshall McLuhan, became for a short time a central figure in the general culture. But he did so not as a New Critic, the role in which he began his career, but as a media guru only tangentially concerned with literature. The educated middle class once looked to Victorian sages like George Eliot and Matthew Arnold to explain it to itself, but now that role has been assumed by sociologists like Philip Rieff and social historians like Christopher Lasch. This transformation had already begun in the fifties, with books like David Riesman's *The Lonely Crowd*, but it has speeded up since then, mainly because of the psychologizing of American

4

culture but also because literary critics voluntarily surrendered the field.

To be sure, cultural criticism is not dead. That can hardly be claimed in view of recent American Studies books like Ann Douglas's *The Feminization of American Culture,* Sacvan Bercovitch's *The American Jeremiad,* Alan Trachtenberg's *The Incorporation of America,* and Jackson Lears's *No Place of Grace.* Other recent works of cultural criticism are Susan Sontag's *On Photography* and Morris Dickstein's *Gates of Eden.* Dickstein's book is interesting as a younger writer's attempt to revive the old New York intellectual style in criticism.

More typical of recent tendencies in academic literary studies have been the writings of Fredric Jameson, Gerald Graff, Edward Said, and Frank Lentricchia. All have polemicized against the political and cultural complacency of academic literary criticism. But their writing, even in attacking academic theorizing, remains more narrowly oriented to the academic literary scene than that of Trilling and the New York critics who were his contemporaries. Trilling may not have been the last American cultural critic, but he seems to have been the last literary man whose views of literature and culture have influenced a large nonspecialist audience as well as students and professors of literature. Some later critics have tried to fashion a style that would bridge the two worlds, but they have not succeeded. The man of letters as a social type has largely vanished with the passing of Trilling and his generation.

Critics on the left, like Fredric Jameson, would seem to have a stake in reaching out to a larger audience than the academic avant-garde that keeps up with new works of theory. In fact, however, Jameson's major work, *The Political Unconscious,* makes no concessions to the common reader. He assumes a knowledge of the major debates within Marxism from Lukács to Louis Althusser and beyond; he expects that his reader will have kept up with the major theories of narrative since Vladimir Propp; and he draws heavily on the structuralist Freudianism of Jacques Lacan, as well as relevant theorizing by Jacques Derrida, Gilles Deleuze, Jean François Lyotard, Roland Barthes, and others. Jameson's book is so difficult that it has already been the occasion of a great number of essays, and even an entire book, devoted to explication and critique. The excitement has been limited to an academic elite, but it is from such cultural elites that new tendencies emerge. Altogether, the cultism that has surrounded this major critical work is like that which once surrounded an epochal creative work like *Finnegans Wake*.

The Dark and Bloody Crossroads

Lionel Trilling was a cultural critic of an earlier generation and of a greatly different kind from contemporary academic theorists like Jameson. It surely makes a difference that Trilling's major work, *The Liberal Imagination*, looks back to Matthew Arnold's *Culture and Anarchy*, whereas Jameson takes his inspiration from works like Lukács's *History and Class Consciousness*. The idiom, the level of generality, the critical project—they could not be more different.

Trilling was born in 1905 and died in 1975, and his most influential work appeared in the forties and fifties, before the decisive transformation of criticism into a kind of philosophic discourse. His criticism is sometimes difficult, but not because it draws, like Jameson's, on Continental theories of interpretation. Trilling's writing is difficult at times because it tries to be true to the complex movements of his own thought, which was "undulating and diverse," as his model, Matthew Arnold, had said criticism ought to be. The difficulty has less to do with philosophical erudition than with the way Trilling defined his critical project and with the style of his mind and the kind of role he invented for himself.

Part of this difficulty has to do with Trilling's mediating impulse, his desire to heal the divisions in criticism and culture in his own moment. In this book I frequently shall have occasion to comment on "the two Trillings," the Trilling who moved in the "uptown" world of academic literary studies and the Trilling who was an important figure in the "downtown" world of New York intellectuals. More generally, Trilling was divided between the university and the general culture. Nowadays, when academic criticism has largely given up its ties to the great world, the inner conflict that proved so productive for Trilling troubles few of his successors.

Trilling was divided between his commitment to liberal politics and his commitment to modernist literature, which was often

6

reactionary in its social attitude. His commitment to modernism was itself ambivalent, as was his liberal belief that the widest possible diffusion of high culture necessarily makes for a better society and more autonomous individuals. Trilling tried to reconcile these various divisions and contradictions. Similarly he tried to reconcile his own drive to the center, which involved accommodation to existing society, with a strong impulse to remain separate, in opposition to all orthodoxies. And in his practice as a critic he tried to reconcile different styles of writing, the style of English men of letters like Matthew Arnold and that of European intellectuals like Ortega y Gasset.

In Trilling's best years the split between a frequently philistine literary journalism and a hypertheoretical academic criticism had not yet appeared, and the gap between all-purpose explainers from sociology and professional specialists in the English department had not yet become as vast as it is today. But during Trilling's career it had already become difficult for a literary man or woman to stand at the heart of the culture, with a totalizing point of view. In part this book is about the difficulty that criticism has experienced in trying to work out a synthesizing perspective on literature and society in the period since the disillusionment with Marxism in the forties. And it is about the difficulty Trilling had, from the fifties on, in carving out and maintaining a role for himself as a critic.

In 1946 Trilling described the middle ground of criticism as "the dark and bloody crossroads where literature and politics meet." He was not encouraging other critics to take up this station. Speaking of the dark and bloody crossroads, Trilling added ruefully: "One does not go there gladly."[3] But a world war had just ended and another, with Russia, threatened. So Trilling did assume the role of the critic at the crossroads, and wound up keeping the vigil until his death thirty years later.

As this book will argue, Trilling did not carry out the work of cultural criticism with uniform success. He seems always to have been ambivalent about his self-imposed burden and never to have resolved his inner debate about life within culture as against life "beyond culture," intellectual struggle as against passive contemplation, the historical mode of understanding as against the aesthetic mode. But the important thing is to see how productive Trilling's doubts and contradictions were. Few critics have thought

7

as long and as seriously about the discontents of civilization. For Trilling those discontents included the sacrifices entailed by his own public role as sentry at the crossroads of his culture. Indeed, his lifelong reflection on the price of culture may be understood as an obliquely autobiographical reflection on the price of his own career in criticism.

There is much to object to in Trilling's social attitudes. In this book I have also registered my impatience with the vagueness and equivocations to which he was prone, especially in the latter part of his career. But I continue to admire the seriousness and dedication with which he set about, from decade to decade, defining his role and his project as a critic. What remains, after the flaws have been noted, is an impressive sense of cultural vocation and a unique way of going at criticism. Trilling's career is an object lesson in the glories and difficulties of being an intellectual in America. And, in the end, it is not his particular attitudes but his way of being an intellectual and his kind of criticism that I have wanted to recommend as an exemplary alternative to the academic criticism we have lately had.

One does not go gladly to the dark and bloody crossroads of politics and literature, Trilling said. But, he added, "it is not exactly a matter of free choice whether one does or does not go."[4] Actually, for other critics of Trilling's time, it turned out to be remarkably easy not to go. The New Critics, in their pedagogical phase as popularizers of "close reading," and then the myth-symbol critics in the wake of Northrop Frye gave academic literary studies examples in the artful dodging of contemporary history. And criticism in the past twenty years has only extended and deepened this indisposition to involve criticism in general questions of culture. "Politics" in recent criticism has been mainly about "the politics of interpretation," in which the fights are about rival theories of reading.[5] This, too, is politics—the question of who will define reality is hardly a trivial one. Yet in much American criticism the debate has been academic in the bad sense. In recent years academic theory has frequently degenerated into a new Alexandrianism, theory for theory's sake.

In this book I shall be discussing Lionel Trilling's specific literary and social-cultural preferences. But they are not my main subject. I am more interested in trying to characterize a certain kind of writing. What, after all, is "cultural criticism"? And what does it mean in the American context to be a cultural critic? For Trilling's overall project in criticism required that he invent a cultural identity for himself. Indeed, the social role that Trilling devised may in fact be his most original contribution. Certainly Arnold and Freud were useful models in this work of self-definition, but their culture was not his. They had their own problems, which didn't include the peculiar "weightlessness" Trilling attributed to American culture.

That weightlessness proved, paradoxically, to be Trilling's heaviest burden. For he had not only to contrive a persona for his writing, he had in a sense to invent the culture itself. The coherent intellectual community and clearly defined cultural situation that Trilling addresses were partly a rhetorical invention. The "we" of his essays was much criticized in his time. Readers thought it stood for an in-group, "the Diors and Schiaparellis of intellectual fashion design," as one outsider said of Trilling's New York circle.[6] But that circle was not as tightly knit as outsiders believed. The society of the *Partisan Review* writers, as Irving Howe has remembered it, was as atomistic and competitive as the larger society,[7] and Trilling was always a little alone, even when he seemed most at the center of things. His style bodies forth a counterhistorical ideal community, a society that did not in fact exist.

That style has its problems, of course. It was never clear in Trilling's writing just what his grand abstractions referred to. He always invoked "the liberals" and "the educated class." Who were these people? And what about "the liberal imagination," "moral realism," "biological reason"? Moreover, what was "the culture" he always talked about? Which culture? Whose culture? If these things did not have a precise existence, it was usually possible to guess at what Trilling had in mind. Perhaps in the end we learn more from his essays about the landscape of Trilling's mind than about American cultural actualities themselves. But that mind was itself an important cultural fact.

In this book I shall be considering Trilling in the context of modern criticism, as a salutary counterexample. Above all I have wanted to see him in the context of *American* criticism and culture. I accept that the writers who influenced Trilling most—such as Austen, Wordsworth, Hegel, Arnold, Nietzsche, and Freud—were all European. But the Europeanizing American, the American who quarrels with his own culture, is himself part of a distinctively native tradition. The "party of memory" as R. W. B. Lewis once called it, is surely as central to American high culture as Ralph Waldo Emerson's "party of hope."[8] A party that includes Nathaniel Hawthorne, Herman Melville, Henry James, Henry Adams, George Santayana, and T. S. Eliot is by no means marginal.

THE CRITICISM WE HAVE LOST

Before trying to characterize Trilling's approach to criticism, I want to indicate briefly his intellectual moment and milieu. Trilling was born in 1905. This makes him the contemporary of the New Critics Allen Tate, Cleanth Brooks, and Robert Penn Warren. It has become something of a cliché to describe the New Criticism as "formalist," but anyone who has read at all in the Russian Formalists knows that American New Criticism was much less purist. The first generation of New Critics was greatly interested in general questions of society and culture, and as Southerners they had a keen sense of region and of history. Allen Tate's *Essays of Four Decades* includes very little in the way of "close reading" but a good deal about the culture of the Old South. And there is also Tate's famous essay on Emily Dickinson, which sets forth a historical thesis concerning the freeing of literary creativity by the decay of religious and cultural orthodoxy. A cultural approach to art as the phosphorescence of decay is the key also to Tate's understanding of his fellow-Southerners Edgar Allan Poe and William Faulkner.

Tate was not alone in his preoccupation with social and cultural issues. Robert Penn Warren all through his life criticized the conception of "pure poetry." Warren's keen interest in the extra-aesthetic is evident in *All the King's Men*, his novel about Huey Long, as Tate's is in his single novel, *The Fathers*. As for Cleanth Brooks, best known for assimilating T. S. Eliot's aesthetic for classroom purposes in a series of influential textbooks, it was Brooks who in his old age undertook a long-deferred labor of love, a book on Faulkner which is as much a hymn to the South as it is an instance of Brooks-Warren close reading.

Introduction: Lionel Trilling and His Tradition

If we turn to Trilling's own literary circle, the New York intellectuals, we see a still clearer case of fascination with the realistic details of American life, as well as a strong taste for social-cultural analysis and polemic. This is obviously true of critics like Philip Rahv, Alfred Kazin, and Irving Howe, all of whom at one time or another argued against American-style formalism. But it's true even of the most formalist critic of the New York school, the art critic Clement Greenberg. Greenberg avoided cultural speculation in favor of close attention to the medium in his writings on painting and sculpture, but he also wrote illuminating cultural criticism on the Jewishness of various Jewish writers and intellectuals.[9] And Harold Rosenberg, Greenberg's major rival as an interpreter of modern painting, is in fact far more brilliant in his satiric observations on trends among his fellow intellectuals than he is in his essays on art. *The Tradition of the New* (1959), Rosenberg's best book, is mainly composed of social and literary criticism rather than writings on art itself.

The Southern New Critics and the New York intellectuals were opposed in their ideologies and in their conceptions of literature and culture, but sociologically they resembled each other. Both groups were driving from the margins to the center. Southerners like Tate might defend marginality in their self-consciously "reactionary" idealization of the antebellum South, but it was just as significant that the best of them were leaving the South for literary journalism or university positions in the North. Their drive to the center was intellectual as well, involving a curious amalgam of traditionalism with modernism, after the manner of T. S. Eliot.

The New York writers' drive to the center and to modernity was a shorter ride. They were escaping the Jewish ghettos of Brooklyn and the Bronx. In crossing the respective bridges into Manhattan, they were making their claim to freedom, worldly success, America, Western civilization. They were entering "the fair courts of life," a phrase that Trilling borrowed from James Joyce. Today, centrality—the ideal of Matthew Arnold, T. S. Eliot, F. R. Leavis, Trilling—this ideal is unfashionable because it has come to be associated with undemocratic forms of political organization. "Centrality" suggests capitalist domination or imperialism. Since America remains politically and culturally the center, this means that insofar as contemporary criticism is interested in politics and culture at all, its interest is deflected toward the Third World, toward whatever is marginal and lacks a voice to speak for itself.

The preoccupation of the Southern and New York critics of the thirties and forties with the national culture does not mark them off from what came before, but it sharply separates them from the academicized criticism that followed. We have only to compare a historical anthology of criticism like Philip Rahv's *Literature in America* (1957) with recent anthologies of criticism to note the turn to abstract philosophical theorizing on the one hand and a technical, hyperacademic formalism on the other. Rahv's selection of earlier American criticism starts with an excerpt from Alexis de Tocqueville's *Democracy in America* and includes James Fenimore Cooper and D. H. Lawrence on Cooper, Emerson's "American Scholar" and John Jay Chapman on Emerson, Henry James on Hawthorne and Ezra Pound and T. S. Eliot on James, a selection from Van Wyck Brooks's *America's Coming-of-Age*, Randolph Bourne's "The History of a Literary Radical," H. L. Mencken's "Puritanism as a Literary Force," Edmund Wilson on Hemingway, Robert Penn Warren and Irving Howe on Faulkner, Trilling on Scott Fitzgerald, and other pieces.

Every one of these essays is informed by a passionate sense of nationality, an intense personal involvement in the question of the relation of the writer to America. Who could say today what Rahv wrote in his introduction in 1957, that our critics have been moved by a "profound sense of the problematical in the American awareness of cultural identity"? For what American critic today can it be said, as Rahv says of the greatest critics of our past, that the American character appears as a "fascinating problem"?[10] Even when Lionel Trilling is most ambivalent about American culture, he manifests a solicitude for it, a public concern, that now seems part of an earlier, more innocent age.

Trilling, though a university teacher for all of his mature life, mediated between the university and the general culture. In making a case for Trilling, I mean to be making a case for that middle ground of literary-cultural reflection of which Philip Rahv's anthology is a monument, and I mean to be tracing the lineaments of an ideal critic who no longer exists.

What Is Cultural Criticism?

Trilling seems to me the single most important cultural critic in this century among American men of letters. Not the most brilliant reader of texts—R. P. Blackmur probably deserves that title; nor the foremost aesthetic theorist—W. K. Wimsatt and Paul de Man might contend for that honor; nor the most curious and wide-ranging literary intelligence—Edmund Wilson remains unchallenged in that respect. What, then, was Trilling's specialty?

His subject, as I understand it, was the relation of culture and personality, and his cultural criticism was chiefly oriented to styles of self-definition. He sums up his approach in an essay of 1961, "On the Teaching of Modern Literature." In that essay he explains how in the fifties he had taught his undergraduate course in modern literature at Columbia:

> Since my own interests lead me to see literary situations as cultural situations, and cultural situations as great elaborate fights about moral issues, and moral issues as having something to do with gratuitously chosen images of personal being, and images of personal being as having something to do with literary style, I felt free to begin with what for me was a first concern, the animus of the author, the objects of his will, the things he wants or wants to have happen.[11]

This statement is the closest Trilling ever came to formulating his "method." But it is very vague. One major aim of this book is to clarify this formulation and to explore its multiple ambiguities and implicit contradictions.

The main problem involves Trilling's idea of the relation of self and culture. The first thing to acknowledge is the imprecision of his phrasing. He sees literary-cultural situations as debates about moral issues, which in turn have "something to do with" choices of personal selfhood. Trilling was not rigorous about these relations; like Matthew Arnold he was cogent without being precise. A curious tautology appears at the heart of this statement, in Trilling's remark about "gratuitously chosen images of personal being." The dictionary defines "gratuitous" as "free," and "choice" as implying "the free exercise of one's judgment." That repetition—can there be choices that are not "gratuitous"?—seems to me a sign not of Trilling's certitude but of fundamental doubt about whether the self really is free in relation to culture.

13

At times Trilling writes as if freedom consists in being able to create the self as if the conditions of existence were not binding. Trilling himself seems to have set out defining his own self as if his cultural circumstances were not determining. His writing differs sharply from that of other intellectuals in his New York circle in reflecting little of his East-European Jewish ancestry. The Trilling we meet in his critical essays is keen on tradition, but it is a tradition that he has patched together, not a tradition that has any clear relation to his personal past. This Trilling who emphasizes the self's freedom to make anything of itself, regardless of the past, is the American Trilling, in the line of Emerson.

But Trilling is better known as a sharp critic of the Emersonian tradition. He believed that American literature is inferior to European literature because American culture does not take sufficient account of "the conditions." In Trilling's view American innocence about limitation has issued in the triviality and "weightlessness" of contemporary American culture. The Europeanizing Trilling argues that the American idea of freedom is a pernicious myth. Our aim should not be absolute freedom but "autonomy," and the self can become autonomous only if it has strong authority to define itself against. The self needs circumstances and limitations that don't give way at the first push.

Strong authority, strong self. Trilling is changeable on this question, but usually the Emersonian self seems to him excessively volatile. Trilling wants a self that is not all air and fire; rather, he imagines a self that is "dense," "perdurable," "impenetrable." What he wants is a certain stability that will enable the self to cohere and endure. Unlike the American ideal of the self as metamorphic and protean, Trilling's ideal is conservative. He looks for a principle of permanence in the self that will allow it to maintain its wholeness amidst the disintegrative tendencies of modern culture.

Trilling's attitude is ambivalent, as it is on so many issues. He is sympathetic to Scott Fitzgerald's Gatsby, who is a wholly ideal construction, born "from his Platonic conception of himself." But Trilling also values the *strong* self, the self that is certain in its "sentiment of being." His model for the self that is strong, single-minded, direct in its relation to other persons and things is the nineteenth-century Englishman. Unlike Gatsby's self, which is a poor boy's dream of genteel success, the well-born

Englishman is the real thing. His selfhood allows for no discrepancy between what it is and what it shows. At its most extreme, Trilling's ideal would allow no self-consciousness at all. Hence the importance to him of Wordsworth's primordial figures in the landscape, like the Leech Gatherer of "Resolution and Independence." Now, there is clearly a difference between these two ideals, Gatsby's American freedom to invent himself, as against the Englishman's strength in his sentiment of his own being. Trilling never decisively chooses between them, and the result is a pervasive ambivalence about a host of related issues.

Another problem centers on Trilling's idea that images of selfhood manifest themselves in a writer's style. In a 1938 essay on John Dos Passos, Trilling says that Dos Passos does not judge the characters in his *U.S.A.* trilogy in terms of the truth of what they say or in relation to the practical effect of their actions. Rather, Dos Passos judges them on the basis of their quality of selfhood, as revealed by their style. We recognize a villain in Dos Passos not by *what* he does but by *how* he does it. Thus, Trilling says, we despise the public relations man J. Ward Morehouse "for the words he uses . . . for his self-deception, the tone and style he generates."[12]

This formulation is clarified by Trilling's statement that he cares about literature mainly as a revelation of the writer's "animus." That animus relates to the writer's wished-for way of personal being. In the Marxist thirties attending to the writer's will meant attending to the collective or class element in his ideology. Trilling shifts that emphasis to the writer's "personal will" as revealed in his style. He wants to reawaken the liberal intellectuals to the idea of the individual's free will and consequent personal responsibility. But his voluntarism has a strongly aesthetic coloration. He envisions the self defining itself not by its choice of actions but by its choice in styles of selfhood. That revision implies a downgrading of political radicalism, which relies on the will-in-action rather than the stasis of aesthetic contemplation. This is a complicated matter to which we shall have to return. But, for the time being, it may do to suggest that Trilling's early emphasis on manners and tone foreshadows his later flight from politics and, more generally, his lifelong ambivalence about history itself as the arena in which selves define themselves.

The Dos Passos essay raises the question also of Trilling's

conception of "politics" as a whole. At the end of that essay Trilling asks: "In the long run is not the political choice fundamentally a choice of personal quality?"[13] Well, yes and no, depending on the reach of that rhetorical question. What it seems to imply in 1938 is a displacement of politics by ontology, putting the question of the self where the idea of political struggle had been.

Trilling of course was being political in relegating political questions to a lesser role. His cultural redefinition of politics was not the typical vagueness of the literary man about the world of class, power, and institutions. It was itself a political act, an attempt to displace the cultural attitudes that accounted for Stalinism's hold on liberal intellectuals. But having succeeded in that revision in the forties, Trilling subsequently kept politics at some distance during the remainder of his career. One has only to compare him with a truly politically minded member of his intellectual group, Hannah Arendt, to see how little Trilling conceived of human destiny in political terms. The New York intellectuals are best known for their political passions and their changing attitudes, over more than five decades, to left-wing politics. Trilling was deeply involved with that group and shared its passions, and it would be misleading to discuss his work apart from the politics of culture. Thus, I shall be discussing Trilling's politics—his early radicalism, his anti-Stalinism, his impulse toward accommodation, his liberal anticommunism, his detestation of "the adversary culture," and so on. But I have been mainly interested in Trilling's politics as I believe he himself was, as they bear on "the choice of personal quality."*

Perhaps the best way of thinking of Trilling's politics is as a politics of the self. He remained enough of an intellectual of his generation to remain preoccupied with the question of ideology. But the ideologies about which he was most interesting were ideologies of personhood. He had certain notions about how the self ought to be affirmed and defined, and about what he once referred to as an "aesthetic of personality." His taste in styles of self-formation is clear in his 1968 essay on James Joyce, in which he expresses his wonder that anyone could have been capable of "so sustained a rage of effectual intention . . . , so ferocious an

---

*William M. Chace's book *Lionel Trilling: Criticism and Politics* (Stanford: Stanford Univ. Press, 1980) offers itself as a critical study of Trilling's politics, but Chace never makes clear in what sense he understands Trilling to have been "political."

ambition" as Joyce's. Trilling says little about Joyce's social attitudes or about Joyce's art. His attention in that essay is almost entirely directed to Joyce's "nearly absolute . . . commitment of himself to himself."[14]

In this book I try to understand Trilling's ideas of the self in relation to his life as well as his work. In chapters 2 and 3 I discuss the 1920s and 1930s, when Trilling tried to found his own cultural identity in terms, first, of "positive Jewishness," and then in terms of Marxism. Chapters 4 and 5 are devoted to Trilling's great decade, the forties, when he carved out his distinctive role as a critic in recoil against the dominant left-liberal values of his New York intellectual milieu. In chapter 4 I take up the essays collected in *The Liberal Imagination*, which turned out to be Trilling's most influential book, and in chapter 5 I analyze the fiction—three stories and a novel—that he wrote in the forties. I interpret that fiction in relation to the positions Trilling was staking out in the critical essays he was writing in the same years. Throughout this first half of the book I am concerned with the theme of "the two Trillings," the drama of a critic always divided against himself and engaged in exhausting but productive self-confrontation.

The second half of the book is concerned with Trilling's struggle to find a new basis for his criticism, and for his role as a cultural critic, from the early fifties on. By that time the theme of "the liberal imagination" had ceased to be sufficient to anchor a general criticism of culture. In chapter 6 I examine some major intellectual tendencies of the fifties and Trilling's new role, as a "figure in the culture." Chapter 7 is also mainly concerned with the fifties. My emphasis here is on the uses to which Trilling put Freudianism and his personal view of Freud himself in working out his conception of the right relations between culture and the self. In chapter 8 I discuss Trilling's conception of modernism—modernism as a literary canon (Dostoevsky, Conrad, Eliot, Joyce, etc.) and the vulgar parody-modernism of "the adversary culture" of the sixties. Chapter 9 is a critique of Trilling's last book, *Sincerity and Authenticity*, a study of changing ideals of personhood. In chapter 10, the conclusion, I extend the discussion of the previous chapter about Trilling's "aesthetic of personality" and discuss the irresolution that continued to mark Trilling's criticism right up to the end. Throughout the second half of the book

I explore Trilling's ever-changing dualistic categories of interpretation. At the end I suggest a cultural explanation for his irresolution in the hope that it may help us better understand his dilemmas and contradictions as a critic and the larger question of the fate of cultural criticism in our time.

Chapter Two

The Gentleman and the Jew*

Wh[W]hat kind of person becomes a cultural critic? Like Matthew Arnold, he will be eager to study the best that has been known and thought. But if he is like Trilling, he will not always limit himself to the best. He will spend much of his time attending to the less than best, because he will characteristically define himself and his position in reaction to fashionable opinion. He will therefore need to read magazines of opinion, as well as the "Great Books," to learn what his fellow intellectuals are thinking. Focusing on "the culture," rather than on literature as such, he starts out with a grievance, a pervasive resentment that his culture has not been adequate to his needs. This feeling does not change a great deal over the course of the critic's career. No culture, not even one that he has helped to bring into being, will ever really be adequate.

Trilling was an undergraduate at Columbia College from 1921 to 1925. These are the years R. P. Blackmur was later to celebrate as the *anni mirabiles*, the miracle years that witnessed the publication of *The Waste Land* and *Ulysses*, Yeats's *The Tower* and Stevens's *Harmonium*, *The Magic Mountain* and most of the separate sections of *Remembrance of Things Past*. The young Trilling was an eager student of the new writing, and yet he was later to recall the *anni mirabiles* as years of drift and boredom for him. For a great literary movement is not by itself a guarantee of an adequate culture—at least as Trilling understood the term. In his early twenties Trilling had not integrated Joyce, Eliot, Mann, and Proust into his own worldview, and the liberal culture of his in-

*I am grateful to Meyer Schapiro and George Novack for conversation and correspondence on the subject of chapters 2 and 3. Both read and commented on very early versions of these chapters. I have previously discussed Trilling's Jewishness in "The *Menorah Journal* Group and the Origins of Modern Jewish-American Radicalism," *Studies in American Jewish Literature* 5 (Winter 1979): 55-67; and "Lionel Trilling, 'Culture,' and Jewishness," *Denver Quarterly* 18 (Autumn 1983): 106-22.

tellectual elders did not mirror the world he knew at first hand. In 1966 Trilling looked back on the miracle years without nostalgia:

> For a young man in the Twenties, the intellectual or cultural situation was an enervating one. The only issue presented to him was that of intelligence as against stupidity, the fine and developed spirit confronting the dull life of materialistic America. With that theme, for what it was worth, Mencken had done all that could be done. I read *The Nation, The New Republic, The Freeman* and hoped that some day I would be worthy to respond to their solemn liberalism with something more than dim general assent. I was addicted to Wells and Shaw but it seemed to me that they spun delightful but fanciful tales about young Philosopher Kings who insisted that their divine right be recognized. I recall my college days as an effort to discover some social entity to which I could give the credence of my senses, as it were, and with which I could be in some relation. . . . I was bored and vacuous because I had no ground upon which to rear an imagination of society.[1]

The rhetoric of "credence" and "assent" in this passage derives from John Henry Newman and points to the question of belief. But as a secular liberal intellectual, Trilling was not really much interested in the problem of poetry and religious belief that exercised many critics in the twenties. The dilemma Trilling evokes is rather different. Nowadays we might call it psychological because it so clearly has to do with the experience of the self. But Trilling is right in thinking of it as intellectual and cultural. He conceives of his personal identity as being intimately involved with his relation to advanced ideas. He wants to be able to "give the credence of my senses" to these ideas or better ones so that society will seem real to him. But the ultimate goal of his quest for an adequate theory remains personal. If society can be made to seem more intelligible and manageable, he will then feel more anchored and real in relation to that society.

Trilling's ideas about the relation of the cultural critic to society are highly nuanced. To begin with, the cultural critic feels himself to be deeply dependent on the sentiments and attitudes of the intellectual class both for his most intimate sense of himself and for his social identity. So it was unfortunate for the young Trilling that American liberal culture in the twenties could only propose as an organizing dialectic the quarrel between the free spirit and commercial-puritan America. This was the stock-in-trade of critics like Mencken and Edmund Wilson and novelists like Sinclair Lewis and John Dos Passos. But it couldn't be the central issue for Trilling and his generation, which came of age after the battle against genteel culture had been largely won.

If the ideas of the previous generation have an important influence on the cultural critic, he is not entirely at their mercy. The cultural critic inherits a "situation" but then sets about revising it and placing himself in opposition to it. The self for Trilling is always a conscious, personal achievement, an expression of free will. We may inherit our genes, but we make our selves. The cultural critic shapes, disciplines, defines his self according to a "gratuitous" choice of a mode of personal being, in the light, that is, of a conscious intention. But he needs to have fresh ideas to direct his will. Otherwise he can only drift.

Trilling's account of himself as a spiritual drifter when young is confirmed by contemporary testimony. In an essay of 1927, "Jewish Students I Have Known," the poet Mark Van Doren, who had been one of Trilling's teachers at Columbia, offers a portrait of his former student. Trilling is identified only by the letter "F":

> F, starting brightly as a freshman, grew more melancholy each year, and more beguiling . . . . [He] spoke diffidently, with a hushed and harmless voice; and though he wrote exceedingly well he found it hard to decide what to write about . . . . He took up this, he took up that, only to let both fall gracefully at his feet . . . . He still is feeling himself out— respectfully, with dignity, and with grace. What he will eventually do, if he does it at all, will be lovely, for it will be the fruit of a pure intelligence slowly ripened in not too fierce a sun.[2]

Van Doren, while conscious of the young Trilling's fineness of mind and temper, seems not to have been certain his former student would ever fully ripen. Certainly at the time Van Doren was writing Trilling was still searching for a direction. In 1926–27 he was a teaching assistant in English at the University of Wisconsin in Madison. But he stayed only a year in the Midwest, returning to New York to take up a teaching position at Hunter College and to write for a bimonthly magazine, the *Menorah Journal*. Teaching at Hunter was mostly unpleasant, but becoming part of the *Menorah Journal* circle helped Trilling to decide on the kind of self he wanted to be.

For Trilling finding a culture and establishing a personal identity were inseparable. Simply being an American or a liberal intellectual didn't give him access to a social entity that as a critic he could do anything with. And so he lacked a personal identity as

21

well. But as a member of a small, obscure, middle-class Jewish subculture, he found a social group to which he could give the credence of his senses. The idea of himself as a Jew sustained him and gave his writing a focus for some five years.

"POSITIVE JEWISHNESS"

The *Menorah Journal* published articles on the Jewish past and on current issues affecting Jews, and also published new work by Jewish poets and storytellers. The purpose of the magazine was to promote Jewish ideals and learning, especially among young nonaffiliated Jews, so as to offset the negative psychological effects of anti-Semitism in the larger society. By demonstrating the interest and dignity of the Jewish past, the magazine encouraged American Jews to accept and identify themselves as Jews, to perceive Jewishness not as a burden or stigma but as a normal condition. The specific cultural-psychological malaise of the American Jew and the *Menorah Journal*'s program of "positive Jewishness" as cure are suggested in an article which appeared in the magazine in 1927:

> The Jew must remain a torment to himself, and an annoyance if not a nuisance to others, so long as he fails to make it part of his ethical consciousness that he has as much right to indulge in the expression of his own nature—without the constant fear of the disapprobation of other peoples—as has the Frenchman or the Englishman.[3]

But what can such a program have meant to a young man who, by his own testimony, had earlier associated Jewishness with awkwardness and vulgarity, and distanced himself from the whole question?* Does the fact that Trilling published twenty-five stories, articles, and reviews in the *Menorah Journal* between 1925 and 1931 necessarily demonstrate a real interest in the "Jewish problem" and a strong sense of himself as a Jew? A writer in his early twenties is usually happy to be published anywhere. In addi-

*Trilling describes his early relationship to Jewishness and the profound impact on him of the *Menorah Journal* in a letter to Elliot Cohen dated December 2, 1929. That letter is in the *Menorah Journal* files of the American Jewish Archives at Hebrew Union College in Cincinnati. There was talk in 1929 of dissolving the magazine, and Trilling's letter is an impassioned plea for its continuance.

tion, the *Journal* paid well, had good contacts with the university world, where Trilling planned to make his career, and allowed his work to appear in the company of such established Jewish writers as Ludwig Lewisohn, Maurice Samuel, Waldo Frank, and Israel Zangwill, as well as non-Jewish writers like Van Doren, Lewis Mumford, and Charles Beard.

Trilling seems to have started out writing for the *Menorah Journal* simply because it was there, only later finding himself involved with Jewish issues and a Jewish definition of his own being. This pattern, of the Jewish acculturation of non-Jewish Jews, was common among the young writers recruited by the magazine's managing editor, Elliot Cohen, who is better known as the founding editor (in 1945) of another Jewish magazine, *Commentary*.

Cohen's circle at the *Menorah Journal* differed from older Jewish intellectuals chiefly by virtue of the irreverence which was the mark of their generation, and they differed from the well-known Jewish intellectuals of the following decade in having been born into comfortable circumstances. They started out more interested in cultural than in specifically political questions. Most, like Trilling, were solidly middle class and had studied at Columbia. What bound them together was mainly contempt for the stiff pretentiousness of official Jewish-American culture, which veered between the extremes of defensive apology for its existence and offensive chauvinism. The deformations of organized Jewish intellectual life in the twenties were not entirely the fault of the Jews themselves, as Trilling's group rather uncharitably implied. Rather, the touchiness of the older generation was the stigma of their second-class status in a still-provincial America that allowed Jewish immigrants and their sons to make money in business but kept them out of mainstream social and cultural life. For Trilling's group the possibility of careers in college teaching was not much less dim than for the earlier generation. Their exasperation, however, was directed not against the gentile culture, whose resistance they took for granted, but against their own elders.

Some of Trilling's contemporaries at the *Menorah Journal*, like Clifton Fadiman, were content to adapt H. L. Mencken's satire on the American "booboisie" to the pretentious middle-class culture of their Jewish elders. But Trilling went further, laying down in reviews he wrote in the late twenties the main lines of a theory of the novel that appears more fully articulated twenty years later in "Manners, Morals, and the Novel." That theory of the novel is also a statement of how culture may best be studied. In "Manners, Morals, and the Novel," Trilling defines the novel as "a perpetual quest for reality, the field of its research being always the social world, the material of its analysis being always manners as the indication of the direction of man's soul."[4]

The distinctive element in Trilling's sense of the real is his emphasis on manners, style, and tone. His 1966 memoir makes clear that his acute sense of manners was honed as a regular reviewer of new Jewish novels in the *Menorah Journal*.[5] But manners as a clue to "the direction of man's soul" only shadow forth a larger category: social class. Again the *Menorah Journal* provided Trilling with the germinal experiences. In his 1966 memoir, Trilling says that seeing how Jews were divided into social classes enabled him to see how society at large was so divided. In time it became the general culture and not the Jewish subculture that would claim his interest. Thus, the long-term effect of the *Menorah Journal* years was not so much to instill in Trilling a positive sense of Jewish identity as to contribute, instead, to his acculturation as an American. As he puts it in his memoir, "The discovery, through the *Menorah Journal*, of the Jewish situation . . . made America available to my imagination, as it could not possibly be if I tried to understand it with the categories offered by Mencken or Herbert Croly."[6] Neither Mencken's *Smart Set* nor Croly's *New Republic*, prestigious as they were in the twenties, provided as useful a point of departure for understanding reality in America as this little-known Jewish magazine.

It may be that Trilling's emphasis in his memoir on the universal category of class blurs the importance to him forty years earlier of the idea of a specifically Jewish identity. For five years, after all, the main theme of his writing was the image of the Jew in fiction. He wrote review after review of new Jewish novels, almost invariably dismissing them for being too simplistic in their representation of Jewish life. Trilling even taught a summer-school course in 1930 on the Jew in English literature from Chaucer to George Eliot. He also wrote a long essay on that topic that he submitted to the *Menorah Journal*, but that only appeared in print after his death.[7] From the start Trilling was preoccupied with cultural issues in relation to the question of the self. In studying how Jews had been seen by others, he seems to have been trying to learn how a modern-day Jew might define himself. He gives the impression of reading all those old English novels and new American ones with an eye to finding a version of Jewishness that he might, "gratuitously," choose for his own mode of personal being.

GENTLEMAN OR JEW?

The most interesting of Trilling's twenty-five contributions to the *Menorah Journal* are his short stories. These pieces reveal even more about the autobiographical origins of his cultural criticism than do his reviews. Trilling's very first contribution to the *Menorah Journal*, a sketch entitled "Impediments," suggests what his letters in the *Menorah Journal* files make even clearer, his ambivalence at the start about accepting himself as a Jew. Trilling was not yet twenty when "Impediments" appeared in the June 1925 issue of the magazine. The sketch is narrated in the first person by an unnamed student who does nothing in the story except fend off the importunities of a less cultivated classmate named Hettner, whom he thinks of as a "scrubby little Jew." The story doesn't amount to much more than Hettner's clumsy attempt at a friendship and the narrator's cold turning him away:

> I felt always defensive against some attempt Hettner might make to break down the convenient barrier I was erecting against men who were too much of my own race. . . . I feared he would attempt to win into the not-too-strong tower that I had built myself, a tower of contemptible ivory perhaps, but very useful.[8]

The narrator is sniffish, also, about Hettner's "hard unmodulated voice" and the threadbare blue serge suit which gives him "the look of a shop assistant." And he has a dread of emotional mess.

> I do not want to know about people's souls; I want people quite entirely dressed; I want no display of fruity scabs and luscious sores. I like people's outsides, not their insides.[9]

Much of Trilling's later development is foreshadowed in "Impediments." The theme that it develops, and that remains central to his thought, is the conflict between sensibility and crudeness. It's curious that Trilling's theme may not be so different from Mencken's as he had thought. Both reflect the American intellectual's anxiety about distinguishing himself from a vulgar mass-democratic society. The anxiety about Jewish vulgarity in the twenties was transposed into anxiety about vulgar liberalism in the forties and then transposed once again, into anxiety about vulgar modernism, "modernism in the streets," in the sixties.

"Impediments" is about the acculturating Jew's uneasiness in relation to the "backward" Jew. To enter the fields of light the narrator must reject this creature who would draw him back. But the story also has a second moment, in which the narrator overcomes the narcissism of small differences and is able to acknowledge his kinship with the "scrubby little Jew" he despises. Hettner, he realizes, is his double, his secret sharer, the negative identity he is fleeing. The reason that he is so anxious to keep his petitioner at bay is that Hettner's insides "would be, probably, too much like mine."[10]

Trilling never entirely repudiates this other, less civilized self. The protagonist of all of the early stories is paralyzingly self-conscious and proper, but he yearns to break free. In his second *Menorah Journal* story, "Chapter for a Fashionable Jewish Novel," the Prufrockian hero imagines himself, self-parodically, as a kind of Jewish Dionysus, come to shock his friends out of their middle-class respectability:

> He began to feel not like a prophet come howling from the wilderness to warn a people defiling holiness, but like a satyr leaped into a respectable home . . . lustfully Hebraic, rowling gloriously, drunkenly, madly, in Jewishness, disgusting the inhabitants by the abandon and licentiousness of his Semitic existence.[11]

Thus, with a comic vengeance, he imagines indulging the expression of his Jewish nature, defying Jews and gentiles alike to disapprove.

The fantasy of the Jew as satyr comes all too close to the anti-Semitic stereotype of the Jew as crude and exhibitionist. It was hardly a comfortable pose for a writer who in the same story has his hero imagining for himself a very different style of selfhood, that of the refined, cosmopolitan Jews in the novels of the

26

Anglo-Jewish writer Israel Zangwill. Trilling was always conscious of the cost to the self of this high refinement, and his conflict over Dionysiac crudeness as against Apollonian refinement is central to his best short story, "Of This Time, Of That Place," which appeared in *Partisan Review* in 1943.

"Of This Time, Of That Place" is far richer thematically than "Impediments," but it builds on the same situation. The "scrubby little Jew" Hettner has become the undergraduate poet-madman Ferdinand Tertan, and Hettner's squeamish fellow student has become Tertan's English teacher Joseph Barker Howe. The Jewish theme, what John Murray Cuddihy has called "the ordeal of civility,"[12] has been refined away, but there is a clear continuity from "Impediments." The teacher's ambivalence toward the lower-class, emotionally expressive Tertan may be read as a later version of the ambivalence of the cultivated Jew of "Impediments" toward Hettner. And there is also the teacher's guilty sense of having betrayed a brother, for both stories conclude with the rejection of the disturbing shadow-self. Both stories are also about the moral cost of assimilation. The narrator of "Impediments" wants to be colorless and conventional so that he will not have to recognize his kinship with his fellow-Jew Hettner. In "Of This Time," Tertan is not specifically identified as Jewish, but it is plain that undue concern for him would endanger Dr. Howe's acceptance in the refined society of his academic colleagues.

"Culture" early became associated in Trilling's thinking with the social ideal of the gentleman. He took over his conception of the gentleman mainly from nineteenth-century English literature, which became his professional specialty. That ideal of the self is illuminated by Maurice Samuel's polemical book *The Gentleman and the Jew* (1950), which tries to demonstrate the incompatibility of the social types named in its title. Samuel sets up a schema in which the gentleman, actually the English gentleman, is moved by a passion for battle and personal honor. He is pagan, competitive, egotistic. The Jew, on the other hand, is presented by Samuel as peaceable, cooperative, and loving. In effect, Samuel sets British imperialism and the human type it produced in opposition to the socialist Zionist ideal.

Some Jewish writers in every generation since Jewish emancipation have responded to the secular culture of the West by drawing back in recoil. There is something of this in Samuel's crude caricature of English-style heroism and his idealization of the Jew as a social type. But Trilling, even in his *Menorah Journal* period, wanted to be both an English-style gentleman and a Jew. The preoccupation with image was strongly marked in Trilling from early on. So was the preoccupation with some impossible ideal whereby antithetical styles and values might be reconciled.

Trilling's feeling both for English refinement and Jewish moral seriousness was common among the literary offspring of the East-European immigrant generation. There were also in Trilling's case unique accidents of family background that may have reinforced the double tendency.[13] His father, a manufacturer of fur coats, had come to America from Bialystok in northeastern Poland. His family in Poland had been noted for its learning, and as a young man the elder Trilling had studied to be a rabbi. Later, in the twenties, as clothier to fashionable men about town, David Trilling came to have a great deal invested in the idea of the gentleman. After the crash of 1929, when his customers could no longer afford the luxury of fur coats, his business went bankrupt and the family's standard of living sank. David Trilling never recovered from the collapse.

Trilling's linking of gentility and culture may have been even more strongly influenced by his mother. Although her parents had been East-European Jews, Fanny Trilling had grown up in London's East End. When she was a teenager her family emigrated once again, to America, but she retained a strong sense of herself as English and brought up Lionel and his younger sister on the English Victorian literature she had herself learned in school. Her dream for her son was that he should receive an Oxford Ph.D.*

*Trilling's success in England far outran his mother's fond dream. He was George Eastman visiting professor at Oxford in 1964–65 and a visiting fellow at All Souls College, Oxford, in 1972–73. That year he was honored by the offer of the Goldsmiths' Professorship in English at Oxford. But by that time he was a University Professor at Columbia, earning much more than the Oxford appointment would have paid. Although he was tempted by the opportunity to remain at Oxford and wavered for some time, he decided to refuse the offer. The low salary and a wish not to leave New York seem to have been the main factors in his decision. For information about the offer of the Goldsmiths' Professorship, I am grateful to Professor John Bayley of Oxford.

CHAMELEON OR PARIAH?

We have considered the young Trilling's sense of culture as opinion, transmitted by magazines and intellectual groups, and we have noted his tendency to identify culture with refinement and gentility. Now I want to take up, in connection with his *Menorah Journal* stories, Trilling's attempt to discover a culture and a personal identity in "positive Jewishness," the ideology of the *Menorah Journal*.

Two of the *Menorah Journal* stories are about the uses of Jewishness in defining oneself in opposition to a bland provincial society. These are the stories based on Trilling's year (1926–27) teaching at the University of Wisconsin in Madison. In "Notes on a Departure," the hero feels that his time in the Midwest has represented truancy from duty. He is disturbed that he has gotten along so well with his university friends and students. A kind of New York-Jewish version of Aeneas, he needs to repel the innocence and friendliness of this provincial community for fear he will assimilate himself too easily to its mediocre standards and default on his cultural mission. Wherever Trilling's young protagonists go, they always secretly want to be part of the group, and at the same time they fight that impulse. They must discipline themselves always to affirm their difference, to say "Thou fool!" to those who might be friends.

Trilling's hero, like Trilling himself, is searching for an adequate culture. He will have to go back to New York not because it has any positive attractions for him, but because it offers the possibility of defining himself through opposition. He needs a culture with rough edges in order to feel real. In this story the hero's main problem is his fear of his own disposition to compromise with second-rateness. He fears that he may be a chameleon, willing to transform himself to fit into any group. And just because he worries so much about his own disposition to enter into everyone's point of view, he insists—to himself—on his difference. Although his Jewishness has meant little to him in New York, among the seductions of the provinces he adopts the most refractory self-image possible. He protects his imperiled sense of himself by insisting that, as a Jew, he is an unassimilable outsider.

But it is hard to resist the feeling that his Jewishness is factitious. It is what he himself acknowledges to be a "hitherto use-less fact" that now has become useful. He exploits it to protect his autonomy. The one thing that is real in this story is not the hero's Jewishness but the vulnerability of his ego. And yet, with all his adolescent self-absorption, he remains capable of irony. Of his re-lation to his Jewishness he reflects that "he had made an angel of that question, a pet angel, and kept it by for a wrestling workout every now and then, so that he could appear in company pale and worn."[14] He is a histrionic fellow, this hero of Trilling's, willing to endure considerable pain in order to maintain his sense of dif-ference. But it is not a perverse kind of snobbery that is at work here; it is a desperate will to survive. The story reveals clearly that "positive Jewishness," at least as Trilling understood it, was any-thing but positive. So factitious a choice of selfhood could not provide the basis for Trilling's own self-identity for very long, be-cause its solution to parochialism is itself parochial. Jewishness as the hero's way of protecting himself against his wish to be at one with the compact majority has the effect only of isolating him.

The isolating implication of Jewish self-consciousness is even more sharply represented in another of Trilling's stories, "Funeral at the Club, with Lunch."[15] This story is another experiment in the *Menorah Journal* program of learning freely to express one's own nature as a Jew. The difficulty arises in knowing what that nature is. "Funeral at the Club" concerns the lone Jew in an English department and his anxiety at a colleague's funeral lest his other colleagues become unified in their grief and turn against him as an outsider. The Jewish instructor is brought face to face with his Jewishness as the chief element in his sense of himself as different, and he is obliged to confront his previously unacknowl-edged wish to transcend that difference. Why, he wonders, should he be branded because of the vulgarity that has been attributed to his race? This question only underlines his deep wish to identify with what he takes to be Christian gentility as against what he re-gards as Jewish crudeness. It turns out that there has been no real ground for his worry about being rejected. His colleagues have not cared much for the professor who died, as in general they show themselves to be incapable of caring much about anything. In their blandly tolerant way they have in fact been accepting of the newcomer despite his own sense of strangeness among them. He has appeared to them much less different than he has appeared to himself.

But with this realization the story turns. The Jewish instructor, irritated by his colleagues' easy liberalism, decides he isn't willing to accept *them*. Noting their passionless response to death, he forms a general judgment of their spiritual emptiness. Their very tolerance and civility damn them in his eyes. From here on, the instructor decides, he will insist on his difference, not seek to mitigate it. He will dedicate himself to aloneness, using his Jewishness to free himself and protect his solitary integrity. Jewishness will be, paradoxically, a "liberating fetter." The role of the self-chosen pariah is uncomfortable and unsociable.[16] That Trilling did not stick to it is not surprising. What is surprising is that he should ever have considered taking it up at all. There are other ways to strengthen personal autonomy, and Trilling would canvas many of them in the five decades that followed "Funeral at the Club."

Anyone acquainted only with Trilling's later writing might well find it surprising that the *Menorah Journal*'s philosophy of positive Jewishness could once have been so important a part of his idea of himself. Trilling had almost nothing to say about Jewishness during the thirties. Then in 1944 he returned for yet another wrestle with his pet angel. A journal, the *Contemporary Jewish Record*, had invited a number of younger Jewish-American writers to comment on their attitude to their Jewish heritage. Amidst the mainly sentimental pieties the symposium elicited, Trilling's statement is notable for its almost totally unqualified negativism. He says straight out that "as the Jewish community now exists, it can give no sustenance to the American artist or intellectual who is born a Jew. And so far as I am aware, it has not done so in the past." Trilling's attack is worth quoting at some length for what it suggests of his drive in the forties to be integrated into mainstream culture.

> Of Jewish cultural movements I know something at first hand, for I once served as a minor editor of a notable journal of Jewish culture [the *Menorah Journal*]. The effort this journal represented was, it even now seems to me, a generous one; but its results were sterile at best. I was deep in—and even contributed to—the literature of Jewish self-realization of which Ludwig Lewisohn was the best-known exponent. This was a literature which attacked the sin of "escaping" the Jewish heritage; its effect, it seems to me, was to make easier the sin of "adjustment" on a wholly neurotic basis. It fostered a willingness to accept exclusion and even to intensify it, a willingness to be provincial and parochial. . . . I know of no writer in English who has added a micromillimetre to his stature by

31

"realizing his Jewishness," although I know of some who have curtailed their promise by trying to heighten their Jewish consciousness.*

Adopting a philosophy that suggested "a willingness to be provincial and parochial" seemed to Trilling in the forties nothing less than a sin against the self. He was deeply committed in those years to a cosmopolitan ideal of culture that had been implicit in his early association of the intellectual life with refinement but that had been suppressed in the twenties and thirties in favor of positive Jewishness and Marxist radicalism.

A WORLD ELSEWHERE

In the forties Trilling's search for an adequate culture led to "the literary imagination," the imagination of life at its highest pitch, especially in the creative writing of the past two centuries. But could an ideal conception like "the literary imagination" serve as an anchor for a criticism of contemporary life? At the start of his career Trilling's struggle to find an entity to which he could give the credence of his senses had been a struggle to find an actual living community in which he might establish a social identity. The young Jewish intellectuals of the *Menorah Journal* in the twenties and the political radicals of Greenwich Village in the thirties were palpable actualities, whereas "the literary tradition" and "the humanist intellectual tradition"—Trilling's positives in the forties—could only be disembodied ideas.

*Trilling's contribution to "Under Forty: A Symposium on American Literature and the Younger Generation of American Jews," *Contemporary Jewish Record* 7 (February 1944): 17. Ludwig Lewisohn, the literary journalist and advocate of positive Jewishness, had begun his career hoping to become a professor of English. But after completing the requirements for the M.A. at Columbia, he was denied admission to the doctoral program—the year was 1905—on the grounds that, as a Jew, the prospect of his ever getting a full-time university position in English was too dim. Trilling nearly suffered the same fate at Columbia three decades later. He was already thirty and an instructor in the English department when he was notified, in 1936, that the department was letting him go. In both instances the department was trying to get rid of a promising young academic because he was Jewish, and they were compounding the insult by assuring him that the decision was for his own good. The sequel in Trilling's case was very different. For Lewisohn's account of his rejection at Columbia and how it ultimately led him to formulate his program for Jewish self-realization, see his memoir, *Up Stream: An American Chronicle* (New York: Boni and Liveright, 1922). I consider Trilling's career at Columbia in chapter 3.

A certain marmoreal quality in Trilling's appeal to the humanistic tradition serves to remind us of the lack of any organic social and intellectual tradition in contemporary America to which he could attach himself. Trilling liked to be part of institutions and communities, but there were no existing groups, in his time and place, in which his ideals were embodied. Even though Trilling sometimes identified himself with the New York intellectuals of *Partisan Review,* he always held himself apart from other members of that circle.[17] He was certain that the self can only realize itself in society, but, like other American writers, he had to create his own ideal society in his writing.

In *A World Elsewhere* Richard Poirier writes that "the great works of American literature are alive with the effort to stabilize certain feelings and attitudes that have, as it were, no place in the world, no place at all except where the writer's style can give them one."[18] It would seem at first that Trilling does not belong to the Emersonian visionary tradition that Poirier describes in his book. Conservative by disposition, Trilling distrusted the Emersonian invention of private, counterhistorical worlds. Rather, he had Matthew Arnold's Oxonian love of great institutions and old traditions and seems always to have been intellectually most comfortable within the ready-made academic humanist culture of Columbia College. But to be happy with a particular intellectual tradition does not necessarily imply being comfortable with the particular intellectuals who claim to embody it.

Trilling's writing and the memories of friends of his at the time make it appear that he became increasingly disillusioned with all social groups as the thirties wore on. Sidney Hook, at that time the leading theoretician of the anticommunist left, remembers the young Trilling as ill at ease amidst the often fractious debates of his radical friends. Trilling's withdrawal from the world of radical politics was only partly compensated by his associations at Columbia. The next chapter shows how little he was accepted by his English department colleagues in those early years. More and more Trilling sought society among the illustrious dead, the authors of the classic humanist texts that he was teaching in the General Honors course at Columbia. He was obliged to make a place for himself in the purely ideal world of thought, amidst Montaigne and Pascal, Coleridge and Mill.

Trilling may have defined himself for well over a decade in

terms of "positive Jewishness" and Marxism because, although these philosophies came to seem obstacles to the kind of selfhood he wanted for himself, in the twenties and thirties they offered possibilities of selfhood that were authenticated by the actuality of like-minded friends with whom he could be in relation. It may be that "Marxism" in the American thirties was as much an abstraction as Trilling's "literary imagination" in the forties, but such as it was, American-style Marxism formed the basis of a culture and social existence for Trilling's contemporaries. That element of actuality helped him to respond to radicalism with something more than dim notional assent. Marxism, like positive Jewishness in the twenties, gave Trilling a ground upon which to rear an imagination of society and, at the same time, a ground upon which to rear an imagination of his self.

Chapter Three

Uptown/Downtown: Trilling's 1930s

The incompatibility of communism and Trilling's ideal of personal being was not as obvious in 1930 as it later became. For intellectuals in Trilling's circle, like Sidney Hook, Marxism was a continuation, not a repudiation, of the Enlightenment liberal tradition, and passing from John Dewey to Leon Trotsky involved no sharp break. Or so it seemed until the end of the thirties.[1]

In 1930, at the start of the Great Depression, it seemed logical for Trilling to hate capitalism. Massive suffering and social dislocation were all about him. But there were personal factors as well. The crisis of the world economic system had impinged on him very directly. His father's business in furs had been totally dependent on the post-World War I luxury trade. With the stock-market crash of 1929, the world that had sustained David Trilling's business disappeared almost overnight. A principal victim was his son, who would have been his heir. Instead, Lionel Trilling, newly married and struggling to establish himself in his career, was also obliged to assume financial responsibility for his parents. For a man in his mid-twenties who had been so thoroughly protected from material cares, the change was inevitably demoralizing.

But the Depression didn't dispose Trilling to renounce his dream of culture and ideal selfhood. Instead he renounced the social-economic system that had betrayed the dream. The capitalist economic system was badly shaken, and capitalist culture was discredited. But, like many European intellectuals of the left, Trilling continued to hold on to solid, nineteenth-century middle-class values. Trilling now believed that socialism might very well succeed where capitalism had so signally failed, in creating a stable social order in which ideal qualities of being might be realized. Before the thirties Trilling had been a cultural radical. His communism after 1930 involved greater risks to his career than that earlier, more innocent radicalism, but his ultimate aim did not

35

change. Through all of the shifting alignments of the thirties, Trilling held on to his dream of culture. He was always more concerned with the implications of a social theory for the individual self than with the more specifically political aims of various left-wing groups.

As in the twenties, Trilling continued to be a man in the middle. As a college instructor and *Menorah Journal* contributor in the late twenties, he had tried to reconcile the ideals of the gentleman and the Jew. In the early thirties he persisted in the gentleman ideal as it had been carried over into academic literary life, but he renounced "positive Jewishness" in favor of Marxism. This chapter is concerned with Trilling's double life in the thirties, as college instructor in English and as political man. It is convenient to consider these separate roles in relation to Trilling's sharply separated worlds, the downtown world (south of 14th Street) of radical politics and the uptown world (Broadway and 116th Street) of Columbia. In the thirties Trilling personally lived out the split in America between the two cultures, the rough-and-ready culture of ideological politics downtown and the genteel academicism of uptown.

MARXIST AND JEW

Nowadays when a radical literary critic speaks of "the system," he is likely to be referring not to capitalism but to the organization of academic literary studies. There is a growing preoccupation with politics among academic critics, but politics for many of them mainly refers to power arrangements within university departments of literature. These critics are asking good questions, about the implications of competing theories of interpretation and about the authorization of knowledge. But the project seems ingrown.

In the 1930s the politics of academic literary study was of little interest to the liveliest critical minds simply because many of the best literary critics did not even hold positions in universities. And for those, like Trilling, who did teach for a living, there existed another world besides the university. Trilling spent nearly the whole of the thirties completing his Columbia University doctoral dissertation on Matthew Arnold while teaching full time as an instructor in English at Columbia. But he was also involved in radical politics, as a communist fellow traveler in 1932–33 and as a member of the anti-Stalinist left for the remainder of the decade. For Trilling there existed social institutions apart from the English department. There were a variety of left-wing committees and political groups, and there was the world of New York literary journalism, itself energized by the political crisis of these years. Trilling was working on his Matthew Arnold dissertation, but he was also writing thirty reviews for the *Nation* between 1930 and 1936, and eleven more essays for the *New Republic* and *Partisan Review* during the last three years of the decade. Some of the most distinctive features of Trilling's later cultural criticism are comprehensible only in the context of this double life as college instructor and political man.

Only a subway ride separated Columbia University from Greenwich Village, but in the thirties no worlds could have been further apart. Columbia had a tradition of great liberals among its humanists, including figures like the philosopher John Dewey, the historians Charles Beard and James Harvey Robinson, and the anthropologist Franz Boas. But the English department had been little affected by the tendency they represented. In Trilling's time, except for younger professors like Mark Van Doren and Joseph Wood Krutch, the English faculty was a bastion of Anglo-Saxon gentility in a city whose temper was determined less by American Protestant ideals than by Jews, Irish and Italian Catholics, and blacks. For some time New York's Jews had pressed especially hard for admittance to the city's dominant social and cultural institutions, and the university's conservative humanists worried that Columbia might become an Ivy League version of City College, whose student body was over ninety percent Jewish.

Through the World War I years American professors of literature had spoken as representatives of a confident dominant class. But by the mid-thirties the dominance of that class had been shaken by two decades of assault on the genteel tradition and the social-economic system that underlay it. During the Depression years Columbia's defenders anxiously guarded the fortress against the new men who had come forward to fill the vacuum of cultural leadership. They were especially offended by what they regarded as the presumption of Jewish intellectuals of the left in undertaking to explain America, its cultural tradition and its present ideological crisis, to old-line Americans like themselves.

That skittishness was by no means limited to gentile academic humanists on the right. As Daniel Aaron has pointed out, radical intellectuals of old-stock antecedents were also often uncomfortable with the style and manners of their Jewish associates. Edmund Wilson was sympathetic to communism in the early thirties but repelled by most communists. In his diary, *The Thirties*, he remarks on his companions in the Writers' Solidarity Delegation who journeyed to Pineville, Kentucky, in February 1932 to interview striking coal miners. They were "queer equivocal anomalous people—mongrel negroes and Jews, thyroid women—who didn't make any sense anyway—also Communists, etc., finally putting it over on you—leading you like lambs to the slaughter." Wilson was never on easy terms with most of the Jewish radicals, not even the anti-Stalinist Jewish literary intellectuals of *Partisan Review*. As Aaron observes, old-stock radicals like Wilson may have "covertly resented the first- or second-generation American's . . . assumption that sharing their political and cultural iconoclasm automatically admitted him to their coterie."[2] Admittance to the friendship of old-stock radicals like Wilson could be as strictly regulated as admittance to the gentleman's club that was the Columbia University English department.

When Trilling began teaching at Columbia in the early thirties, he was the first Jew ever to teach in the English department, and his position was far from secure. His reviews showed, although often obliquely, communist sympathies, and in 1936 he was nearly denied reappointment. The reason, a departmental spokesman explained, was that it was thought that "as a Freudian, a Marxist, and a Jew" Trilling would be "more comfortable" elsewhere.[3] Trilling was able to persuade his colleagues to let him stay on, and soon after this episode he completed his dissertation and received the promotion that made his appointment permanent. It is true that Trilling had been proceeding very slowly on his dissertation, which may have contributed to his colleagues' doubts about him. But it does appear that his being a Jew and his radical politics were the main factors in the move to get rid of him.

If the English professors were guardians of the tradition of genteel culture, the Greenwich Village radicals carried on their own tradition, the cultural and political radicalism of magazines like the old *Masses*. Trilling, like other young writers in his circle, felt the pull of the Village. He married Diana Rubin, a Radcliffe graduate, in 1929,* and his first apartment was on Bank Street. Moving there from his parents' apartment on the Upper West Side was a symbolic gesture by which, as he wrote many years later, "I signalized my solidarity with the intellectual life."[4] Edmund Wilson, then the literary editor of the *New Republic* and most recently the author of *Axel's Castle*, lived across the street. He was a living token of Trilling's own ambition to become not merely a professor but a man of letters and ultimately a figure in the culture.

The Village in the early thirties, the years of Trilling's involvement with communism, was different from the bohemian literary scene of the twenties. Although Wilson lived across the street, Trilling's friends downtown were mainly Jewish. They were the onetime cultural radicals of the *Menorah Journal* who had quit the magazine and regrouped under the banner of the newly organized National Committee for the Defense of Political Prisoners (NCDPP). Elliot Cohen, formerly the managing editor of the *Menorah Journal*, had resurfaced as executive secretary of the NCDPP, with essentially the same team as before.

The NCDPP had been organized by the Communist Party in 1931 to exploit the reputations of sympathetic writers and intellectuals. As in other Communist Party auxiliary organizations, the idea was to use well-known figures like Theodore Dreiser, Lincoln Steffens, and John Dos Passos to win favorable publicity while obscure younger intellectuals like Trilling and his wife carried out the day-to-day administrative chores. The old stars would interview coal miners and union organizers in Kentucky as newspaper photographers took pictures, but it was the young, unknown former *Menorah Journal* writers back in New York who kept the NCDPP going.

It is often difficult for members of a later generation to get a clear fix on just what intellectuals of the Old Left actually *did*. What did their political activism amount to? The intellectual debates of groups like Trilling's probably had less impact on the general public than the marches, demonstrations, and sit-ins of the radical movement of the 1960s. But it is difficult to measure practical effectiveness. Certainly the Old Left dissipated much of

*The Trillings had one child, James, who was born in 1948. He received a Ph.D. from Harvard in 1980 in art history.

39

its potential force by acting as if New York were St. Petersburg in the last years of the Czar and trying to do everything according to the model of the Bolshevik takeover of power. But if the Old Left was undone by the success of the New Deal and by its own failure to make contact with the American masses, it did achieve a major success in forging something like an American intelligentsia.

Trilling's phase of fellow traveling was very brief, only ten months in 1932 and 1933, up to the time of his resignation from the NCDPP. But this fact by itself is misleading, for Trilling was a communist sympathizer for some time before joining the NCDPP; and when he resigned he did not overnight turn back into a liberal. It is very difficult to be certain about Trilling's politics in the thirties because he left few traces. But it appears, from his writing and associations, that he was involved with revolutionary Marxist thinking for at least two or three years after quitting the Communist-controlled NCDPP in 1933. Altogether, Trilling's adherence to revolutionary politics probably lasted about four years, even though his actual membership in a Communist front organization lasted less than a year. Even then, after 1936–37, Trilling's anti-Stalinism was grounded in an independent socialist position, not to be confused with the liberal anticommunism of the fifties.

But why this concern with dating? My purpose is not to "expose" Trilling or argue for his political virtue or lack of it. Rather, I want to emphasize the seriousness of his involvement with radical politics because the evolution of his cultural criticism only makes sense against the background of that involvement. Trilling's criticism is always reactive and dialectical, and his recoil from positive Jewishness was nothing compared to his lifelong recoil from the radicalism of the thirties. Trilling stopped being a Marxist, but he continued to define himself in relation to Marxism.

REVOLUTIONISM TO HUMANISM

Already in 1930, in a review of "proletarian" novels by Edward Dahlberg and Nathan Asch, we find Trilling writing: "There is only one way to accept America and that is in hate; one must be close to one's land, passionately close in some way or other, and the only way to be close to America is to hate it."[5] Of the lumpenproletarian heroes of Dahlberg and Asch, Trilling says:

> They are sure, very sure, that their world is against them. And they are right: their world is *for* nobody. . . . There is no person in the United States, save he be a member of the plutocratic class, who is not in a direct line with [them], not one who is not tainted, a little or much, with the madness of the bottom dog, not one who is not in a sympathy of disgust and hate with his fellows.

These negative emotions, Trilling writes, are "the universally relevant emotions of America."[6]

Another essay of the same year, on D. H. Lawrence, reflects Trilling's radicalization and his inner tumult. In an essay in the *Nation* marking Lawrence's death, Joseph Wood Krutch had summed up the twenties' view of Lawrence as "essentially an anarchical individualist," with "no political interests and no social program." In challenging that orthodoxy, which Krutch had recently summed up in his book *The Modern Temper*, Trilling speaks in the name of an insurgent younger generation. "For us," Trilling writes, "Lawrence's deepest significance must be as a poet of rebellious social theory,"[7] which tells us that "our system has taken from us the body and its joy and knowledge."[8] That system, capitalism, has succeeded where Christianity failed, in subduing self-assertion, masterfulness, pride, and passion. All that remains of an older heroic masculinity is a feminized tenderness and dutiful submission.

During the next few years Trilling was a communist in his sympathies although, as with most of his intellectual circle, not a Communist Party member. Disillusionment with the Party arose over the refusal of American Communist lawyers to appeal the cases of non-Communist political prisoners, such as Wobblies and Trotskyists, who had been arrested alongside Communists. Abroad, in Germany, according to the analysis of Trilling's circle, an even more self-defeating sectarianism, involving the Communists' refusal to ally with the Social Democrats, had allowed Hitler to come to power.

Trilling's break with the Communists in 1933 didn't become public until the next year, when he and twenty-four others, including Edmund Wilson and John Dos Passos, as well as most of the old *Menorah Journal* group, signed an "Open Letter" to the

Party that appeared in its periodical, the *New Masses*. Communist bullies had broken up a mass meeting at Madison Square Garden called by the American Socialist Party to honor the Austrian Socialist workers killed by the anti-Marxist Dollfuss regime. For the Communists in their ultraleft Third Period, these Socialists were not allies but "objectively social-fascist." By the tortured logic of sectarian leftism, anyone on the left who didn't belong to the Party was indirectly giving aid to the fascist enemy.

The "Open Letter" bitterly attacks the Party for undermining the possibility of a "united front," but it is in no sense a "liberal" rejection of the revolutionary movement or of communism as an ideal. The signers were obviously disillusioned, but they were not shifting their support to Norman Thomas's reform-minded Socialist Party, much less to the New Deal. As independent radicals, some of the signers withdrew from formal association with any wing of the communist movement. But most in Trilling's circle moved toward one form or another of Trotskyism. They still regarded themselves as communists if not Communists, as an outlawed faction which carried on the ideals of the October Revolution, which the ruling clique in Moscow had betrayed. A few actually joined the Trotskyist organization, the Communist League of America, while others—including Trilling—joined the Non-Partisan Labor Defense, which had been organized in protest against the Stalinist-dominated NCDPP.

From this point on Trilling's radicalism manifested itself mainly in arguing with the Stalinists about cultural matters. The Communist Party held a near-monopoly on revolutionary agitation, and Trilling was discovering he had little taste for active militancy in any case. But he remained within the radical fold. He regarded the Trotskyists as accurate in their analysis of the political situation; at the same time he regarded them as unlikely to achieve political power.* By this time Trilling had very little involvement in organizational politics. The Moscow Trials of 1936-38, in which Nikolai Bukharin and other first-generation Bolsheviks were victims of a Stalinist frameup, provoked a great crisis on the American left and completed Trilling's disillusionment with the Communist Party. It did not, however, inspire deeper involvement in the Trotskyist movement. In 1936, along with others in his intellectual group, Trilling was a member of

*Trilling, unpublished letter to Jacques Barzun, July 26, 1935, at Columbia University Library. Access restricted.

the American Committee for the Defense of Leon Trotsky, which sponsored an inquiry into the charges made against Trotsky during the Moscow Trials. But he had nothing like the involvement of his friend Herbert Solow, who had direct contact with the "Old Man" in Mexico, or of another friend, George Novack, who became a lifelong official and ideologist of the Trotskyist movement.[9] By 1937 Trilling seems to have been much less interested in Trotsky's political program than in opposing Stalinist influence on literature and culture.

In later years Trilling commented bitterly on the radical thirties, on their "dryness and deadness" and on "the dull unreverberant minds and the systematically stupid minds that had been especially valued."[10] But he had himself been a part of that radical milieu even if he had not been a radical activist after 1933 and even though his distaste for confrontation and extremism distinguished him from others better adapted to the temper of the time. Trilling was an uncertain, self-divided man through most of the thirties. His dilemma was that the radical political stance he shared with his downtown friends was not really compatible with his uptown literary-cultural attitudes. He would be able to move ahead only when he finally found a way of resolving that tension. His struggle to find himself amidst those antinomies consumed a whole decade.

It's possible to trace the evolution of Trilling's criticism by comparing three successive essays of his on E. M. Forster, in 1934, 1938, and 1942. In the first of these, a review of Forster's biography of his friend G. L. Dickinson, Trilling is still using the familiar left-wing jargon of the thirties. He attacks the "merely liberal-humanitarian view" of Dickinson and others whose liberal idealism had made them "the tools of the interests they truly hated." Trilling concedes that the liberal virtues, such as understanding and tolerance, are still valuable in personal relations, but he warns against being taken in by the merely personal. "In political life," he says, "history has proved [understanding and tolerance] to be catchwords that becloud reality in the service of the worst 'passions and interests.' "[11] In short, Trilling's revolutionary politics require him to depreciate the characteristic liberal virtues. It was only later, in the forties, that Trilling reversed the strategy, using those same liberal moral-cultural values as the standard for judging left-wing politics.

By 1938 Trilling was somewhat less apologetic about

liberalism. Reviewing a new critical study of Forster, Trilling comments favorably on the revival of liberal humanism as a cultural fact. But then he pulls back, adding that "as a political portent" that revival is "saddening, for it is in large part the result of a retreat to the uncritical acceptance of the old slogans of liberal democracy."[12] Trilling was by no means ready yet to join politically with the Norman Thomas Socialists, much less the liberals. At the same time, his aesthetic and moral attitudes clashed with his leftist politics. It was only a question how long he could go on assuring himself and his downtown audience that he was keeping the radical faith while at the same time avowing moderate and centrist impulses in regard to literature and culture.

A letter from Trilling to Sidney Hook in 1938 reveals how divided he was. The main news is that Trilling's doctoral dissertation on Matthew Arnold had been enthusiastically received at Columbia. This might have been unalloyed good news inasmuch as only two years earlier Trilling's senior colleagues had tried to have him dismissed. His future at Columbia continued to be dependent on the good opinion of these colleagues. But the letter is anything but cheerful. Trilling tells Hook that he is dismayed by his success. It makes him wonder if he has not soft-pedaled his radicalism. The disapproval of his antiradical colleagues would have reassured him about his fidelity to his political " 'direction.' " He wonders how his readers can have missed his point of view and worries that, in trying to be " 'understanding' with his complex material," he may have overdone it—"to the point of causing myself to be misunderstood."[13]

Of course we have to take account of the receiver of this letter. In 1938 Hook was still the leading Marxist theoretician among the New York intellectuals. All through the thirties he had been the single greatest influence on Trilling's political attitudes. If now, in 1938, Trilling was slipping free of Hook's influence, he might well have wished to reassure his mentor that nothing had changed. Whatever Trilling's intention, he does affirm himself still a radical, even if a radical with doubts about Marxism itself. He writes, he says, because Hook knows his political attitude and can judge whether he has "falsified" it. He seems to be setting up Hook as a political tribunal, in the hope that he will be cleared.

But what is the crime? Ideological deviation? Or is it the will to succeed? For Trilling seems to be apologizing not only for possibly compromising his political position but for winning the approval of his uptown colleagues. Regardless of their intellectual qualifications or political virtue, Columbia's English professors were the agents of respectable society. They had the power to confer the acceptance that Trilling, or at least part of Trilling, craved. There is no question of vulgar "opportunism" here. If Trilling muffled his radicalism, the reason would appear to be that he was genuinely ceasing to believe in radicalism. We might speak of "inauthenticity" except that Trilling *was* being true to himself in his dissertation in modulating his leftism. He just could not acknowledge that modulation to Hook, a contemporary who stood in the role of mentor to Trilling by virtue of his political experience and self-assurance.

The issue, I think, is not politics alone but "growing up," the subject of Trilling's important essay on Wordsworth's "Immortality Ode" in 1941. Of course, "growing up" itself is a complicated idea, involving not only some abstract notion of "maturity," but also acculturation and the acquisition of power and the means of pleasure. Trilling worried that question a good deal in the decade to come, notably in his 1943 short story "Of This Time, Of That Place," and in his 1948 essay "The Princess Casamassima."* He continued to worry the question of success, usually with great indirection, right up to the end of his career. Small wonder, then, that Norman Podhoretz, who had been a kind of spiritual son to Trilling as his student in the late forties, should have written his precocious autobiography, *Making It*, to affirm explicitly the son's wish for success that the father-figure seems not to have been able fully to acknowledge in himself. Trilling's ambivalence made it hard on those who followed him.

In general, however, Trilling's position was firming up. His third essay on Forster, in 1942, reveals nothing of the apologetic tone of this letter or the 1938 review. It is one of Trilling's most confident, most poised critical performances, containing in embryo all the major themes he developed the next year in his full-length monograph on Forster. The 1942 essay differs from the earlier ones in that Trilling no longer feels obliged to make obeisance to

_____

*I discuss the Wordsworth essay in chapter 7, "Of This Time, Of That Place" in chapter 5, and the essay on *The Princess Casamassima* in chapter 4.

the politics of the left. He deals with the problem by implying that his left-wing credentials are beyond reproach—they needn't be insisted on. With his political virtue taken for granted, Trilling can go on to stress Forster's tone, temper, style, moral attitude, cultural stance—everything but his politics.[14]

Earlier Trilling had tripped over his own contradictions, especially in connection with the clash between personal and political values. Now, in 1942, he makes a virtue of contradiction. Forster's "addiction to ambivalence" is not a disabling flaw, as it would have seemed to a radical in the thirties. Rather, it is a term of praise. Trilling's Forster is exemplary precisely *because* of his feeling for irony, paradox, ambiguity, complication. His imagination of good-and-evil as an "inextricable tangle" distinguishes Forster from the liberals, for whom simple good is always arrayed against an equally simple, monolithic evil.

At this stage I want to consider not Trilling's new "imagination of complication," which is the subject of chapter 4, but how he arrived at it. That means considering the influence on him of the gentleman-humanist ethos of Columbia College. Trilling's uptown colleagues were by no means deluded in recognizing the author of *Matthew Arnold* as one of their own. The young instructor they had tried to fire in 1936 would come to embody, far more fastidiously and cogently than they themselves, the values of the College.

HUMANISM AT COLUMBIA

More has been written about Trilling's life downtown among the radical intellectuals of the thirties than about the influence on him uptown of a distinctive Columbia University tradition of humanistic education. But that academic tradition seems to me to have been at least as important in shaping his cultural criticism as the debates conducted in *Partisan Review*. Over the course of the thirties Columbia effectively replaced Marxism as Trilling's cultural context. He found a new self-identity as an academic humanist in a distinguished Morningside Heights tradition.

An important aspect of Trilling's uptown intellectual life was his association with the Columbia historian Jacques Barzun.[15] This intellectual association was closer and longer-lasting than

Trilling's friendships with any of the downtown intellectuals. The Trilling-Barzun relationship, which continued up to the time of Trilling's death in 1975, began in 1934, when they were both instructors at Columbia and were assigned to teach a joint colloquium in the General Honors course in the College. This course, in which juniors and seniors studied the classics of Western civilization, became famous when it was carried to the University of Chicago by a former Columbia undergraduate, Mortimer Adler. But the originator of the "Great Books" idea was not Adler or Robert Hutchins but a Columbia professor of English named John Erskine.[16]

Erskine was a typically conservative American continuator of Matthew Arnold. As John Henry Raleigh has shown, Arnold's use of literature to inculcate moral values remained an influential tendency in the teaching of the humanities in American colleges well into the twentieth century.[17] At Columbia College this tradition dominated all others in the 1920s, when Trilling was an undergraduate, and it continued to be strong throughout Trilling's career, long after it had faded in the English departments of other major universities. The question arises as to why this particular tradition of literary study should have persisted at Columbia long after professional specialization and the New Criticism had made such powerful inroads at most of America's great universities. How was it that in New York, a city ablaze with new fashion in every other sphere, such traditionalism should have flourished for so long? One obvious explanation would be the personal interests of the individuals there, who perpetuated themselves, as academic departments are wont to do, by promoting and recruiting like-minded persons. But it may also be that the humanist tradition at Columbia was as conservative as it was precisely *because* of its geographical setting and the university's desire to act as a brake on the new.

New York was and remains the symbolic heart of capitalism, with its irresistible drive to dissolve old traditions in the service of continual innovation. Besides being the symbolic center of American capitalism, New York was also the port through which millions of non-English-speaking immigrants poured into America between 1880 and 1920. Acculturation was an immediate and pressing problem, nothing less than a crisis, as we may judge from the frightened reaction of old-line Americans like Henry James and Henry Adams to the polyglot confusion of the Lower East Side. The respectable citizens of New York conceived a special role for Columbia. Part of that role, as I have already indicated, was maintaining the racial purity of the city's dominant class. This meant, specifically, avoiding the examples of City College and New York University, which had admitted large numbers of Jewish students. But that special role meant, more generally, investing the university with a traditional and civilizing mission in the midst of an alien, philistine society.

In 1897 the university moved to its present site, atop Morningside Heights on Manhattan's Upper West Side. In dedicating the new site, the university's president, Seth Low, appealed to a familiar image of America as a city on a hill. Columbia, the university on a hill, was to fulfill the same redemptive mission as America itself. How else was Columbia to justify its proud name?

> A university that is set on a hill cannot be hid. . . . If New York is taunted in the years to come with being a city wholly given up to the love of money, she may well point to this eminence . . . and say: "These are my jewels; these are the things my children care for more than they care for money. . . ."[18]

Such a mission needs missionaries, humanists who conceive of their role in public terms. John Erskine was typical of the civic-minded academic who acts as an exponent and embodiment, so to speak, of the humanities in a vulgar mass democracy. Erskine's immense energy—he was a prolific novelist, essayist, and anthologist—has not saved him from the obscurity of countless genteel Arnoldians like him. But one essay, "The Moral Obligation to Be Intelligent," became a great influence on gentleman humanists who succeeded him at Columbia.

Erskine himself was following in a distinctive literary tradition at Columbia. In 1897, when the university moved to Morningside Heights, two of its most highly regarded humanists were the literary critic and poet George Edward Woodberry and the drama critic Brander Matthews, whose anthologies, editions, surveys of the drama, novels, collections of essays, and sundry other productions occupy about one hundred separate entries in a university library card catalog. Matthews was the archetype of the Columbia humanist: various, fluent, anglophilic but at the same time proud to be identified with the artistic and cultural life of New York City. Like Trilling many years later, Matthews looked to England for his cultural standards but was assiduous in noting the development of an independent American literature, American language, American code of manners. One of Matthews's books is called *Americanisms and Briticisms*, and he was as interested in the emerging difference between American and British speech as Trilling was to be in the difference between American and British styles of selfhood. *

From Matthews and Woodberry there is a line that runs to John Erskine and down to the classicist Gilbert Highet, the poet-essayist Mark Van Doren, and Trilling's colleague Barzun.[19] The title of one of Barzun's many books, *Teacher in America*, sums up the self-conception of these Columbia humanists, all of them generalists and popularizers, all of them devoted, as Trilling himself, was, to *refining* American culture. Trilling seems to me a much larger figure than Matthews and Erskine, but he shared with them a certain conception of his social role. Inevitably that sense of his role was at odds with his self-identification as a New York intellectual. As a *Partisan Review* writer, Trilling was committed to opposition to the established order; as a humanist at Columbia, he participated in a project of acculturation.

In an autobiographical lecture that he presented in 1971, Trilling comments on the indebtedness of John Erskine's General Honors course to the Renaissance-humanist conception of an education appropriate to an aristocratic ruling class. Trilling took seriously the notion that he was educating young men—he was never much concerned with the education of young women—who

---

*Trilling, however, was contemptuous of Matthews's kind of urbanity, dismissing him as "a man of club lounges and theater greenrooms . . . who held his University post with some irony and gave the same amusing lectures from the same set of notes year after year." Trilling appears to have identified much more closely with Woodberry, whom he describes as "not a religious believer, but . . . a man of great natural piety for whom the spiritual life was everything." Trilling himself became the Woodberry Professor at Columbia in 1965, holding that chair until 1970, when he was appointed University Professor. See Trilling, "The Van Amringe and Keppel Eras," in *A History of Columbia College on Morningside Heights* (New York: Columbia Univ. Press, 1954), 24, 25. I am grateful to Gerald Graff for calling my attention to this essay.

would, as he put it, be "responsible for the welfare of the polity." It was not consonant with the obligation to educate a ruling class that Columbia's subway scholars should all be transformed into *Partisan Review* intellectuals. Trilling had another aim in view that owes more to Aristotle's *Ethics* than to Marx or any other great adversary mind. He was concerned to encourage his students to a certain largeness of spirit, or magnanimity, which is likely to be destroyed in a mass democracy. The idea of "the vulgar" sums up a great deal of what Erskine, and Trilling after him, wanted to overcome.

As Trilling says in his autobiographical lecture, "the Columbia *mystique* was directed to showing young men how they might escape from the limitations of their middle-class or their lower-middle-class upbringings by putting before them great models of thought, feeling, and imagination."[20] To be sure, many Marxist revolutionaries share humanism's appreciation of the usefulness of great models. But Trilling does not consistently emphasize the adversary implications of this theory of education. Although he is equivocal on the matter, he often tends, as here, to conceive of "culture" not as a critical attitude but as a sanctuary, a great good place to which young candidates for civility might escape from the parochialism and vulgarity of their families. Trilling's tone can sometimes suggest that culture is a fixed possession that one might acquire, an alternative style of selfhood that brings with it higher status.

Columbia's humanistic ideal of moral-aesthetic refinement had as its social counterpart a conception of the university as a bulwark against political radicalism. We have only to consider the keynote address at the Morningside Heights dedication ceremony in 1896. New York's mayor, Abram S. Hewitt, was plainly worried about social disorder. Hundreds of thousands of foreigners had arrived in the previous twenty-five years, turning New York into a scene of political unrest. Columbia's task was to defuse that threat:

> So far as the City of New York is concerned the Columbia University must be made the fountain-head of knowledge, the centre from which will flow the conservative and recuperative principle of social progress. . . . Against its walls the waves of communism and anarchy will then beat in vain.[21]

Trilling adapted both parts of the Columbia ethos—its concern with refinement and its opposition to radicalism—to the critique of "the liberal imagination" that established his reputation in the forties. It is not really strange, in view of the university culture in which Trilling had his being, that this revolutionary of the early thirties should have become, by the end of the decade, a cultural critic still nominally identified with the left, whose arguments, however, had the effect of defusing radical passions.

MATTHEW ARNOLD AND THE DIALECTIC

Trilling's story in the thirties is that of a man who changed his mind. At the start of the decade he was enough of a Columbia man to settle on Arnold for his dissertation topic and to conceive of his project as a critical history of Arnold's ideas. Trilling's dissertation director, Emery Nef, had written on Thomas Carlyle and John Stuart Mill from the point of view of their ideas, and this approach was standard in the Columbia English department. Where Trilling differed from his mentors was in planning to found his theory of Arnold's intellectual development on a philosophically rigorous conception of Marx's dialectic. According to Sidney Hook, who first became involved in the project in 1931, Trilling's attitude toward Arnold at that time was much more critical than in the final version. The Marxist dialectic which was Trilling's original framework included such ideas as development by contradiction, triadic progression by phases, the necessarily progressive character of such change, and the centrality of class struggle. What happened is that as the years wore on and the manuscript went through successive revisions, Trilling found himself renouncing Marx's idea of the dialectic and interpreting Arnold positively in Arnold's own terms.

But the concept of the dialectic remained. Now, however, the word had a new meaning and implication. Trilling was not alone in having changed his mind about the Marxist dialectic by the end of the thirties. The validity of the concept had also been challenged by other onetime Marxists, among them Hook, Max Eastman, and Edmund Wilson. *To the Finland Station*, Wilson's major book of the thirties, experienced a sea-change like Trilling's *Matthew Arnold*. Midway through the decade Wilson repudiated communism. The effect is that his study of the European socialist tradition ends rather less enthusiastically than it begins. For his part, Hook believed that under Stalinism the dialectic had become a quasi-religious dogma and that, in any case, "dialectic" as a word had accumulated so many different meanings that for philosophical purposes it had become useless and ought to be discarded.[22]

For Trilling this ambiguity about "dialectic" constituted its appeal. T. S. Eliot had complained about the vagueness of many of Arnold's key terms. The same objection might be made against Trilling, but it is important to see the uses of this vagueness. Many of Trilling's most important essays are exercises in definition (e.g., "The Meaning of a Literary Idea"), and an essential strategy of his criticism is to redefine key terms used by his adversary, to wrest these words from the Stalinists. In the case of "dialectic," Trilling was taking an honorific term in Marxist writing and using it for anti-Marxist ends, using Marxism against itself. At the same time—by virtue of his familiar idiom—he was able to present himself as a man of the left.

What Trilling means by Arnold's "dialectical" method is illustrated by his account of Arnold's attitude toward the French Revolution. According to Trilling, it cannot be said that Arnold held any fixed view of the Revolution. His judgment of it shifted. At any particular moment of his career, Arnold's view "was determined, first, by his notion of the historical context in which [the Revolution] had occurred and, second, by the particular historical moment in which he was writing."[23] It appears that in Trilling's view the second context, the present, is far more important an influence on Arnold's judgment than the first, the past. Although Trilling praises Arnold's sense of history, the Arnold he presents is not very historically minded. Rather, his approach to criticism, and Trilling's after him, is therapeutic and pragmatic. What is good is what the present situation requires. As Trilling reads Arnold, the French Revolution might be judged good or bad according to how much of the "revolutionary principle" Arnold decided England needed at the moment he was writing.

The dialectical mode of judgment as Trilling himself practiced it encourages relevance rather than consistency. Trilling is even more changeable than Arnold. Writing in 1935 about the novelist John O'Hara, Trilling laments O'Hara's incapacity for general ideas. But in 1956, in an introduction to the Modern Li-

brary collection of O'Hara's short stories, Trilling celebrates
O'Hara's knack for social detail and verisimilitude. The documentary specificity that had been a limitation in 1935 has become a
positive in 1956.[24] What had happened over the years? In the
thirties American literature could boast many documentary talents
but few writers capable of creating abstractions out of the welter of
particulars. Hence the appeal in these years to European examples
like André Malraux and Ignazio Silone, with their generalizing intelligence. In the mid-fifties things had changed. There were
plenty of novelists all too eager to generalize experience, but few
had O'Hara's eye for detail. So his observation might be praised
and his mindlessness overlooked. But what of O'Hara himself,
O'Hara the writer as against O'Hara the cultural portent? The fact
is that he had not changed much as far as his fictional mode is
concerned, and by the mid-fifties, when Trilling was recommend-
ing him most wholeheartedly, O'Hara was not writing as well as
in the thirties.*

Trilling's self-chosen role from the late thirties on was to
mediate between uptown and downtown, between literature and
politics, between the left intellectuals' new spirit of accommodation to American values and their residual sympathy for Marxist
ideas. Trilling's "historical-dialectical" view of Arnold is a case of
a later critic's reinventing himself in the image of his precursor,
but also of a "strong reading," that is to say, a misreading
whereby the later critic interprets his precursor to accord with his
own present needs. Trilling's Arnold is a version of his own
idealized self as man in the middle. The passage that follows is
Trilling's revisionary reading of Arnold's "dialectical" view of the
French Revolution:

---

*Another instance of Trilling's changeableness involves his estimation of
William Dean Howells. In 1945 Trilling was depressed, even appalled, by
Howells's blandness. Only six years later, in "William Dean Howells and the
Roots of Modern Taste," Trilling recommends Howells as just what the culture
needs. In that essay Trilling praises Howells for precisely the qualities—his
benignity and moderateness—he had earlier found depressing. On the new cultural situation that helps account for Trilling's changed estimate of Howells,
see chapter 6. Trilling's earlier remarks on Howells appear in an unpublished
letter of his to Jacques Barzun. The letter, dated August 24, 1945, is part of
the Trilling material at Columbia University Library to which access is restricted.

Arnold, like his father, lived in the shadow of the French Revolution and of the Reign of Terror. He welcomed the new democracy but he suspected it. He welcomed rationalism but feared its effects. He was far from being at one with established religion yet he feared the void which its disappearance would leave. He saw old institutions crumbling and was glad, but he was uneasy lest their fall bring down more than themselves. He wanted progress but he feared the "acridity" which would characterize the forward movement. Consequently he found it necessary to formulate a point of view which, while it affirmed the modern spirit with its positive goal and scientific method, would still allow him to defend the passing order. Arnold's criticism was, in effect, his refusal to move forward until Burke and Voltaire compounded their quarrel, bowed to each other and, taking him by either hand, agreed on the path to follow.[25]

In their political implication, these nicely turned sentences are simply paralyzing. Anyone who waits to move forward until Burke and Voltaire compound their quarrel isn't going anywhere. It is true that one can reasonably take something from each, but Trilling's balanced clauses have the effect of canceling each other out, leaving us in a charmed condition of inaction. They create an effect Trilling especially admired, of stasis, of equilibrium, of all willing suspended. That taste for stasis sharply separated Trilling from the left-wing critics in his New York circle. It will appear in a variety of guises in the chapters that follow, as in the impulse to truancy that struggles against Trilling's commitment to watch over the culture, and in the aestheticism that conflicts with his commitment to life in history.

In his study of Arnold, Trilling most frequently associates the dialectical way of thinking with historical and cultural relativism. But the more important sense of the dialectic for him is that of unresolved dualisms. Once you arrive at a view of culture as divided, however, you next have to decide how you feel about the fact of division. And Trilling decided that he preferred the continued existence of oppositions to any program for resolving them. Inevitably, given this preference, "dialectic" lost its association with dynamism and the active will. In Trilling's hands the dialectic ceased to be a doctrine of historical progress by means of revolutionary struggle. Indeed, it ceased to have any connection with change at all. Instead, dialectic now referred to a static doctrine of sustained tensions.

It is possible to see how nicely this theory complements the more exclusively literary theory that the New Critics were working out in the same years.[26] Trilling's dialectical method is like the "tension" and "irony" by which, in New Critical theory, the contraries of a poem are bound together in an organic unity. Not surprisingly, then, one of the New Critics, Robert Penn Warren, found much to praise in his review of Trilling's *Arnold*. By 1946, when Diana Trilling was writing in praise of Warren's novel *All the King's Men*, there was not a great deal to distinguish the liberal conservativism of Warren from the increasingly conservative liberalism of Trilling.* The major difference, apart from obvious differences in their approach to the literary text, concerned religion. Trilling affirmed no sense of the redemptive. For him there was no unity, organic or otherwise, no transcendence. There was *only* conflict and complication.

*Warren's review of Trilling's *Matthew Arnold* appeared in *Kenyon Review* 1 (Spring 1939): 217–21. Diana Trilling reviewed *All the King's Men* in the *Nation* 163 (August 24, 1946). There she praises Warren for exploring issues similar to those that engaged the Trillings themselves in the mid-forties: "He is questioning the absolutes of good and evil which are so much the assumption of a large part of our present-day political morality" (220). In the same year both Trillings reviewed *The Bitter Box*, a parabolic novel by Warren's wife, Eleanor Clark, about life in the American Communist movement. Diana Trilling praises Clark's novel for its "serious, funny, and truthful picture of Communist doings in this country" (*Nation* 162 [April 27, 1946]), and Lionel Trilling calls it "a distinguished book, both in its conception and execution." His review appeared in *Kenyon Review* 8 (Autumn 1946): 658-67.

Chapter Four

The Imagination of Complication

In the late thirties, trying to fight his way free from Stalinist orthodoxy, Trilling worked out the stance that would characterize his writing during the next four decades. His essays of the forties, later collected in *The Liberal Imagination* (1950), are trenchant expressions of that stance. In these essays Trilling appears as the liberal critic of liberalism, the critic of the left from within its ranks. His stance is summed up at the start of *The Liberal Imagination* in his praise of Hawthorne's "dissent from the orthodoxies of dissent."[1]

But orthodoxies of dissent are always changing, and as they change so do Trilling's positions. His stance is consistent but his opinions are not. These latter depend upon what, in his view, "the culture" needs. In the forties the liberal intellectuals were sunk in a drab and soulless materialism, so Trilling argued for vivacity and variety, for wit and style. In the sixties the orthodoxy of dissent had become "the adversary culture," which Trilling saw as a mindless parody-version of the older adversary culture of high modernism. So Trilling shifted course, arguing now for reason and expressing skepticism about the literary values he had once celebrated as a corrective for an excessively rationalistic liberal culture.

There is no point in denying the ambiguities that result from Trilling's dialectical relation to the left. It is not only recent critics, like Mark Shechner, who remark "the elusive Lionel Trilling."[2] Contemporary reviewers of *The Liberal Imagination* were also unsure of the direction of his thought and where, finally, he stood. For example, in *The Liberal Imagination* Trilling praises modernist literature as a corrective to the dullness of liberalism. At the same time, however, he shows himself to be wary of modernist extremism and seems more comfortable with Henry James and E. M. Forster than with Joyce and Kafka. Are we, then, to regard Trilling as antimodernist in his taste? He praises T. S. Eliot's moral imagination of culture and quotes from Reinhold

Niebuhr on the evil nature of man. Does that mean he approves of the postwar religious revival? It is clear in *The Liberal Imagination* that Trilling regards as shallow the moral outlook of American progressivism, an intellectual tradition that goes back to the utopian communities of the 1830s and 1840s and comes up to John Dewey and "the revolt against formalism" in the early part of the twentieth century. Does Trilling's disdain for the progressive tradition imply a conservative social attitude?[3]

None of these questions can be answered simply. Indeed, not having a fixed, easily summarized position is for Trilling itself a kind of position. It is his way of rebuking the simplifications of the left. As Jacques Barzun says, Trilling responded to the ideological certitudes of Stalinized liberals with this characteristic rejoinder: " 'It's complicated. . . . It's much more complicated. . . . It's very complicated.' "[4] It's important to see that Trilling makes no claim to be offering either a worked-out doctrine or a new position. Rather, on every occasion he reminds the liberals of the complexity of moral fact. He stands coolly aloof from the enthusiasms of the intellectuals in order to recall them to what he takes to be old, timeless truths. His mind works dialectically, not as the Marxists understand the dialectic—to bring about historical change—but to keep the culture on a steady course and maintain an always threatened equilibrium.

That means Trilling may well appear to contradict himself in connection with a specific writer, like O'Hara, or large literary-cultural movement, like modernism. He is not chiefly committed either to literature as such or to a particular view of society. His opinions on literature and society fluctuate because he is concerned above all with the health of "the culture." But what is "the culture"? In practice this phrase stands for the sentiments, attitudes, and morale of the intellectual class. As Delmore Schwartz said in an essay of 1953:

> Mr. Trilling is interested in the ideas and attitudes of the educated class, such as it is and such as it may become: it is of this class that he is, at heart, the guardian and the critic. . . . As the prestige and problems of that class change, Mr. Trilling's literary opinions and social views also tend to change, and quite rightly, given his essential purposes.[5]

Schwartz might have added that Trilling is not so much interested in ideas as in the intellectuals' *relation* to their ideas. He is never more effective than when he exposes the inauthenticity of the intellectuals' relation to their fashionable ideas.

But it is not enough, in trying to define Trilling's cultural criticism, to note his satiric reflections on the inauthenticity of the intellectual left. Trilling also had positive aims. Above all, he was trying to achieve a sane and steady overview. He wanted, like Arnold, to achieve a totalizing vision and thereby provide readers with an "intellectual deliverance." Trilling was our last Victorian sage. His zeal for making sense of life as a whole has largely disappeared from literary criticism.

In *Matthew Arnold,* Trilling writes: "When a man sees life under the aspect of a distinct and illuminating idea, all things become interrelated and it is no step at all from the investigation of Homer to the investigation of elementary schools."[6] For the Arnold of *Culture and Anarchy,* that illuminating idea was the insufficiency of English middle-class culture. Arnold was writing in the 1860s. Trilling adapted Arnold's critique to the educated class—"the liberals"—of the American 1940s. I shall have more to say in the next chapter about Trilling's theory of society in the forties. Here I want to take up his cultural attitude. That attitude is summed up in the phrase "the liberal imagination," which has about the same place in Trilling's cultural critique as "philistinism" had in Arnold's.

Of course the world had changed a great deal in the eighty years between *Culture and Anarchy* and *The Liberal Imagination.* One difference is that it had become far more difficult in midcentury America than in the British 1860s to achieve a sane and steady overview. Since the 1940s, the continually accelerating rate of cultural change and the bewildering proliferation of art and ideas have made it even more difficult to achieve an intellectual totalization. Trilling managed it in the forties, but he never achieved anything like the same unity and trenchancy in the following decades. Nowadays critics are urged not even to try. We are instructed to value fragmentation, heterogeneity, marginality. Whatever the usefulness of that strategy in Europe, where the idea of totality has been tainted by its association with political totalitarianism,[7] its effect in America has been mainly to confirm us in our present cultural confusion. In the forties literary critics, like the great modernist writers they admired, were still trying to make the fragments cohere, to reveal a pattern or entelechy. The world might still be held together, if only in the mind.

COMMUNISM AS KITSCH

The dream of totality among left intellectuals of the forties was a dream of the reconciliation of avant-garde politics and art. The most important magazine to espouse this position was *Partisan Review*, which tried to combine a program of independent radicalism (independent, that is, of the Communist Party) and aesthetic modernism. Trilling, who had always been less radical than other *Partisan Review* writers, both in his literary taste and his social views, shared their dream of a union between the deep places of the imagination and political fact. In practice, however, his best criticism was written out of a steady sense of the contradictions, complications, and complexities that made any such resolution unlikely. And as the dream of a marriage of modernism and Marxism came to seem increasingly unlikely in the forties, it was contradiction itself that became the basis of Trilling's totalizing view.

The central problem of *The Liberal Imagination* is summed up in Trilling's 1946 essay "The Function of the Little Magazine," which had originally been published as the introduction to a collection of essays from the first decade of *Partisan Review:*

> If . . . we name those writers who . . . are to be thought of as the monumental figures of our time, we see that to these writers the liberal ideology has been at best a matter of indifference. Proust, Joyce, Lawrence, Eliot, Yeats, Mann (in his creative work), Kafka, Rilke, Gide—all have their own love of justice and the good life, but in not one of them does it take the form of a love of the ideas and emotions which liberal democracy, as known by our educated class, has declared respectable. So that we can say that no connection exists between our liberal educated class and the best of the literary mind of our time.[8]

This passage, like so much of Trilling's writing of the forties, requires glossing. It is not self-evident forty years later what ideas Trilling has in mind in speaking of "the ideas which liberal democracy . . . has declared respectable," or who made up the group Trilling calls "the educated class."

As everywhere in *The Liberal Imagination*, Trilling is reacting against an orthodoxy of the left. The political-cultural situation he addresses is the vastly expanded influence of Stalinism among liberal intellectuals following the promulgation in 1935 of the new Communist policy of the Popular Front. In the early thirties the

Communist program had been sectarian and extremist, emphasizing class struggle and social revolution. As such it was uncongenial to most middle-class intellectuals. In the late thirties, however, Stalin was less concerned about Marxist doctrine than about enlisting Western nations as allies against Hitler. Instead of agitating for revolution, or even for socialism, Western European and American Communist parties shifted to presenting themselves as the vanguard of democracy in the struggle against fascism. In the United States, Communism altered its image and offered itself as "Twentieth Century Americanism." As the leader in the battle against fascism, the Party was able to attract a substantial number of fellow travelers moved by a powerful if diffuse yearning to be on the side of virtue.

The Popular Front in America was not merely a political position. For many liberals, as Trilling observed at the time, it provided an ethics and a culture. That culture calls for some attention here because Trilling's characteristic way of going at criticism was worked out in dialectical response to it. The high value Trilling gives to style, his idea of "moral realism," his invocation of "variousness" and "complexity," the special polemical use he makes of modernist literature—all of these elements of Trilling's cultural criticism only make sense in terms of his struggle to destroy the foundations of Stalinist cultural influence.* In the fifties Trilling's anticommunism became the dominant position among liberal intellectuals. But in the late thirties, when he worked out that position, it was still a minority position and remained such through most of the forties.

The Communist Party's greatest success in the late thirties was in creating a climate of opinion which became pervasive, deeply affecting writers and intellectuals who were not politically minded and who previously had had nothing to do with left-wing causes. Hemingway's *For Whom the Bell Tolls*, which Trilling reviewed in 1940, was one of many novels of the period that showed the influence of the Popular Front. But a more characteristic product of the new mood was John Steinbeck's *The*

*For Trilling Stalinism was not essentially a mode of social organization or type of politics but rather a cultural portent. In a letter of May 12, 1946, to the drama critic Eric Bentley, Trilling says that, in order to prevail, Stalinism as a political force requires "the death of the human spirit." Trilling believed that this corruption and death of the spirit were increasingly evident among American intellectuals. I am grateful to Professor Bentley for making available to me the relevant passages from that letter.

Grapes of Wrath, which appeared in the same year. Steinbeck's novel, which Trilling loathed on account of its sentimentality, was typical of the new fiction of social protest that had displaced the "proletarian novel" of the early thirties. *The Grapes of Wrath* was one of the first of the new protest novels to achieve a great commercial success. It was followed by many novels of a similar kind, as well as by Hollywood films reflecting the same mix of kitsch and liberal sentimentality.

Trilling's exasperation was directed as much at its audience as at the new protest fiction itself. Many of the middle-class liberals who sympathized with the suffering of the poor Okies of *The Grapes of Wrath* bowed to Stalinist propaganda in justifying the murder of millions in Stalinist purges. At the behest of the Popular Front, the American liberal imagination betrayed itself by whitewashing Stalin's crimes. Communist propaganda made for a liberal culture that was both sentimentally mindless and brutally repressive.

Trilling's response to the Stalinists is a literary man's response. The antidote he offers for vulgar Popular Front liberalism is "the literary imagination":

> To the carrying out of the job of criticizing the liberal imagination, literature has a unique relevance . . . because literature is the human activity that takes the fullest and most precise account of variousness, possibility, complexity, and difficulty.[9]

These key words are obliged to carry the weight of Trilling's argument, for he provides no sustained counterargument that will function as a substitute for Stalinism. Instead of a theory, Trilling advocates a certain *temper* that will serve as the context or anchor of an Arnoldian "criticism of life." Trilling's "variousness, possibility, complexity, and difficulty" are the equivalent for the American 1940s of Matthew Arnold's "disinterestedness." The key quotation, which Trilling cites many times, is from Arnold's essay "The Function of Criticism at the Present Time":

> [Criticism] must be apt to study and praise elements that for the fulness of spiritual perfection are wanted, even though they belong to a power which in the practical sphere may be maleficent. It must be apt to discern the spiritual shortcomings or illusions of powers that in the practical sphere may be beneficent.[10]

This formula allows Trilling to commend the "moral" vision of various conservative writers, such as Burke, Coleridge, and T. S. Eliot, while disavowing the implications of their thought for the "practical sphere," that is, politics.

It is an extraordinary balancing act. Trilling insists that he is a man of the left. Yet the disinterestedness that is the chief virtue of "the literary imagination" can only have the effect of defusing (radical) political passions, for no politics can appear as anything but degraded set against the Arnoldian standard of "spiritual perfection." It turns out that "the literary imagination" has the same neutralizing effect on politics as Arnold's "culture" and "criticism." It is an impossibly high standard against which to judge existing parties and States.

Trilling offers the literary imagination as a cure for the simplifications of the liberal imagination. In the preface to *The Liberal Imagination* he contrasts the "primal imagination" of liberalism with its "present particular manifestations." The function of the literary imagination in the American present is the work of retrieval, "to recall liberalism to its first essential imagination of variousness and possibility."[11] Trilling's essentialism is part of the generally idealist tendency of his thought. The story he has to tell is of a fall from a Platonic idea of liberalism to a corrupted political embodiment. The literary imagination will help to restore liberalism to its original, pure form. But, really, given Trilling's idealism, any political embodiment would represent a fall. It follows from this purism that the function of criticism is literally to "refine" liberalism, to clear away the material dross of Stalinism and progressivism.

Moral Realism

But Trilling is nothing if not dialectical. His idealism, derived from Arnold and Victorian moralism, is at odds with his realism, derived from Freud and the modernist revolt against Victorian idealism. He attacks the drab materialism and scientism of Stalinist liberalism in the name of the greater spiritual awareness of various conservative moralists in the line of Burke ar.. Coleridge, but at the same time he attacks writers like Sherwood Anderson for not being materialistic enough. Trilling's project of "refining" American liberal culture involves him in a number of confusing distinctions. It turns out that there is the right kind of materialism (Santayana's) and the wrong kind (Dreiser's), the right kind of idealism (Arnold's) and the wrong kind (Parrington's), the right kind of realism (Forster's) and the wrong kind (Anderson's).

Trilling's cultural politics in the forties involved a great fight about words, above all about who will define "reality." Realism was the dominant tendency in American literature and social thought; every right-minded liberal claimed to be a "realist." As the forties began, the Stalinists were generally thought to be the legitimate heirs of the realist revolt of the twenties and thirties against formalism and gentility. The opponents of the established left were dismissed as ghosts in flight from the real in their ivory towers. Trilling's self-assigned task in the forties was to redefine "reality" so as to wrest it from the Stalinists.

Trilling's polemic against the corrupted imagination of American liberalism is summed up in the phrase "moral realism." The phrase first appears in his writing in 1938 in an essay on E. M. Forster. There Trilling contrasts the American "hard-boiled" novelists deriving from Hemingway, who (Trilling says) are tough on the surface and sentimental within, with Forster, whose "work looks soft but inside is hard as nails."[12] Trilling attributes Forster's appeal to his "absolutely ruthless moral realism." This praise of toughness is toned down five years later in Trilling's book on Forster. There he glosses moral realism in these terms:

> All novelists deal with morality, but not all novelists, or even all good novelists, are concerned with moral realism, which is not the awareness of morality itself but of the contradictions, paradoxes and dangers of living the moral life.[13]

In short, "moral realism" is the imagination of complication.

"Moral realism" has a whole host of meanings, as it must to carry the burden of Trilling's message in the forties. Trilling links Forster's feeling for the complexity of moral fact with his "worldliness." Unlike the American realistic novelists who are his contemporaries, Forster is "too worldly to suppose that we can judge people without reference to their class." Trilling's celebration of Forster makes him sound like Balzac. He is credited with understanding "the way things go." He has "the sense of what houses, classes, institutions, politics, manners and people are like."[14] Trilling develops this sense of moral realism in 1948 in "Manners, Morals, and the Novel." The Stalinists, he says, had made it appear that morality was a simple affair, reducible to supporting a specific political party (the Communists). Using the classic European social novel as his model, Trilling argues for a very different idea of morality involved with money, class, and snobbery, in which manners and tone reveal a far more complex reality than Communist sloganeering.

Trilling uses "moral realism," as he does "liberalism," to suggest a large tendency, a medley of sentiments rather than a specific, clearly defined doctrine. In general, the phrase stands for the tragic sense of life. Trilling has in mind Freud's sense of the intractable conditions of existence and Niebuhr's idea of radical evil, but he also means to praise the ironic spirit of Austen and Henry James and the *brio* of Mozart and Stendhal. Probably the best way to understand this protean term is as the summation of everything that was missing in American literature in the thirties and forties. Trilling supplies our clue when he says, in his introduction to the second edition (1964) of *E. M. Forster*, that he wrote the book in 1943 as part of "a quarrel with American literature as at that time it was established." It was "against what seemed to me its dullness and its pious social simplicities [that] I enlisted Mr. Forster's vivacity, complexity, and irony."[15]

"Reality in America," the first essay in *The Liberal Imagination*, begins with a fierce attack on the simplistic conception of reality in a once-popular work of liberal cultural history, V. L. Parrington's *Main Currents in American Thought*. Parrington was a Jeffersonian progressive rather than a Marxist, but he had influenced a number of Marxist critics of the thirties, like Granville Hicks. Trilling very shrewdly relates Parrington's crudely simplistic conception of reality to a certain "political fear of the intellect." On the one hand, Trilling writes, Parrington is sure there is "a thing called *reality*; it is one and immutable, it is wholly external, it is irreducible." On the other hand, "he meets evidence of imagination and creativeness with a settled hostility the expression of which suggests that he regards them as the natural enemies of democracy."[16]

The same connection between a mistaken politics and a mistaken metaphysics is developed in the second part of "Reality in America," which contains Trilling's famous demolition of Theodore Dreiser. As is common in Trilling's criticism, he approaches

Dreiser through his commentators. The liberal critics prefer Dreiser to Henry James because of the former's awkwardness and dullness:

> His books have the awkwardness, the chaos, the heaviness which we associate with "reality." In the American metaphysic, reality is always material reality, hard, resistant, unformed, impenetrable, and unpleasant. And that mind is alone felt to be trustworthy which most resembles this reality by most nearly reproducing the sensations it affords.[17]

The liberal mind in America makes a cult of direct experience and a fetish of "reality." And yet, as Trilling observes, the more American writers and intellectuals seek the real, the more it eludes them. Trilling's example is Sherwood Anderson, whose reputation has never recovered from Trilling's 1941 essay:

> Anderson's affirmation of life by love, passion, and freedom had, paradoxically enough, the effect of quite negating life, making it gray, empty, and devoid of meaning. . . . His praise of the racehorses he said he loved gives us no sense of a horse; his Mississippi does not flow; his tall corn grows out of the soil of his dominating subjectivity.*

THE HERO OF CULTURE

What, then, is "moral realism"? Flexibility of mind, objectivity, a feeling for the importance of social class and manners, the tragic sense of life. Not surprisingly, given its many associations, the phrase comes to seem a little fuzzy at the edges. Still, it's always possible to catch the drift of Trilling's criticism if we keep in mind that it is reactive. And what he was reacting to in the forties was the pious simplicities of the left. He was always saying to his fellow liberals, "It's more complicated."

Trilling was always writing in opposition to the domination of intellectual life by the dispiriting categories of politics. He was "political," that is, in always writing against the influence of a simplifying politics. If his denunciation of Dreiser was unchar-

---

*"Sherwood Anderson," in *The Liberal Imagination* (New York: Viking Press, 1950), 28. Trilling's critique of "dominating subjectivity" in the novel has influenced a number of critics, among them John Bayley, in *Tolstoy and the Novel*, and Quentin Anderson, in his interpretation of classical American writing, *The Imperial Self: An Essay in American Literary and Cultural History*. I have discussed Anderson's book in the *New York Review of Books* (September 23, 1971).

acteristically fierce, the reason might be that in the early forties Dreiser was not just a novelist. He was also a figure in the culture with an important symbolic role in left-wing literary polemics. Trilling was not just responding to texts but to Dreiser's involvement in Communist propaganda campaigns in the thirties and the use that was made of him in the forties by Stalinist literary criticism.

It is in response to Dreiser the figure as much as to Dreiser the novelist that Trilling proposes, in "Reality in America," his counterideal of the writer as dialectician. Unlike Dreiser, Trilling's literary exemplars—he mentions Hawthorne, Melville, and Henry James—"do not submit to serve the ends of any one ideological group or tendency." Trilling's characterization of the American writer as moral realist suggests his own ideal image of himself as culture critic. Moral realism appears here as a totalization founded on ambivalence:

> In any culture there are likely to be certain artists who contain a large part of the dialectic within themselves, their meaning and power lying in their contradictions; they contain within themselves, it may be said, the very essence of the culture. . . . It is a significant circumstance of American culture . . . that an unusually large proportion of its notable writers of the nineteenth century were such repositories of the dialectic of their times—they contained both the yes and the no of their culture, and by that token they were prophetic of the future.[18]

The writer as culture hero contains within himself the essence of the culture, but as a dialectic rather than an undifferentiated monolith.

This passage calls to mind Trilling's long passage, which I quoted earlier, about Matthew Arnold and the French Revolution, in which Trilling imputes to Arnold an extraordinary vision of Burke and Voltaire moving forward hand in hand. Of Arnold's conception of the marriage of the best parts of Enlightenment liberalism and Romantic conservatism, Trilling had written: "From each [Arnold] desired to conserve the best, and consequently he gets his drubbings from all parties. . . . He sought to conciliate epochs and that is something that history but no single man can successfully do."[19] Trilling was engaged in a no-less-impossible task of conciliation. The only way he was able to sustain his totalization was, paradoxically, by raising his own contradictions to the level of an explanatory principle. Ambivalence and irresolution did not have to be seen as negatives but as evidence of negative capability. Negative capability, moral realism, the dialectical imagination: these are alternative terms for the double vision that is Trilling's distinguishing trait. One sentence of Scott Fitzgerald that Trilling quotes might serve as the epigraph to *The Liberal Imagination:* "The test of a first-rate intelligence is the ability to hold two opposed ideas in the mind, at the same time, and still retain the ability to function."[20]

Trilling's short essay on Fitzgerald in 1945 is a trial run for his much more ambitious essay on Keats six years later. The poet appears in that essay as the quintessential hero of culture, his heroism consisting in his ability to take "the dialectical view of any large question, . . . his refusal to be fixed in a final judgment." This, too, is self-portraiture, for Trilling's own faith consists in being able to do without a positive faith. Keats viewed Coleridge as an example of "irritable reaching after fact and reason." Unlike Keats himself, Coleridge lacked negative capability. He was incapable, Keats says, of "remaining content with half-knowledge."[21]

It's possible to see why Trilling should have praised a worldview that dignified and legitimized his own uncertainties. I have remarked on Trilling's double life, the division between uptown and downtown, literary humanist at Columbia and political man south of 14th Street. That ambivalence appears also in Trilling's blend of Victorian high-mindedness and modernist demystification, refinement and polemic, traditionalism and insurgency, gentleman and Jew. Later he would rationalize his ambivalence in terms of philosophical dualisms such as Schopenhauer's will and representation, Nietzsche's Dionysus and Apollo, Freud's Eros and Thanatos. These oppositions come to a focus in his last book, *Sincerity and Authenticity,* which does not unambivalently decide in favor of either.

The extraordinary thing is that Trilling was able to use his uncertainties for positive ends. His difficulty in making up his mind helped him to speak for an entire literary generation. In the thirties the writers and intellectuals who commanded attention were those who were most dogmatic. Complicated minds like those of William Faulkner and R. P. Blackmur were mainly ignored. Liberal intellectuals flocked, instead, to unresonant and simplifying minds like those of Granville Hicks and the left-wing playwright Clifford Odets. But as the liberals moved away from the radicalism of the thirties, Trilling's complicated blending of modernist sensibility and enlightened politics provided just the "modulation"—a favorite word of that postradical decade—an entire generation was seeking. The educated class was ready, after two decades of simplistic rallying cries, to consider that things might in fact be more complicated than they had once believed. A new kind of cultural hero appeared on the left. The self-divided intellectual, who had been the butt of Communist ridicule in the thirties, now replaced the revolutionary proletarian as possible redeemer of society. Trilling's best essay of the forties, on Henry James's novel *The Princess Casamassima*, is also his fullest statement of that enabling myth, of the self-divided man as cultural hero.

The Autobiographical Myth

The essay on *The Princess Casamassima* has been praised by Joseph Frank as "among the finest performances of contemporary criticism."[22] It is certainly a brilliant performance, but it tells more about Trilling's preoccupations in the forties than it does about the novel that Henry James wrote. James's story is a plausible pretext but, finally, only a pretext for Trilling.

Since I want to compare Trilling's reading of *The Princess Casamassima* with my own, it will be helpful to have in mind some details of the plot. Hyacinth Robinson, the young hero of the novel, is the illegitimate son of a French dressmaker from the lower classes and an unknown Englishman, thought to be a lord. Hyacinth grows up poor but respectable, his early life shadowed by the death in prison of his mother, who had been sentenced for killing his putative father. The boy has artistic ability and is apprenticed at an early age to a bookbinder. Through his work Hyacinth becomes involved with a circle of anarchist terrorists, and on one fateful night he pledges himself to commit whatever act of terrorism—including assassination—he may be ordered to carry out by the anarchist leadership. In the meanwhile, however, Hyacinth has been initiated into the very different world of the Princess Casamassima. Without intending it, the beautiful princess is responsible for Hyacinth's conversion to the cause of "civilization," so that he now wants to save the wonderful things rather than destroy them.

"Civilization" in this novel stands for the world "raised to the richest and noblest expression." For Hyacinth, as for James himself, the supreme expression of civilization is art, which includes beautiful manners as well as magnificent buildings and artifacts. The novel is structured about a double reversal. Just as Hyacinth has been converted from his revolutionism to a conservative appreciation of the world as it is, with all its injustice, the Princess has moved in the opposite direction, finding her reality not in the privileges of her own class, which Hyacinth now wishes to preserve, but in the aspirations of the disadvantaged. The Princess takes up with Paul Muniment, a working-class friend of Hyacinth and a most implacably single-minded revolutionary. Hyacinth finds himself betrayed in his affections by the man who is his closest friend and the woman who is his inspiration. Feeling himself bound by his commitment to the anarchists but disillusioned with their program, Hyacinth commits suicide.

James's canvas is crowded, as befits a London novel in the Dickens manner, but the meaning is as clear as the novel's hourglass shape. James seeks an effect like that of his later novel *The Ambassadors*, another novel of aesthetic initiation with the same hourglass structure. In *The Ambassadors*, Lambert Strether has been sent on a mission to rescue young Chad Newsome from the enticements of Paris. Chad's mother wants him back in Woollett, Massachusetts, to take up his place in the family business. Strether hopes to marry the grand matriarch, and his own future is bound up with the success of his ambassadorial mission. When he arrives in Paris, he discovers that young Chad is quite ready to leave his older mistress and come home. But in the meanwhile the older man has himself been enchanted by Chad's lover, who symbolizes for him the beauty and high civilization of the Old World. In the novel's reversal, the ambassador from the New World finds himself, at the risk of his own future, urging the young prodigal *not* to go home. The structure of the plot is similar to that of *The Princess Casamassima*, and the symbolic role of Madame de Vionnet is like that of the Princess. Strether resembles Hyacinth in his discovery of the glory and grandeur of "civilization." But, again like Hyacinth, this hero of sensibility comes to his aesthetic initiation too late; his heightened capacity for moral-aesthetic appreciation costs him his future.

The Princess Casamassima is a hybrid novel, a blending of James's grand theme of aesthetic initiation with the determinisms, hereditary and environmental, of Zolaesque naturalism. The mix does not work because the form of the art novel and the theme of radical politics are at odds. In contrast, *The Ambassadors* limits itself to the play of Strether's sensibility—it is an instance of the art novel pure and simple. What appears poignant in the awkward eagerness of Lambert Strether appears as mere fecklessness in Hyacinth Robinson. Like his name, Hyacinth is too flowerlike for his world; he is a Jamesian passionate pilgrim lost in the harsher circumstances of Dickens and Zola. *The Princess Casamassima* has its incidental beauties—no novel of Henry James is a complete failure—but Hyacinth is impossible as the protagonist of a political novel, and he is without weight as a hero of tragedy.

It is extraordinary to see what Trilling makes of this seemingly unpromising material. His essay is a *tour de force* of different critical approaches, but its most extraordinary feature is the way Trilling uses Hyacinth's story to forge his autobiographical myth. Hyacinth becomes a version of Trilling's own idealized self as a hero of culture. The major themes are all here: the outsider's dream of high culture, the legend of the Young Man from the Provinces come to conquer the great world, the sense of a special fate, the fastidious gentleman thrown among vulgar radicals, the impulse toward renunciation. These central themes of Trilling's career find better expression here than in *The Middle of the Journey*, the novel he was writing at about the same time. It is curious how Trilling's creative exuberance could be liberated in the form of the critical essay, when he could play off a pre-text, whereas in his fiction he appears terribly abstract, essayistic, and constrained.

What, then, does Trilling make of *The Princess Casamassima*? He celebrates James's novel as an "incomparable representation of the spiritual circumstances of the modern world." It turns out that these spiritual circumstances were essentially Trilling's own in the mid-forties: the struggle between the rival claims of social justice and the glory of high civilization, the conflict between mass-democratic values and art. Trilling's preferences are obscured by a flurry of those balanced sentences that we have found to be his hallmark. Hyacinth emerges not as a merely sensitive victim but as the Trillingesque "hero of civilization," an exemplary figure caught between two rights, as in Hegel's view of tragedy. He appears as a figure of immense symbolic importance who pays the price of his life in assuming the contradictions of his culture. I quote at length from Trilling's account of Hyacinth because this passage so clearly exemplifies Trilling's own dialectical habit of mind and because it apotheosizes the Trillingesque central man, the hero-martyr of culture:

> By the time Hyacinth's story draws to its end, his mind is in a perfect equilibrium, not of irresolution but of awareness. His sense of the social horror of the world is not diminished by his newer sense of the glory of the world. On the contrary, just as his pledge of his life to the revolutionary cause had in effect freed him to understand human glory, so the sense of the glory quickens his response to human misery. . . . And just as he is in an equilibrium of awareness, he is also in an equilibrium of guilt. He has learned something of what may lie behind abstract ideals, the envy, the impulse to revenge and to dominance. . . . But if the revolutionary passion thus has its guilt, Hyacinth's passion for life at its richest and noblest is no less guilty. It leads him to consent to the established coercive power of the world, and this can never be innocent. One cannot "accept" the suffering of others, no matter for what ideal, no matter if one's suffering be also accepted, without incurring guilt. It is the guilt in which every civilization is implicated.
>
> Hyacinth's death, then, is not his way of escaping from irresolution. It is truly a sacrifice, an act of heroism. He is a hero of civilization because he dares do more than civilization does: embodying two ideals at once, he takes upon himself, in full consciousness, the guilt of each. . . . By his death he instructs us in the nature of civilized life and by his consciousness he transcends it.[23]

This is very eloquent, but more revelatory, I think, as Trilling's idealized conception of himself than as an interpretation of Henry James's novel. The sensitive plant Hyacinth has become a fearfully portentous figure, a world-historical figure like Antigone in Hegel's theory.

What Trilling responds to most keenly in James is the novelist's feeling for the infinite complexity of consciousness and his affirmation of disinterested aesthetic contemplation at the expense of the active will. This aesthetic consciousness Trilling calls "love." It is an "intellectual love," making no claim on its object; it is static and intransitive, an alternative to the political realm of practice and struggle. Robert Boyers, in his valuable discussion of

Trilling's essay, remarks on Hyacinth's tendency to respond to the world "in the spirit of the passionately disinterested connoisseur who is too good to be violated by a practical idea of what had best be done."[24] This attitude, more appropriate to the artist than to the political actor, accounts for the reader's sense that not only Hyacinth but the novel itself are at odds with themselves.

Trilling discusses moral realism as a kind of intellectual love in his account of the Princess. That self-deluded lady brings ruin upon the hero by her mistaken belief that reality is "a thing, a position, a finality, a bedrock." Unable to hold two opposing ideas in her mind at the same time, the Princess wants to locate and possess reality once and for all, in the revolution, so that in identifying herself with the poor she can redeem the frivolity of her previous life. For Trilling, the Princess' folly anticipates that of the Stalinist fellow travelers of the forties. As with Nancy and Arthur Croom of *The Middle of the Journey,* the punishment for her corrupted will and mistaken conception of the real is to be condemned to perpetual unreality.

For Trilling the antitype of the Princess is her creator, Henry James. Trilling describes James as nearly godlike in his sublime disinterestedness:

> For the novelist can tell the truth about Paul and the Princess only if, while he represents them in their ambiguity and error, he also allows them to exist in their pride and beauty: the moral realism that shows the ambiguity and error cannot refrain from showing the pride and beauty. Its power to tell the truth arises from its power of love.[25]

Trilling finds an analogy for this disinterestedness in the imagined father of many children, who loves them all but without illusions as to their virtues and faults, who loves them "not because they are faultless but because they are they." Trilling's idea of the novelist's feeling for his characters as that of the ideal father for his children helps explain his preference for Tolstoy over Flaubert. He remarks on the "irritability" with which "Flaubert's objectivity is charged," contrasting it with the "affection" that accounts for "the unique illusion of reality" created by Tolstoy's writing.[26]

But the Henry James of *The Princess Casamassima* is a very long way from the Tolstoy, say, of *War and Peace.* Tolstoy was a great historical novelist as well as the loving father of his vast tribe of fictional characters. Trilling discusses *The Princess Casamassima* as if it belongs to the same genre. He reads it not as a novel of personal relations or as an American novelist's romance of "Europe" but as a great allegory of modern culture, based on the collision of social classes and great ideological demands. Trilling would place James's novel alongside *Lost Illusions* and *The Red and the Black* and *Sentimental Education* and other great European novels of society.

It is true that the "glory" to which Hyacinth responds, like the glory Strether perceives in Madame de Vionnet, is precisely historical. That history is manifested in great houses, great art, great personalities. But this is a connoisseur's experience of history, history as a museum, a collection of wonderful "things." The American artist can arbitrarily rearrange these things because, after all, there is no necessity about this history; it is not his. *The Waste Land* and Pound's *Cantos* are just such instances of artwork as museum; they are works founded on "traditions" which do not belong to any single culture or nation but are more or less arbitrary assemblages, homemade worlds. This is history as art, history as romance. Henry James has no place in the studies of the European novel of society that Georg Lukács and Raymond Williams have written. For in the European social novel, history is always living history, a set of processes that continue to operate in the present. Hyacinth Robinson is the hero of a very different kind of fiction, an American romance in which European history is rendered as the object of an aesthetic passion. He strives for, and achieves, a timeless vision, which, once achieved, leaves him little to do but die. Hyacinth's view of reality is altogether richer than that of the Princess, but, like hers, it is static, fixed, complete.[27]

In his fine appreciation of *The Princess Casamassima*, Trilling reveals his own unregenerate Americanness. Even in arguing for James's novel as a brilliant account of modern politics, Trilling reveals his own ambivalence about politics and, more generally, his ambivalence about history as the medium in which the self has its being. James's famous contrast of America and Europe implies the competing claims of art and history. Ambivalence about those claims appears in nearly every phase of Trilling's career. It appears with great insistence especially in the last few years of Trilling's life, when he seemed to be groping about for the ground theme underlying the various binary oppositions he had proliferated over the course of his long career.

The Imagination of Complication

I deal with the art/history opposition in some detail in this book's last chapter, but in the next chapter I turn to the novel and the three short stories Trilling published in the 1940s. My purpose is not so much aesthetic evaluation as interpretation of the social preferences revealed in those fictions. I read Trilling's fiction as a continuation of his cultural criticism, with this difference: his critical essays on the novel in the forties could be organized about the large, abstract dialectical oppositions I have considered in the present chapter, but his own stories and novel were obliged to dramatize and test those abstractions in particular situations. Trilling inevitably revealed more in his fiction than in his critical essays on fiction about the specific social preferences implied by these abstractions.

Chapter Five

Fiction as Criticism

N
ear the end of his life Trilling addressed a graduate seminar in literary criticism at Purdue University. To students who wanted to know how Trilling had come to criticism he began by saying, "I am always surprised when I hear myself referred to as a critic."[1] He had set out in the twenties, he said, not to be a critic but to be a novelist, and that early ambition had determined the direction of his criticism when, later, he abandoned the writing of fiction. Here is how, in 1971, Trilling defined "the nature of my work in criticism":

> I shall not attempt to be more specific about this than to say that my conception of what is interesting and problematical in life, of what reality consists in and what makes for illusion, . . . was derived primarily from novelists and not from antecedent critics or from such philosophers as speculate systematically about the nature and function of literature. . . . In remarking that my work in criticism took its direction from the novel, I have it in mind to point to its tendency to occupy itself not with aesthetic questions, except secondarily, but rather with moral questions, with the questions raised by the experience of quotidian life and by the experience of culture and history. . . .[2]

Trilling calls the Purdue seminar not the "appropriate" occasion for explaining why he gave up the writing of fiction. He goes on to say, rather mysteriously, "and perhaps such an occasion will not ever present itself."[3] But it seems clear from what he does say that he only came to a sense of himself as a critic fairly well along in his career. It is true that he had done a great deal of reviewing in the thirties. But it would have been possible to think of reviewing as only a sideline, done to make money or avoid working on a doctoral dissertation that was giving him trouble. Trilling's large-scale critical work *Matthew Arnold* may have been written out of his heart's desire as well as to satisfy a professional requirement, but it seems significant that after completing it he returned to writing fiction and never again attempted a similarly sustained work of criticism.

By the summer of 1939 he had written six chapters of a

77

novel. Shortly after that he abandoned the novel, but by June 1940 he had completed a *nouvelle*. In the introduction Trilling wrote for the reissue of *The Middle of the Journey* in 1975, he describes that novel as having begun as a *nouvelle*. Possibly the six abandoned chapters and the *nouvelle* that he completed in 1940 but never published became the basis of the later novel. In that case the writing of *The Middle of the Journey* would appear not as a sport amidst Trilling's mainly critical writings of the forties, but as the central project of that decade.* His career has a different shape than in our usual view of it if we conceive of Trilling as very much occupied with his own fiction in the twenties and forties, and only diverted from the path he had originally marked out for himself by his need in the thirties to establish himself in his academic career.

My purpose is to emphasize the importance in Trilling's early years of his sense of himself as a novelist rather than as a full-time critic, and the influence of his experience as a novelist on his later criticism. As he implies in his Purdue seminar, most American critics have looked to philosophy for their models. Trilling certainly had a philosophic mind—he was always exploring large questions such as those of fate and free will—but his primary education came not from philosophy but from novels. His feeling for manners and tone, for style as a manifestation of "quality of being," his satiric observation of the intellectual as a social type, his sense of art as a tissue of contradictions—these sensitivities belong to the novelist in him.

The essays in *The Liberal Imagination*, the most important of which concern novelists and the theory of the novel, served Trilling as blueprints for his own fiction. These essays, which established Trilling's reputation in the larger intellectual community, can be regarded, then, as grist for the fiction-writing project that culminated in *The Middle of the Journey*. But that novel, when it

*As earlier chapters of this book suggest, Trilling was slow in finding himself. Similarly, all of his major book projects were slow in maturing. *Matthew Arnold* (1939), *The Middle of the Journey* (1947), and *The Experience of Literature* (1967) each had a gestation period of nearly a decade. The seeming exception, *Sincerity and Authenticity* (1972), which he wrote quickly, is in fact the summation of an argument that had been implicit in his writing for at least twenty years. My speculation about the composition of *The Middle of the Journey* is based on unpublished letters of Trilling to Jacques Barzun at Columbia University Library to which access is restricted.

finally appeared, was a critical failure. Trilling never explained why, but he appears never to have attempted a long fiction after *The Middle of the Journey*. His success as a critic may explain his abandonment of fiction as much as the failure, with the public, of his novel. He was increasingly being confirmed in his new identity as cultural critic. It may well be, of course, that in the fifties and sixties he attempted stories that he later abandoned or that he completed stories that he decided not to publish. In any case, he published no new stories or novels after 1947.

But perhaps it was not necessary for him to write fiction to use his novelistic talents. He was able to harness those talents to his criticism. His biographical (and obliquely autobiographical) essays, on Henry James (1948), John Keats (1951), and Isaac Babel (1955), and later on James Joyce (1968), have the passion and personal intuitiveness that he could never tap in his own fiction. As a critic, that is, Trilling has the virtues of a novelist. Conversely, despite his limitations as a writer of fiction, that fiction remains valuable as criticism.

It is valuable, first of all, as literary criticism. His highly mannered style and fine-spun moral crises are an indirect criticism of the crudeness of the protest fiction that was the dominant form in the forties. But more importantly for my purposes, Trilling's situations and characters constitute a criticism of the cultural attitudes that were commonplace on the left. These stories might be read, without taking account of the cultural context in which they were written, as moral parables about the need to grow up to an acceptance of the limited and conditioned nature of human life. But the stories are not timeless fables and parables. The passage from innocence to experience is always embedded in a realistic social situation, and the tension between the abstract moral theme and the concrete social implication makes in each case for the interest of the story. For the tragic consciousness to which Trilling's protagonists grow up is like that of Hyacinth Robinson; it implies an accommodation to unjust society. These are very American stories, about the price of success.

"OF THIS TIME, OF THAT PLACE"

The first of these stories, "Of This Time, Of That Place," was published in 1943, but it dramatizes a situation that goes back to the mid-twenties. We have already considered it, in chapter 2, in relation to "Impediments," Trilling's first published story. Like "Impediments," it concerns the relationship between an emotionally distraught, lower-class character and a coolly controlled middle-class person to whom he comes for help. Both stories turn on the reaction of the rational man to the claim on him of the psychologically disintegrating man. The theme of madness always proved compelling for Trilling. Around the same time as "Of This Time, Of That Place," he took up the question of madness and creativity in one of his best essays, "Art and Neurosis," and twenty-five years later, at the end of his last book, *Sincerity and Authenticity*, Trilling came back to the same theme, in a biting attack on the British psychiatrist R. D. Laing. Madness was too serious, too real, for ideologically motivated sentimentalizing.

In "Impediments" both characters are undergraduates; in "Of This Time, Of That Place" the man of reason is a young college English teacher who must decide what to do about a brilliant but psychotic student. Ferdinand Tertan, the mad student, seems at first glance to have nothing in common with his teacher Joseph Barker Howe. Tertan is separated from Howe by his excessive emotionalism, his foreign-sounding name, and his manners and dress. In turn Howe's squeamishness about Tertan's threadbare suit and "musty odor" is one of the ways by which Howe himself is characterized. Despite his impulse to distance himself from Tertan, Howe agonizes about him. He befriends the disturbed student and acknowledges him as a fellow poet, but Howe sees that something is wrong with Tertan and knows that ultimately something will have to be done. The obvious solution is to turn the matter over to the Dean, but Howe feels a loyalty to his student that he can't rationally explain. He feels "he must not surrender the question to a clean official desk in a clear official light to be dealt with, settled and closed." The story's climax is Howe's almost involuntary overcoming of that scruple: "It would always be a landmark of his life that, at the very moment when he was rejecting the official way, he had been, without will or intention, so gladly drawn to it."[4] The story inquires into the significance of Howe's turning the case over to the Dean. It's a question for Howe himself as well as for the reader.

There is another student in Dr. Howe's class, a senior named Blackburn, who helps to fill out the drama and account for its resonance. Blackburn is a creature of "telegrams and anger," in E. M. Forster's famous phrase. A typical Forster public-school bully translated into an American college setting, Blackburn tries to blackmail Howe in quest of a better grade. When that doesn't work, he gets down on his knees and begs to be passed. Howe wonders if Blackburn isn't more insane than the clinically certifiable Tertan, but at the end of the story it is Blackburn who receives his degree and the Dean's blessing while Tertan, expelled from the college, stands outside the magic circle in his terrible isolation.

Trilling spells out the point of his story in his anthology *The Experience of Literature,* in which "Of This Time, Of That Place" is reprinted along with Trilling's commentary on it. In his commentary Trilling says that "there are kinds of insanity that society does not accept and kinds of insanity that society does accept."[5] Tertan is an instance of the former, and thus he must be institutionalized; Blackburn is an instance of the latter, and thus he can go on to reap society's rewards. As Trilling describes the moral of his story, it becomes yet another slap at the shallowness of American liberal culture. Trilling recalls that when the story was first published, it was difficult for his readers to accept that Tertan's fate was irreversible. They wanted to see Blackburn cast out. But Tertan's madness is very different from Blackburn's because it suggests irredeemable desolation. Tertan is "on the way," Trilling says, "to being beyond the reach of ordinary human feelings."[6]

Since characters in fiction suffer at the behest of their creators, the reader may wonder why Tertan has to be represented as beyond help. The answer is that only irreversible damage, not inequities that can be ameliorated, allows Trilling to make his familiar point about the incapacity of "our educated class" to face the facts of ruin and death. The story is arranged to make this point. The unwillingness of Trilling's original readers to accept that Tertan is indeed beyond help only reveals liberal shallowness, by exposing "our modern anxiety at confronting a painful fate . . . which cannot be said to result from some fault of society."[7] The story has a second polemical point. Trilling wants to rebuke popular notions about madness as the basis of poetic genius, as in Edmund Wilson's influential book of 1941, *The Wound and the Bow,* to which "Art and Neurosis" is a rejoinder.

But if we attend to Trilling's story itself, rather than to what he says about it, we see that it is more interesting than the teller's moralizing interpretation. Perhaps the best way to approach the story, and Trilling's fiction generally, is by way of the critical essays he was writing around the same time. Thus Trilling's conception of the culture hero, first developed in "Reality in America" and elaborated in his essay on *The Princess Casamassima*, provides a useful schema for understanding "Of This Time, Of That Place." In his essay on James's novel, Trilling describes the coexistence within Hyacinth Robinson of his egalitarian political ideal and his sense of the glory of the world with all its injustice. Joseph Howe can hardly be described, as Trilling describes Hyacinth, as a full-fledged "hero of civilization," but he is like Hyacinth in summing up in himself a large dialectical opposition. He embodies two ideals at once.

I remarked earlier on the ways Howe differs from Tertan. It is just as important to note their similarities. Although Howe casts Tertan in the role of the other, an alien who brings with him "the stuffy sordid strictness of some crowded, metropolitan high school," Howe is like Tertan in feeling alienated from the smug provincial society of Dwight College. As a new member of the faculty, Howe has few friends at Dwight. Moreover, his new book of verse has recently been savaged as "precious subjectivism" by a middlebrow critic much admired by his colleagues. To be sure, Tertan is a Romantic visionary in the manner of Blake or as depicted by William Collins. The poet as "rich-hair'd Youth of Morn" is a long way from Dr. Howe's private ironies, but by virtue of their intellectual seriousness both teacher and student are marginal in relation to the genteel philistinism of the college community. And so it is hard for Howe to turn his back on Tertan, for in some sense Tertan is Howe's double, his "secret sharer."

John Bayley has made the point that as a writer of fiction Trilling is never completely himself.[8] His stories are full of reminders, verbal and thematic, of the fiction he admires. His most important debt in the present story is to "The Secret Sharer," Joseph Conrad's mythic tale of a young sea captain's initiation, which is included, with Trilling's commentary, in *The Experience of Literature*. In his own story Trilling describes the young instructor's mood as he faces his first class of the fall semester in terms that echo the foreboding of Conrad's young sea captain as he assumes his first command: "The lawful seizure of power he was about to make seemed momentous." Conrad's story concerns the young captain's initiation into the mysteries of authority. This initiation occurs by way of the captain's curious relationship with his shadow, a romantically lawless seaman named Leggatt (legate), whom the captain hides in his cabin and sets free only after he has successfully piloted his ship through his first near crack-up.

Joseph Howe's relation to Tertan is part of *his* initiation. Tertan, too, is a dark, threatening double. One difference from Conrad, revelatory of Trilling's work as a whole, is that the romantic extremist Tertan is disavowed, not integrated into Howe's identity as the outlaw Leggatt is integrated into that of Conrad's young captain. As a result, Howe's initiation is shadowed by guilt and self-doubt. For his initiation has consisted in letting the Dean do society's dirty work. Howe's turning his student over to the Dean has not been an act of courage but of accommodation. This is not to say that he has acted in a brutally self-seeking way, but that his chameleon adaptation to the customs of the country have led him "to consent to the established coercive power of the world." And, as Trilling says of Hyacinth Robinson, "this can never be innocent."

According to Trilling's moralizing gloss, Howe has to learn that, although Tertan is sincere, dedicated, even brilliant, he is also irredeemably damaged. Despite his gifts and love of literature, Tertan is beyond help. The teacher's innocence must give way to experience. Thus the story is about Howe's accession to tragic knowledge. This is indeed part of the story, but a Hawthornesque tableau at the end suggests a more complex meaning. The story closes with the ritual of commencement. Howe appears at the ceremony arm in arm with the Dean and Blackburn in what amounts to a parody of social order and a grotesque emblem of the price of Howe's initiation into the Dwight College community. We learn that Blackburn, who should have failed Howe's course, has been the first man in his class to get a job and that Howe has been promoted to assistant professor. Meanwhile, Tertan hovers, a blighted figure, some distance away. He is outside the magic chain of human sympathy, as Hawthorne would have said. There is another Hawthorne touch when Howe has his photograph taken at commencement by the Dean's teenage niece, Hilda, whose name suggests *The Marble Faun* and its theme of the Fortunate Fall.

The story is complicated by plotting which balances Howe's success against Tertan's failure. Howe has acquired in the Dean a friend in power; he has been admitted to the inner circle of the college community; and his initiation has been confirmed by his promotion. Howe's life as a man is commencing; he is on his way to success. But that success is shadowed by the teacher's sobering knowledge of irreversible loss. At the end Tertan's "isolation made Howe ache with a pity of which Tertan was more the cause than the object, so general and indiscriminate it was." Howe grieves not only for Tertan but for his own lost youth and innocence. The story dramatizes an idea about growing up that is central to Trilling's essay two years earlier on Wordsworth's "Immortality Ode": "Inevitably we resist change and turn back with passionate nostalgia to the stage we are leaving. Still, we fulfill ourselves by choosing what is painful and difficult and necessary, and we develop by moving toward death."[9]

Trilling characteristically raises issues up to a high moral elevation, but Howe's ambivalence about growing up has a specifically social aspect. At the end he turns back in a halfhearted attempt to extricate himself from the Dean's grip so that he may go over to Tertan. But Tertan slips away and Howe never sees him again. The stage Howe has been leaving is the stage of identifying with this blighted boy. In turning away from his own marginality, Howe may be moving toward death, but he is more obviously moving toward assuming a place for himself in the great world.

Given that "Of This Time, Of That Place" is a story of the rise of Joseph Howe, it is more complacently solemn than it needs to be. But it won't do to deny its poignancy. Dr. Howe's moral pain is not as grievous as Tertan's emotional desolation, but it is real enough. That pain is involved with Howe's deep contradictions, his wanting to be both bohemian and respectable, poet and professor, adolescent and grown-up, outsider and insider. The key to the power of the story is the perilous balance of these contradictory impulses, one trend associated with "a sense of the social horror of the world," and the other with "a sense of the glory of the world." It's hard not to surmise that the ambivalence was Trilling's own, caught between the claims of his generation's vision of social justice and his powerful craving for success, acceptance, and assimilation into the larger society. Trilling in the forties was close to midpoint, as alive to one claim as to the other. The balance was delicate, but while it lasted Trilling produced his best work. "Of This Time, Of That Place" suggests that by 1943 the balance was already tilting toward assimilation, acculturation, accommodation.

"The Other Margaret"

Tertan in "Of This Time, Of That Place" may have been modeled to some degree on Bartleby the scrivener in Melville's story, which is also included, with Trilling's commentary, in *The Experience of Literature*. Trilling's next story, "The Other Margaret," calls to mind another Melville story, "Billy Budd," with its theme of motiveless malignity and metaphysical evil.* The good Margaret in Trilling's story, a sensitive, thirteen-year-old middle-class child, is as radically innocent as Billy Budd, and "the other Margaret," the black maid who cleans house for the good Margaret's parents, represents evil incarnate, like Claggart. Little remains of Joseph Howe's middle-class guilt as Trilling neatly divides up moral virtue according to social class. "The Other Margaret" belongs to 1945. It is as if, with the triumph of the democracies in World War II, Trilling had decided it wasn't any longer necessary to apologize for middle-class aspirations and values.

Margaret Elwin's father, Stephen, is the story's point-of-view character. At forty-one, Elwin is a successful publisher of scientific books. His sensibility, however, is more like that of a humanist intellectual than a scientist or businessman. He is a typical Trilling hero in that his thoughts are engaged almost exclusively with questions of conscience. "The Other Margaret" mainly concerns Elwin's reflections on two related themes: wisdom and heroism. Wisdom is summed up for Elwin in a Hazlitt quotation that he has puzzled over since he memorized it in high school: "No young man believes that he shall ever die." And heroism is symbolized for Elwin by the famous Roualt painting of a king,

---

*"Billy Budd" figures importantly in the plot of Trilling's novel, *The Middle of the Journey*. The reaction of different characters to Melville's story allows Trilling to make his point about the essential equivalence of ideological Stalinism and the reactionary religiosity in which some ex-communists, like Whittaker Chambers, were finding refuge in the 1940s.

blackbearded and crowned, facing in profile to the left, holding a spray of flowers in his hand. The story begins with Elwin standing in front of a reproduction of that painting which he has recently purchased. He imagines the king as one who has come to wisdom through suffering, who "has passed beyond ordinary matters of personality and was worthy of the crown he was wearing."[10]

As in a novel by E. M. Forster, the incidents that lead to Elwin's moral illumination are fairly trivial. Riding home on a Fifth Avenue bus, he sees an old conductor keep a young boy from boarding the bus. The boy is left in the street wounded by his experience of the world's cruelty. Here, as elsewhere, Elwin represses his anger despite his obvious identification with the "carefully reared child." Remembering all the advantages he himself has had and the conductor has missed, Elwin "tried to know the weariness and sense of final loss"[11] that explain the old man's cruelty. Instead of being angry, he is merely elegiac, recalling a better time when such things did not happen. When he gets home, he finds that his wife's experience of the lower orders has been no better. She tells about another bus conductor who had that day tried to insult a woman by pretending she was Jewish. And then, to make the day complete, there is trouble with the black maid, who has the same name as the Elwins' daughter. The maid has once again, apparently deliberately, smashed a piece of the Elwins' favorite china.

Mrs. Elwin has none of her husband's diffidence about anger toward social inferiors. She flatly declares that Margaret "is a thoroughly disagreeable person, a nasty, mean person."[12] Her daughter, the good Margaret, is scandalized by her mother. She has been taught in her progressive school that poor people are not responsible for their misdeeds; it's all the fault of society. At this point Stephen Elwin breaks into the discussion to challenge his daughter. He demands to know why "the other" Margaret shouldn't be considered responsible for her acts? Elwin now has a revelation. The meaning of the Hazlitt sentence he had pondered these many years is disclosed to him and transfigures his moral landscape. He now sees that, in the aspect of the knowledge of death, all people are equal in their responsibility, Elwin himself and his wife and daughter, the two bus conductors, the boy enraged against the conductor's injustice, Margaret the maid: "all of them, quite as much as he himself, bore their own blame. Exemption was not given by age or youth, or sex, or color, or condition of life."[13]

The good Margaret can only accept her father's wisdom after the maid has maliciously smashed on the floor a ceramic lamb the child had made in school as a birthday present for her mother. With that act the young Margaret is shocked out of her own lamblike innocence into experience. As Elwin now understands, his child, in resisting the idea of "the other" Margaret's responsibility, has been resisting the acceptance of her own. The story makes the same point as Gerard Manley Hopkins's poem "Spring and Fall," about another Margaret who must learn that "it is Margaret you mourn for." The story concludes with the hurt of the child's disillusionment and her father's inability to assuage that hurt.

"The Other Margaret" is clearly intended to be a poignant story about parenthood, about a father's pain in the face of his child's first intimation of mortality. But the effect of the story is very different. Stephen Elwin exemplifies a connoisseur's aesthetic relation to the moral life. His moral fineness, an assumption the story never questions, is demonstrated not by anything he does but by his fine sensitivity to various aesthetic objects—the Roualt painting, the family china, the daughter's ceramic lamb, even the "well-shaped head" of the schoolboy who is kept off the bus. With his dandified consciousness and complicated renunciations, Elwin resembles Eliot's Prufrock, but without any of Prufrock's self-irony. For Trilling is too identified with Elwin to see through him.

Elwin's solemnity is complemented by his wife's middle-class self-righteousness. Trilling seems blind to the unattractiveness of this feckless, self-absorbed husband and his blunt-spoken wife. His characteristic ability to see the complexities of a situation may have been sacrificed in this story to his polemical intention. The peculiar unpleasantness of "The Other Margaret" would seem to owe a great deal to Trilling's wish to take a slap at a certain kind of liberal sentimentalism that was rife in the mid-forties. The story was rejected by the *New Yorker*, which had lately been publishing a great number of social-protest stories about the cruelty of strong people in relation to the weak. Earlier in the same year Trilling had complained, in a review of Richard Wright's *Black*

Boy, about the tendency of protest fiction to represent the victims of the dominant culture as exempt from the flaws of their oppressors. The middle-class reader, Trilling says, is being "morally entertained by poverty, seeing it as a new and painful kind of primitivism which tenderly fosters virtue, or, if not virtue, then at least 'reality.' "[14]

The fiction that was written during World War II *was* mostly second-rate, infected equally by a dilute version of thirties liberalism, wartime propaganda, and the influence of Hollywood. And Trilling had a point, although it seems a small point in view of the moral issues raised by the war. The problem is that the pointedness that makes for effectiveness in his criticism proves in this story to be incompatible with the negative capability or "moral realism" that he elsewhere praises. In response to the simplifications of protest fiction, Trilling produces his own countersimplifications, flattering the reader rather less subtly by projecting an image of middle-class refinement and decency in a world in which everyone else is vulgar and threatening.

Despite all its moralizing about death and "wisdom," "The Other Margaret" is mainly about social class and may best be read as a gloss on Trilling's essay "Manners, Morals, and the Novel." In that essay, as in his essay on Scott Fitzgerald, Trilling insists that his emphasis on social class and manners by no means implies an endorsement of hierarchically organized class society. He argues that differences of class and manners are important in our actual lives, and it is therefore disingenuous to brush away these facts in our novels "even though to do so may have the momentary appearance of a virtuous social avowal."[15] By foregrounding social class, Trilling presents himself as a tough-minded realist. He is only showing the way things are, not taking sides or endorsing the present system of domination. But "The Other Margaret" dissolves this fine distinction by exposing Trilling's undifferentiated view of the lower classes as anarchical and depraved, and his uncritical identification with the refined middle-class character who resembles himself.

Trilling's social attitude in "The Other Margaret" is essentially a domestication, for American purposes, of Matthew Arnold's. In Elwin, Trilling presents one of Arnold's "remnants," the sensitive, artistic middle-class intellectual whom we know from "Dover Beach" and similar poems. In the bus driver and the black maid Trilling gives us the mindlessly brutal lower classes, Arnold's "populace." The basic situation pits the refined middle-class intellectual against the vulgar world.

"THE LESSON AND THE SECRET"

Stephen Elwin has a cultivated liberal consciousness and comfortable income, but he is not rich. In Trilling's next story, "The Lesson and the Secret," which also appeared in 1945, he takes up the very rich, the American counterpart of the class Matthew Arnold had called "barbarians." Scott Fitzgerald had thought that great wealth made for a difference of spirit that separated the rich from everyone else. He famously remarked to Ernest Hemingway: "The very rich are different from you and me." Hemingway, as we know, was unimpressed. "Yes," he countered, "they have more money." Trilling usually argues for Fitzgerald's view, but in "The Lesson and the Secret" he is not so sure. The American rich in that story are only a pale counterpart of the permanent and hereditary British aristocracy that Arnold had in mind.

In his essay of 1948 "Art and Fortune," Trilling says that the novel as an art form has as its work "the investigation of reality and illusion . . . in relation to questions of social class."[16] These questions of class, Trilling continues, have "in relatively recent times [been] bound up with money." But, he adds, "money and class do not have the same place in our social and mental life that they once had. . . . Money of itself no longer can engage the imagination as it once did; it has lost some of its impulse, and certainly it is on the defensive." In Trilling's view, the prestige of intellect had risen, and the prestige of wealth had declined. In this new situation, money, in order to be justified, had to be involved with virtue and with "the virtuous cultivation of good taste in politics, culture, and the appointments of the home."[17] Trilling appears to have been hoping that, with the revival of capitalism and with the postwar boom in culture, there might yet be a reconciliation of America's rich and powerful with America's intellectuals.

Similar thoughts are on the mind of Vincent Hammell, the hero of "The Lesson and the Secret." Hammell teaches an adult-education class called "Techniques in Creative Writing," in which all of his students are women of wealth and leisure. He hopes devoutly that his rich ladies will perceive the need to justify their wealth by "the virtuous cultivation of good taste." Unfortunately, however, his students care only about "the secret of selling." Their idea of the secret of art is the secret of "selling themselves" to the commercial magazines. Hammell is disappointed. He has an exalted view of the opportunities of the rich and can only lament his students' "meagerness," their lack of "the imagined appearance of wealth, the serenity and disinterestedness to which wealth is supposed ideally to aspire."[18]

Hammell's notions about the rich are bookish. Aristocracy for him means what Trilling says it did for Fitzgerald, "a kind of disciplined distinction of personal existence." For Hammell, that is, wealth is an aesthetic fact. It has nothing to do with power, everything to do with style. Hammell looks at society as an aesthetic spectacle, in which virtues and vice manifest themselves as manners and taste. His students fail him not because they are bad but because they are petty. They wholly lack the loftiness of conception of a true aristocracy. Tocqueville believed that although aristocrats are often very tyrannical in their actions, they are rarely small-minded in their thoughts. Dr. Hammell's ladies are altogether petty. They manifest America's failure to produce a true aristocracy or the large-souled personalities that such a class is supposed, ideally, to make possible.

"THE MIDDLE OF THE JOURNEY"

In "The Lesson and the Secret" Trilling takes up the philistine rich. In his novel of 1947, *The Middle of the Journey*, he examines the philistines in the American educated middle class. Nancy and Arthur Croom represent Trilling's major effort to represent the Stalinist fellow traveler as a social type. *The Middle of the Journey* is unsuccessful as a novel, but it is interesting as Trilling's portrait of the self-deluded liberals in opposition to whom his best criticism of the forties was written.

In the preface to the 1975 reissue of his novel, Trilling explains that he had tried to "draw out some of the moral and intellectual implications"[19] of the liberal intellectuals' attraction to communism. Those implications are formidably abstract. The story takes place in the second half of the 1930s, when radical intellectuals were arguing about the Party's new Popular Front strategy, the Moscow Trials, the defense of Trotsky, and the Spanish Civil War. Yet not one of these debates of the time is mentioned. It is possible to make out that Arthur and Nancy Croom are fellow travelers, but they have little existence apart from certain moral and cultural attitudes—about responsibility, the working class, the future, death, etc. We learn nothing of what Communist Party front groups they have worked in, what sectarian struggles they have fought, or what radical magazines they read or have written for. And because it is summer and they are staying at their vacation house in rural Connecticut, we do not get any sense of their normal everyday life.*

What Trilling is striving for is a fiction of ideas, like *The Magic Mountain*, and for that purpose he stages his drama far from the centers of ideological struggle. The Crooms' pastoral retreat is no sanitarium, but Trilling's protagonist, John Laskell, has just recovered from a near-fatal illness and is visiting the Crooms to convalesce. Like the Crooms, Laskell has flirted with communism, but now, as with some of Thomas Mann's heroes, his spiritual life is liberated by the disease of his body. His nearness to death awakens him to life and strengthens him in resisting the inhuman ideologies that would claim him for their own. Apart from Mann, the main influence on Trilling's conception is probably E. M. Forster and the sentence from *Howards End* that is Trilling's preeminent touchstone for thinking about the moral life: "Death destroys a man but the idea of death saves him."

In the middle of his journey John Laskell is initiated into the state of doubt but finds his freedom sickening. Standing at the train station waiting for the Crooms to pick him up, Laskell experiences a "vertigo of fear" that will never leave him. That irrational terror, coming upon him totally unexpectedly, is "the worst experience he or any man could have." Laskell's experience is like the echo in the Marabar cave in Forster's *Passage to India* that de-

---

*Diana Trilling's complaint about Eleanor Clark's novel *The Bitter Box* (1946) might be directed against *The Middle of the Journey*. Amidst her praise of Clark's novel, Mrs. Trilling faults it for not "actually naming its parties, newspapers, and magazines, instead of dealing with them in anonymity or pseudonymity" (514). See p. 55, above. Eleanor Clark and Lionel Trilling steered away from naturalistic detail for similar reasons, associating it with the social-realist fiction that was the counterpart in literature of a corrupted liberalism in politics.

stroys old Mrs. Moore's will to live. One difference is that Trilling's symbol of nullity has contracted to the dimensions of a shiftless handyman named Duck, who works for the Crooms. Duck's failure to pick up Laskell at the station, as he had promised to do, becomes for the stranded convalescent a symbol of the terrible vacancy at the heart of things. It is a fairly heavy load of symbolic baggage for so small a character.

Duck becomes associated in Laskell's mind with the image of "the corpse of a huge white moth." Trilling draws here on a powerful tradition in American literature of imagining a universe without God as a terrible blankness. But in Melville ("The Whiteness of the Whale" chapter of *Moby-Dick*), Frost (the poem "Design"), and Poe (*The Narrative of Arthur Gordon Pym*), that ghastly whiteness is an attribute of Nature. In *The Middle of the Journey*, as in "The Other Margaret," the nihilism of the universe is associated with a particular social class: the working class. But if for Laskell Duck symbolizes nullity, for the Crooms he is reality itself. He is "a manifestation of ordinary life and as such he gave them moral pleasure." The Crooms admire Duck's skill with his hands and his coarseness of speech, and, despite their own comfortable family life, they romanticize "his resistance to the claims of domesticity, his outspokenness about these claims and his rejection of his wife's gentilities."

If the Crooms are sentimental about the working class, they are totally incompetent in the face of death. They are embarrassed by Laskell's illness and what they take to be his morbid preoccupation with it:

> If Laskell's preoccupation were looked at closely and objectively, they seem to be saying, might it not be understood as actually an affirmation of death, which is, in practical terms, a negation of the future and of the hope it holds out for a society of reason and virtue. Was there not a sense in which death might be called reactionary?[20]

The Crooms, then, are Trilling's philistines. But just as Trilling's American aristocracy differs from Arnold's paradigmatic barbarians in *Culture and Anarchy*, so do his philistines differ from Arnold's. In the British 1860s, the enemies of Arnoldian culture were legion. In religion they were dissenting, in ethics utilitarian, in economics laissez-faire. Altogether, Arnold's philistines represented the dominant tendency of the British middle class. By the time we get to Trilling, philistia has shrunk. At least, Trilling is taking on a smaller part of it than Arnold did, for in his writing the philistines are all liberal intellectuals. Cultural criticism has been obliged to narrow its focus since the Victorian heyday of this kind of writing. Whereas Arnold or Ruskin could address themselves to the English nation as a whole, Trilling could speak only in the name of one group of left intellectuals, a minority group, to another, more dominant group. Trilling and his group had little influence in the forties on intellectual circles outside of New York and even less impact on the national polity. To be sure, British cultural criticism lost some of its scope and confidence in the Edwardian period, but enough remained still to offer considerable contrast with Trilling's work in the forties.

The narrowing of focus is clear if we compare *The Middle of the Journey* with E. M. Forster's novel *Howards End*. In Forster's novel the Wilcoxes and Schlegels represent the opposing parts of the great British middle class. The Wilcoxes are entirely without intellectual interests. At their best they have "character" and carry on the solid virtues of the Victorian administrative-commercial middle class; at their worst they are stupid and violent, without any sense of an inner life. The Schlegels, on the other hand, live on their ideals and inherited capital; they represent Forster's own Cambridge-Bloomsbury culture. Trilling's version of the conflict between opposed parts of the middle class limits that conflict to an internecine battle between liberal intellectuals, some fellow travelers and others ex-fellow travelers.

But Trilling has done something new with the scheme he has taken over from English liberal humanism. Duck Caldwell is recognizable as an updated version of the working-class Chartists who alarmed Matthew Arnold. But he is also an early study of totalitarian mass-man, a potential fascist in the American countryside. Hannah Arendt and Norman Mailer would soon do more with this type in *The Origins of Totalitarianism* and *The Naked and the Dead*. And Kermit Simpson, the novel's rich left-wing magazine publisher, is no simple instance of Arnold's "barbarians." Rather, Simpson is a study in radical chic; he seeks absolution for the sin of being rich by entrusting his moral life to Gifford Maxim, the revolutionary who shocks his fellow-traveling admirers by renouncing revolutionism.*

Otherwise, all the major characters are middle-class intellec-

*Trilling writes very interestingly in the preface to the 1975 reissue of *The Middle of the Journey* about Whittaker Chambers as the real-life model for Maxim.

tuals, distinguished one from another not by class but by their ideas. The Crooms, Gifford Maxim, and John Laskell represent, in a fairly schematic way, the major possibilities of belief for intellectuals in midcentury America who had been affected by the experience of communism. The emphasis on ideology is central to Trilling's conviction that the novel of the future would take account of the diminished concern, after the 1930s, with class and class conflict. Instead of conceiving of characters in terms of their social class, the novelist would conceive of them in terms of their ideological affiliations: "Ideological society . . . has nearly as full a range of passion and nearly as complex a system of manners as a. society based on class."[21]

This passage, from Trilling's 1948 essay "Art and Fortune," shows how he was trying to substitute cultural categories for the political categories of the thirties, displacing Marxist materialism with his own emphasis on ideas. Trilling was inventing his own kind of criticism—cultural criticism—as he went along. The invention of that project was itself his most original act of criticism.

Not everyone appreciated it. *The Middle of the Journey,* which otherwise attracted little attention, did receive one review that raised serious questions about Trilling's capacity as a novelist that bear also on his practice as a critic of literature and culture. Since Robert Warshow's devastating review may have been a factor in Trilling's abandoning the writing of fiction, it deserves some consideration. Warshow's specific criticisms come back to Trilling's inveterate abstractness of mind, his incapacity to deal with experience as experience. Warshow observes the oddity that Trilling the Freudian should show such "surprisingly little interest in the deeper layers of motivation." As Warshow says, Trilling "makes it appear as if the surrender to Stalinism or its rejection was mainly a matter of philosophical decision."[22] Warshow is equally acute on other contradictions. Trilling takes his stand as a historically minded critic, yet the characters in his novel "exist in a kind of academic void of moral abstractions, without a history." Such a fictional strategy must be misleading, Warshow says, because "Stalinism was in the fullest sense a historical experience, a particular response to particular historical pressures."[23] In the end, Warshow argues, Trilling has not escaped the ideological habit of mind—he has merely reversed the valences. Trilling "reduces the whole problem of modern experience to a question of right and wrong opinion."[24]

Warshow's argument is mainly valid. Although Trilling praises Tolstoy for his disinterested love of his characters, he himself is unable to render character in anything like its existential variousness and complexity. In general, he is too concerned to judge his people. Trilling's characters *are* their ideas. When, as in the case of the Crooms, those ideas are inadequate, when we discern the shallowness of the Crooms' view of the working class and of death, we have seen all there is to see about them. Their interest is exhausted in our judgment of their sentiments and opinions. Trilling's critical essays are improved by their novelistic virtues; the fiction, on the other hand, is excessively schematic, and the characters live only in their moral passions.

But *The Middle of the Journey* is more interesting than this criticism suggests. For, in emphasizing the "question of right and wrong opinion," Warshow neglects the most original element in Trilling's critique of the intellectual class: his displacement of interest from ideas in themselves to the way those ideas are held. If the Stalinists suppress "gratuitous manifestations of feeling" for the sake of ideological correctness, anti-Stalinists will need to define themselves differently. And that new mode of self-definition will not reduce simply to a question of different opinions but will involve the *manner* in which opinions are held. What is at stake is authenticity. The main charge against the Crooms is not stupidity or evil but bad faith.

Warshow's critique says nothing about the question of *style*, which more and more tended to displace the question of right and wrong opinion in Trilling's writing. We have seen Stephen Elwin reflecting on his Rouault in "The Other Margaret." Similarly, in *The Middle of the Journey* Laskell's superiority to the Crooms is shown as much by his rapt appreciation of the shape of teacups and bowls as by his unillusioned perception of Duck Caldwell. It is as if Trilling were saying that politically "correct" opinions, like those of the Crooms, may serve as a mask for envy or the will to power, whereas aesthetic sensibility is a truer index to the quality of a person's being. The present chapter has been about the critical implications of Trilling's fiction, and so I have largely neglected his style. But style itself was increasingly playing a central role in his evolving cultural attitude.

Trilling's own style, rather than the play of ideas as such, is the most interesting feature of *The Middle of the Journey*. There is one effect, in particular, which Trilling found exemplified in Allen Tate's novel, *The Fathers*, when he reviewed it in 1938: "the strong tension of [Tate's] style which comes from the brutality of the 'abyss' being set against the narrative's delicacy and control."[25] Trilling himself achieves this stylistic effect by means of nuance and indirection. John Bayley describes it finely in the most intelligent appreciation Trilling's novel has received. The subject of *The Middle of the Journey*, as Bayley says, is the characters' preoccupation "about how to live, how to shape and face the future." But the art of the book "is in love with the past and on the side of death."[26]

The cool judiciousness of Trilling's prose is perfectly in accord with the displaced and empty feeling John Laskell has as he recovers from his nearly fatal illness. Nothing in the novel is as real or as profoundly felt as Laskell's love affair with the flower in his sickroom. His sub-Lawrentian sex play with Emily Caldwell is pallid in comparison with his romance with death. The quality of being implied by Laskell's wish for perfect passivity has little to do with politics of any kind. It suggests, rather, a will to remove the self from ideological turmoil, from struggle, from history, if not from life itself. Much more obviously than in the case of the Marxists whom Trilling attacks, this style implies a wish to be released from the burdens of conditioned existence, indeed from the burden of having a self at all. This sense of the self as puzzle and burden would become the central theme of Trilling's writing in the 1950s.

Chapter Six

The Disintegrative Process

The post-World War II decade was a time of readjustment for all the New York intellectuals. Some, like Philip Rahv, found themselves "homeless radicals," rendered superfluous by Stalin's betrayal of their revolutionary faith. In his 1946 essay "Arthur Koestler and Homeless Radicalism," Rahv says that "the political-minded individual who is so unfortunate as to have been deprived of his faith is sure to find himself in the predicament of having virtually lost his historical identity."[1] John Laskell, in Trilling's *The Middle of the Journey*, is suffering just such a crisis. He, too, endures "the supremely painful experience of locating himself anew in a world now strangely drained of value."[2]

But Laskell is not Trilling. By 1946 Trilling himself was no longer a political leftist, except in some obscure, ultimate sense. His postwar writing is mainly concerned with a spiritual malaise of which politics is only one element. In his essay "Art and Fortune" (1948) Trilling alludes to that malaise in the course of a discussion of the decline of the novel as a literary form. He ascribes the diminished vitality of the novel to the collapse, after Hitler and Stalin, of the idea of progress. The novel had developed in a culture that held in tension a belief in human goodness and a belief in human depravity. But now, Trilling says, "society's resistance to the discovery of depravity has ceased. . . . Indeed, before what we now know the mind stops; the great psychological fact of our time which we all observe with baffled wonder and shame is that there is no possible way of responding to Belsen and Buchenwald. The activity of mind fails before the incommunicability of man's suffering."[3]

Although this is the only direct reference to the Holocaust in Trilling's postwar writing, the Nazi crimes against humanity and Stalin's comparable barbarities are the major facts of which his essays try to take account. But the terror of recent history appears only in highly mediated ways. Mainly Trilling reacted against the

97

cultural-ideological moves of others who were responding more directly to the war. Thus Trilling frequently noted in essays written between 1948 and 1952 how evil had achieved a new glamor among literary men. He commented with some coolness on "those desperate perceptions of our life which are current nowadays among thinking and talking people."[4] Nearly twenty years before it became commonplace to attack the Waste Land view of modernity, Trilling had already taken account of the way in which a certain "desperate" idea of modernity was already turning into a cliché.

In his most important essay of the postwar period, "William Dean Howells and the Roots of Modern Taste" (1951), Trilling cites the following passage from Hannah Arendt's *The Origins of Totalitarianism,* which had just been published:

> To yield to the process of disintegration has become an irresistible temptation, not only because it has assumed the spurious grandeur of "historical necessity" but also because everything outside it has begun to appear lifeless, bloodless, meaningless, and unreal.[5]

Trilling relates Arendt's idea of the disintegrative process to the glamor of evil in modernist literature. That glamor, he says, is dangerous because a culture that overvalues the awareness of evil and extremity will become insensible to the possibilities of goodness such as Howells imagined them. Such goodness, the goodness of quotidian life, will come to seem "lifeless, bloodless, meaningless, and unreal."

In reaction against the connoisseurs of disintegration Trilling attempted in the postwar years to rehabilitate the imagination of life's possible goodness. The attempt to recover the lost imagination of happiness was a serious project. If Trilling was not adequate to it, neither was any other writer of the fifties. What had been lost was not so easily recovered. Trilling tried to encourage a more balanced view of the human condition by recalling his readers to the solid virtues and sociable sentiments of nineteenth-century middle-class culture. But William Dean Howells, after all, was no real alternative to the modern imagination of evil. "Desperate perceptions" could not be answered by Howells's flaccid perceptions or his bland domesticity. Neither could they be answered by privatism, or biologism, or various other solutions Trilling proposed in the fifties.

Neither could the imagination of extremity be the all-purpose

clue to the fifties as Stalinism had been Trilling's clue to the forties. For whereas Trilling had struggled against Stalinism with all
his being, he was more than half in agreement with the spirit of
disillusionment of the fifties that he sometimes lamented. Indeed,
one of the main arguments of *The Liberal Imagination* had been
the need for intellectuals to recover the sense of tragedy. Trilling
only objected to the emphasis on human wickedness in the early
fifties as it became ideologized and thus an obstacle to fresh
thought. He never attacked the influential theologian of Original
Sin, Reinhold Niebuhr, nor did he question the turn to religion
among many literary intellectuals.

But Trilling's essential agreement with the tendency that in
some respects he lamented was not the only reason that the imagination of evil and extremity could not serve him as the single
"distinct and illuminating idea" to unify his cultural criticism.
For the emphasis on evil was only one theme among many in a
complicated, fluid cultural situation. The collapse of left-wing
politics and the "progressive" culture that had supported it had
ushered in a new age of multiplicity. William Phillips, the editor
of *Partisan Review*, has in his recent memoir described the postwar situation in which intellectuals like himself were obliged to
find their bearings. He says that the most striking characteristic of
the postwar period has been "its kaleidoscopic quality, its shatter-
ing into literally dozens of currents, its endless contradictions, its
amnesia, its cultism—on the whole, its appearance of dispersion,
like a galaxy of stars moving in all directions."[6]

What Phillips is describing is the end of a literary-
intellectual culture unified by Marxism. For many ex-radicals of
the thirties there never was a new substitute-faith. There was only
leftover life to live, to be spent in quarreling with and later
mourning former friends and in undertaking a seemingly endless
inventory of losses. Trilling's situation following the collapse of
the left was not as dire, because he had been less fully committed
to revolutionism in his youth. His confusions had less to do with
communism as "the god that failed" than with the loss of
Stalinism as a steady, dependable object of his polemic.

Inasmuch as Stalinism became nearly totally discredited
among intellectuals in the Cold War years, Trilling's battle against
it can be said to have ended in unconditional victory. Yet, as it
turned out, the loss of the old enemy was a deprivation from

which his criticism never recovered. In the preface to *The Liberal Imagination* Trilling refers to John Stuart Mill's wish that liberals like himself might always have the benefit of testing their ideas against a powerful and cogent adversary. What Mill says, in his essay on the conservative Coleridge, Trilling might well have said in relation to the Stalinist left: "Their weakness is what fills us with apprehension, not their strength."[7] For Trilling was a reactive critic, and without a clear-cut position to define himself against he became vague and rudderless. His criticism had previously relied upon a situation in which sharply focused political alignments could be taken for granted and used as a launching pad for cultural reflection and recommendation. Now, with the collapse of the left, Trilling had difficulty finding a new organizing idea. American culture and society had always been heterogeneous and fragmented, but in the forties Stalinism and the struggle against it had made social life seem less amorphous. With the fifties and "the end of ideology," the fragmented quality of American culture came to seem its most characteristic feature. In the thirties and forties Trilling's writing had cohered about a single major book project; in the fifties he published only essays and introductions, each one a new beginning. It was not until the sixties that he hit upon a theme ("the adversary culture") that caught on as "the liberal imagination" had in the forties.

The fragmentation of Trilling's criticism in the fifties is evident in the two very different critical roles and personae he assumed. The author of the essays Trilling wrote in the forties for *Partisan Review* was still an avant-garde intellectual writing for a very small audience of similarly marginal high-culture intellectuals. The introductions that Trilling wrote in the fifties for selections of the Readers' Subscription book club was a very different figure, the image of the urbane belletrist. The new role expresses at least a partial repudiation of the avant-garde heritage he had previously celebrated as a corrective to the simplifications of cultural Stalinism. The avant-garde intellectual was supposed to be alienated, agonized, intransigently adversary in temper. The book club persona that Trilling projected was relaxed, comfortable, at ease in the world.

But the Trilling of the book club introductions coexisted with another persona, which one finds in the longer essays Trilling wrote between 1950 and 1954 and which are reprinted in *The*

Opposing Self. In those longer, more ambitious essays Trilling registers the demoralization of the time. He is not the friendly, confident guide of the book club essays but a deeply pessimistic critic increasingly disenchanted with social existence and detached from the political-cultural controversies to which he had been so attentive in the essays of *The Liberal Imagination.* This other Trilling becomes ever more abstract, aspiring, it would seem, to the historical criticism of consciousness in the Hegelian manner rather than the concreteness and shorter views of the practical man of letters we meet in the book club essays.

Still the two Trillings have a good deal in common. In both the book club introductions and the longer essays he is in retreat from an earlier conception of the critic as sentry at the crossroads, highwire equilibrist, scapegoat who assumes the contradictions of his epoch. That is to say, Trilling is in retreat from radicalism in all its forms, cultural and political. The fact that all but one of the essays in *The Opposing Self* concern nineteenth-century authors suggests his retreat from literary modernism; and his praise of middle-class family life and middle-class values in general suggests his retreat from politics. There is much to say about Trilling in the fifties, when, as Irving Howe has recently observed, he was "the most subtle and perhaps most influential mind in the culture."* In the present chapter I mainly discuss Trilling's modulations as they bear on society. In the next chapter, which also concerns the fifties, I focus on Trilling's use of Freud and his increasing attention to ideas of "the self."

THE CRITIC AND THE INSTITUTIONAL LIFE OF LETTERS

After World War II, as after World War I, Americans of all classes had a fierce appetite for normalcy. Sharing in that postwar mood, one after another of the ex-Marxist intellectuals renounced his characteristic posture of alienation from American middle-class society in favor of a considerable degree of accommodation. A *Partisan Review* symposium of 1952 celebrating "Our Country

---

*Irving Howe, *A Margin of Hope: An Intellectual Autobiography* (New York: Harcourt Brace Jovanovich, 1982), 229. The lack of attention to Trilling or any other literary intellectual is a major weakness of Richard Pells's otherwise useful recent book, *The Liberal Mind in a Conservative Age: American Intellectuals in the 1940s and 1950s* (New York: Harper and Row, 1985).

and Our Culture" marked the new mood. In his contribution Trilling does not quite say that the American cultural situation had become "really good," but he clearly welcomes the change and affirms that, "as against the state of affairs three decades ago, we are notably better off."[8] It's hard to think of the early fifties as a good time for poetry and fiction—there was nothing like the creative exuberance of thirty years earlier, when Cummings, Hemingway, Fitzgerald, and Dos Passos were emerging on a scene already crowded with figures like Eliot, Pound, Williams, and Stevens. But it is certainly true that criticial intellectuals like Trilling and his contemporaries at *Partisan Review* were better off.

The reasons for the improved situation of the intellectuals were partly political. The United States had survived the war relatively unscathed. The war had resuscitated the economy, and the country was now politically and militarily the most powerful nation on earth. As part of the Cold War competition with the Soviet Union, America sought to legitimize its political power by demonstrating a corresponding greatness in culture. Trilling was involved in that project as a contributor to *Encounter*, the British magazine financed by the CIA, and another magazine, *Perspectives USA*, a quarterly launched in 1952 by the Ford Foundation with the aim of dispelling old European stereotypes of American cultural sterility.

At home the expansion of a culturally ambitious middle-class audience made the fifties a good time for Trilling, whose message was specifically directed to that class. A number of Trilling's former students, now established in the New York publishing world, helped him to reach that expanded audience. At Doubleday and Company, Jason Epstein pioneered in the publication of quality paperback editions. One of the first books in the new Doubleday Anchor line was *The Liberal Imagination*, which proceeded to sell over one hundred thousand copies before going out-of-print. Two other former students, Gilman Kraft and Sol Stein, managed the Readers' Subscription and the Mid-Century Book Society respectively. These were highly influential new book clubs whose offerings were selected by Trilling, together with his coeditors Jacques Barzun and W. H. Auden. At the end of the decade, yet another former student, Norman Podhoretz, became editor at *Commentary*, in which position he solicited Trilling's contributions.

America in the fifties was a better place for literary critics in general. Professors in the humanities enjoyed greater social status and received more attention than ever before. This was the period Randall Jarrell aptly called "the age of criticism," when the mystique of the critic came close to displacing that of the creative artist. Almost all the best critics, except for Edmund Wilson, now had regular positions in the universities. The independent man of letters was still a familiar type in the American thirties, but by the fifties he had been replaced by the academic critic. Critics moved to the universities because it had become harder to survive on literary journalism than previously, but the main reason is that the old academic prejudice against criticism had diminished and more jobs were available. By the end of the fifties most of the critics who had previously been free lances—including Tate, Blackmur, Rahv, Howe, and Kazin—were teaching full time in university English departments. Trilling profited as much as anyone from the new prestige of the humanities. A wider diffusion of culture and a generally conservative mood made just the situation for which he was adapted. The newly educated middle class needed a mentor, and it was in that context that Trilling established himself not merely as one literary critic among many but as a figure in the culture.

The idea of the writer as "figure" first appears in Trilling's essays of the early fifties and reveals something about his ambition for himself in those years. He touches on this theme in two important essays, "William Dean Howells and the Roots of Modern Taste" (1951) and "George Orwell and the Politics of Truth" (1952), both of which are reprinted in *The Opposing Self*. Neither Howells nor Orwell was first-rate as a novelist, but Trilling is more interested in the roles they played in their respective cultures than he is in their creative achievements. Howells exemplifies for Trilling the decent republican culture of the American nineteenth century, when a boy growing up in a primitive Ohio town might decide on a career in literature and when his community was sufficiently enlightened that it "respected his enterprise and encouraged him in it." Trilling emphasizes the important public position to which Howells acceded as the most gentle but also most effective of literary patriarchs. As such Howells became a convenient target for iconoclastic critics of a later generation like H. L. Mencken, who became a patriarch in his turn. "And since Mencken," Trilling says, "no such figure has arisen."[9]

Orwell was also a figure, one of those writers, Trilling says, "who live their visions as well as write them, who *are* what they write, whom we think of as standing for something as men because of what they have written in their books."[10] Trilling identifies Orwell with "simple, direct undeceived intelligence"— intelligence, as against the abstract intellectuality of the self-deceived upper-middle-class radicals of the British thirties whom Orwell despised. In Orwell's time the middle-class normalcy of the institutional life of letters in the nineteenth century had been replaced by ideological sectarianism. For Trilling, Orwell's left-wing politics are less to the point than his traditionalism, the way he embodies the virtues of "an older and simpler time." Trilling's Orwell appears as a cultural conservative, a defender of family and nation. Against the tendency to see Orwell as a radical, Trilling associates him with "the old, reactionary Anglican phrase that used to drive people of democratic leanings quite wild with rage—'my station and its duties.' " According to Trilling, "Orwell would very likely have loathed that phrase, but in a way he exemplifies its meaning."[11] Thus Orwell is linked with Howells as a spokesman for solid, premodern, middle-class virtues, the decency, seriousness, orderliness, and sense of responsibility that, in Trilling's view, needed to be rehabilitated in the postwar period.

One last passage suggests Trilling's idea of the writer as figure in the culture. The passage occurs in the essay, "Why We Read Jane Austen," which he was writing in the last year of his life. In the essay on Austen, Trilling defines "figures" as

> creative spirits whose work requires an especially conscientious study because in it are to be discerned significances, even mysteries, even powers, which carry it beyond what in a loose and general sense we call literature, beyond even what we think of as a very good literature, and bring it to as close an approximation of sacred wisdom as can be achieved in our culture.[12]

Once again the writer is conceived not primarily as an artist in language but as a hero of culture.

The writer becomes a figure by becoming associated with "wisdom." And just as Stephen Elwin pursues wisdom in Trilling's short story "The Other Margaret," so did Trilling himself pursue wisdom and seek to embody it. The peculiar intensity of his readers' relationship to him in the fifties is a measure of his success in persuading those readers that he had succeeded in that high ambition. We miss the point of Trilling's work if we define it in exclusively literary terms. He sought a central role in the culture as explainer and guide to the perplexed, a conception of the teacher's role that brings him closer to Victorian sages like Newman and Arnold than to academic literary theorists of more recent years.

REFINING TASTE

Trilling's main link to the general culture in the fifties was his involvement as an editor and judge at two important book clubs, the Readers' Subscription from 1952 to 1959 and the Mid-Century Book Society from 1959 to 1962. For eleven years Trilling wrote short essays, of 1500-2500 words, introducing the monthly selections of these clubs. Writing on a more regular basis than he ever had before, Trilling published fifty short pieces in the *Griffin* and the *Mid-Century*, the magazines that announced these clubs' selections. A number of Trilling's introductions are included in *A Gathering of Fugitives*, a collection which he published in 1956, a year after *The Opposing Self*. Few commentators have noted Trilling's book club essays, just as few have taken seriously his time-consuming textbook projects of the sixties. This is unfortunate because some of Trilling's best writing is to be found in the book club pieces and in the short commentaries he wrote for his undergraduate reader, *The Experience of Literature*.

The book club editorship was Trilling's major effort in the fifties to influence a large public. In his contribution to *Partisan Review*'s symposium "Our Country and Our Culture," Trilling says that since the war "intellect has associated itself with power, perhaps as never before in history, and it is now conceded to be in itself a kind of power."[13] The established kinds of power—social, financial, political—are now, in Trilling's view, deferring to intellect. The point has arrived in the history of American culture "at which wealth shows a tendency to submit itself, to some degree, to the rule of mind and imagination, to apologize for its existence by a show of taste and sensitivity."[14]

The problem for a highbrow critic was how to take advantage of this new situation without becoming compromised in the process. The first question, then, was what books to offer. Trilling and his coeditors were careful to avoid certain kinds of books: most topical social criticism (too low), most works from university presses (too specialized), and most new fiction and poetry, especially from publishers like New Directions (too experimental). Typical forms were the letters and biographies of great men, classics in minor genres, and reprints of old favorites. It was always a question of what was "appropriate," a favorite word of Trilling's.

He registered his sense of the appropriate in a new style that was carefully calibrated so as to be not too high nor too low. His manner is altogether more relaxed, more familiar than in the essays collected in *The Liberal Imagination*. Even the titles point to the difference. Here, for example, are the titles of three book club pieces that Trilling reprinted in *A Gathering of Fugitives* in 1956: "A Ramble on Graves," "Profession: Man of the World," and "Adams at Ease." In the first of these, Trilling begins, "Robert Graves has been very pleasantly in and out of our minds for some thirty-odd years."[15] The second piece is an urbane tribute to an urbane but decidedly minor Victorian, Monckton Milnes. And the third, an essay on a new edition of Henry Adams's letters, also shows Trilling trying to avoid the academic or the solemn: "It isn't possible to identify ourselves with Adams for very long. One's parsnips must be already buttered, as Adams's were, before one can despair as wholeheartedly as he."[16]

In these essays Trilling is very self-consciously trying to shed the burden of modernity, with its uncompromising dedication to what is difficult and problematic. The persona of these Readers' Subscription pieces is that of an old-fashioned gentleman remembering how much better things had been ordered in his day. The tone is only rarely acerbic. It is more that of the cultivated bookman putting in his hours in the library, gracefully evoking the charm of the past but not losing his temper about the follies and vulgarity of the present. The tone is highly considered as it projects an image of "Trilling at ease."

A staple of Trilling's book club essays is the contrast between an old, dignified classical modernism and its later, vulgar derivatives. Thus, in an essay on Henry Miller, Trilling places Miller in relation to his master, D. H. Lawrence. Both Miller and Lawrence were "on the side of the angels," Trilling says, having in mind their shared desire for a much freer sexual life than modern society allows. But Trilling makes clear that for him there are angels and there are angels:

> When it comes to angels, my taste had been formed by D. H. Lawrence. The angels he was on the side of were swift, imperious, and very neat about their persons. . . . My predilection for Lawrence's fastidious angels ruled out Miller's. The latter are ill-conditioned creatures; they give no appearance of having come from a Good Home.[17]

By putting "Good Home" in capitals, Trilling distances himself from his own fastidiousness. His ruefulness about Miller and, by implication, about the unruliness of a culture that appreciates him is lightened by self-irony. No criticism can be made of Trilling's decorous tone that he has not anticipated—and defused. The style itself makes a statement. It registers a certain discomfort with the vulgar present, but the discomfort is not enough to affect the writer's equanimity. It is a well-fed, comfortable kind of discomfort. Trilling's disdain for vulgar modernity is not at all incompatible with the satisfaction he had expressed in 1952 about the newly enhanced role of the intellectual in American life. His style bodies forth the taste and sensitivity before which, presumably, wealth and power were expected to bow.

THE DISINTEGRATIVE PROCESS

But there was another Trilling in the fifties. Apart from the suave gentleman-humanist of the book club introductions, there was the disconsolate, uncertain figure who stands behind the more ambitious, longer essays of *The Opposing Self*. The author of that book does not sound like a once-dissident critic now enjoying the pleasures of his newly acquired establishment status. Rather, the essays of *The Opposing Self* take as their themes disillusionment and fatigue. These essays are much more literary and concerned with psychological themes than those of *The Liberal Imagination*. Whereas in the forties Trilling frequently wrote about large social-cultural issues, now he devotes himself to biographical studies of individual writers. In almost every case his attention to their lives reveals a personal crisis: Keats is dying, Dickens is suffering a midlife crisis, Henry James is mourning the death of his mother, and so on.

The Opposing Self is haunted by a sense of futility and waste that defines itself in terms of a revulsion against worldliness. In the early forties Trilling had been writing a novel, which may have turned into *The Middle of the Journey*, about a young man who had on his dresser three books: *Père Goriot*, *The Red and the Black*, and *Sentimental Education*. The hero of each is a Young Man from the Provinces who sets out to conquer the worldly world. In the fifties Trilling was disposed to emphasize not the ardor and ambition of these young men but the renunciation to which their various careers lead them. It is a monkish Trilling, the antithesis of the urbane Trilling of the book club essays, who now recommends the literature of will-lessness, a literature which shows "the will seeking its own negation—or, rather, seeking its own affirmation by its rejection of the aims which the world sets before it."[18]

Trilling never fully emerged from this crisis of the fifties, never recovered the relative high-spiritedness of *The Liberal Imagination*. Trilling's essay of 1953 on *Little Dorrit* is typical of his new mood. It evokes a middle-aged Dickens who feels "that he has passed the summit of life and that the path from now on leads downward."[19] Trilling gives the impression in his writing of feeling the same way. He was only in his late forties when he wrote the essay on *Little Dorrit* and the other essays collected in *The Opposing Self*, but in his writing he seems much older. In his essay on Dickens, as in those on Wordsworth and Austen and Flaubert, Trilling imagines a condition of supernal peace and rest, beyond culture, outside of time. He is much drawn to a vision of self-abnegation, such as he attributes to the middle-aged Dickens, whose imagination, he says, "is directed to the transcending of the personal will, to the search for the Will in which shall be our peace."[20]

The fullest representation of Trilling's consciousness as it appears in *The Opposing Self* occurs in a work of fiction, not by Trilling himself but by Thomas Mann. The story is "Disorder and Early Sorrow," about which Trilling writes one of his most illuminating commentaries in *The Experience of Literature*. Mann's hero is a professor of history and a victim of the massive social dislocations brought about by a world war. Mann's Professor Cornelius is a bourgeois-humanist German intellectual whose life has been shattered by Germany's defeat in World War I. The professor is only forty-seven, but the social upheaval of the Weimar period has made his upper-middle-class consciousness obsolete. He finds himself nostalgic for abandoned aristocratic graces, in love with lost causes, and on the side of death as against fresh life. Nothing is complete or perfect in his eyes until it is past. His deepest impulse, as a father and historian, is "hostility against the history of today, which is still in the making and thus not history at all, in behalf of the history that has already happened—that is to say, death." Trilling quotes these words of Mann in his commentary.[21]

Although the dislocations experienced by American intellectuals in the post-World War II period may seem minor compared with the situation of the middle class in Germany after World War I, Trilling reacted with some of the same yearning for stasis that characterizes Professor Cornelius. He was responding, as I have suggested, to an international crisis of civilization brought on by the Nazi death camps and Stalinist mass purges. The essays of *The Opposing Self* may take traditional nineteenth-century literary figures as their occasions, but their true subject is the impact of totalitarianism on our conception of what it means to live a human life. In the next chapter I shall have more to say about other essays that Trilling wrote in the fifties, but here I want to focus on one essay, "William Dean Howells and the Roots of Modern Taste," as an instance of his strategy of using a comfortable, old-fashioned writer as a way of addressing a new, unprecedented moral crisis.

It says something about Trilling's central concerns in the early fifties that in his long essay on Howells he does not quote a single line of that writer. Instead, he takes his key passages from a political theorist, Hannah Arendt, and a Freudian psychoanalyst, Bruno Bettelheim, both Central European Jews who had fled Hitler's Europe and written important works on the human condition under totalitarianism. I have already quoted the Arendt passage on "the disintegrative tendency" that Trilling glosses in his Howells essay. He quotes the following passage from Bettelheim:

> A fight for the very survival of civilized mankind is actually a fight to restore man to a sensitivity toward the joys of life. Only in this way can man be liberated and the survival of civilized mankind be assured. Maybe a time has come in which our main efforts need no longer be directed toward modifying the pleasure principle. [Dr. Bettelheim is speaking of the practice of psychoanalysis. —Trilling's note.] Maybe it is time we became concerned with restoring pleasure gratification to its dominant role in the

reality principle; maybe this society needs less a modification of the pleasure principle by reality, and more assertion of the pleasure principle against an overpowering pleasure—denying reality. *

The author of *The Rise of Silas Lapham* is all too slight a figure to offset the grim implications of modern history, and he fits oddly in the company Trilling has arranged for him: not only Arendt and Bettelheim but also Hegel, Kafka, and Proust. But Trilling likes hard cases and on occasion will go out of his way to find examples to offend the pieties of the intellectuals. So he recruits the bland and passionless Howells to exemplify the correct relation to the pleasure principle that a culture besotted with visions of extremity has lost. Howells proves a recalcitrant witness, compromised in the eyes of disenchanted modern intellectuals by his unfortunate statement, in an essay on Dostoevsky, that the "smiling aspects" of life are "more American." But Trilling is determined to do what he can for those "smiling aspects" and for those moderate virtues of Howells that were especially out of fashion in the postwar years.

Howells becomes valuable as a reminder of a better time and as a corrective to modernism's masochistic attraction to suffering and death. In Trilling's view, Howells's hopefulness could "at least serve . . . to bind us to the earth, to prevent our being seduced by the godhead of disintegration."[22] Trilling is arguing against a specific conception of the modern. I take up this conception in greater detail in chapter 8. Here it may be enough to say that the modern as Trilling conceives it is not a specifically literary phenomenon that emphasizes stylistic innovation and difficulty. Rather, it is a movement of "spiritual militancy" founded on a rejection of bourgeois humanism and committed to what Trilling calls "the negative transcendence of the human." Trilling stresses its perversity and morbidity, its romance with nihilism and despair. He writes in an essay on Wordsworth in 1950: "We are

*Quoted in *The Opposing Self* (New York: Viking Press, 1955), 102. Another German-speaking Jewish writer to whom Trilling might have appealed on this theme is the Frankfurt School critic Theodor Adorno, whose *Minima Moralia: Reflections from Damaged Life* was published in Germany in 1951. Adorno's book is a collection of philosophical fragments, in the Nietzschean manner, which he wrote between 1944 and 1947, when he was in exile in America. Like Bettelheim and Trilling, Adorno mourns a lost *promesse de bonheur*, but he is sharply separated from them, as from Arendt, by his Marxism.

in love, at least in our literature, with the fantasy of death. Death and suffering, when we read, are our only means of conceiving the actuality of life."[23]

All through the forties Trilling had himself been putting forward the view of human sinfulness that became fashionable in the fifties. But it was in the logic of his position as enemy of all orthodoxies that he should disavow any stance, even his own, once it had become widely espoused. Thus, by defining modernism in very extreme terms, and positing that idea of modernity as a new conformity, Trilling could then advance the most rear-guard middle-class pieties as, in some sense, "radical." In Trilling's essays of the fifties middle-class pieties and routines, even middle-class foibles, are made to seem almost exotic. Confronted a half-century earlier by the multiplicity of modern culture, Henry Adams sought a binding principle in the Virgin of Chartres. Trilling finds *his* unifying principle in the middle-class ordinariness of Howells—"the common, the immediate, the familiar, and the vulgar elements of life,"[24] as Trilling puts it.

The Howells essay is polemical, to be sure, as yet another of Trilling's attacks on advanced literary intellectuals for the extremity of their opinions, which often have little connection with the way they actually live. But that essay, like the essays on Keats and Wordsworth that Trilling was writing at about the same time, is also a kind of prayer. It is a prayer for a certain kind of selfhood, a certain kind of being. That kind of being is suggested by Trilling's praise of Howells for his "passionate wish to speak out for the benign relaxation of the will, for goodness and gentleness, for 'life,' for the relaxation of moral judgment, for the charm of the mysterious, precarious, little flame that lies at the heart of the commonplace."[25]

But what, in Trilling's moment, is the cultural reference of this plea for "the relaxation of moral judgment"? The charm for Trilling of Howells's last novel, *The Vacation of the Kelwyns*, is its "theme of general pardon." But who had sinned and who needed to be forgiven? The Holocaust was a shock with which the imagination was not ready to deal so soon after the events themselves. My sense is that Trilling was thinking less about the war itself than about the excesses of the radical will in the American thirties and forties. It was necessary to bury the communist past. The pardon, then, would be for Trilling himself, for his own earlier involvement with radical politics. Even the opponents of Stalinism might feel that their hands were dirty. They, too, if only briefly, had supported a regime that was responsible for the murder of millions.

The main impression one forms in reading *The Opposing Self* is of a man struggling to come to terms not so much with totalitarianism or modernism or some other large impersonal fact or idea, but struggling to come to terms with himself, or, rather, struggling to get on better terms with himself. The best hope for a writer who had once committed himself to what he now regarded as a murderous, inhuman ideology might lie in coming into touch once more with being as it was exemplified in the unthinking, routine rounds of daily life. As Wordsworth, one of Trilling's favorite poets, had come to believe in the aftermath of the French Revolution, sin inheres in the practical will and in abstract rationality, which leads on to ideology and the crimes committed in its name.

HOWELLS AND "THE CONDITIONED"

The crisis of the fifties is manifest also in the structure of Trilling's major essays. He now vacillates a great deal about the large questions he takes up. His essays become distended as he keeps coiling new loops around the armature of his argument. As a result his point gets lost amidst a proliferation of qualifications and revisions. An essay of 1951, "Wordsworth and the Rabbis," is typical of Trilling's indecisiveness in these years. He begins by positing a link between Wordsworth and Christian thought but soon proposes a new thesis, that Wordsworth's temper is like that of the ancient Pharisees. Then Trilling abandons that analogy as well and settles down to making a point that doesn't require *either* Christianity or Judaism. What Trilling wants to say is that Wordsworth is a valuable corrective to modernist spiritual militancy by virtue of his praise for acquiescence and relaxation of the will. But his essay bogs down in to-ing and fro-ing.

Trilling's uncertainties reflect the general crisis of culture. This was a decade in which Kierkegaard's *Either/Or* was a favorite text of the intellectuals. Not without reason, for America was more than ever an either/or culture. There was, on the one hand, the isolated privatized "self" and, on the other, a projection variously named God or myth or symbol. As far as literature was concerned there was nothing in between. In criticism the middle ground of ethics, society, and politics disappeared. Trilling continued to write cultural criticism, but it now reflected the general turning away from society and history. His famous essay on Keats in 1951 is an example of that turning. Trilling praises Keats for his geniality in his social relations, but his essay largely skips over Keats's social-cultural context to place him in relation to his infancy and his fatal illness. Trilling had complained about the perversity and morbidity of postwar literary culture, but his own essay is death-haunted. It is as if, amidst the fog of American culture in the fifties, Trilling could only locate reality in the ultimate confrontation of the self with its extinction.

Without an overarching theoretical critique, Trilling could only reproduce, not explain, the contradictions of the larger culture. Above all, his essays reflect and confirm the polarization between fact and spirit, between the solitary individual and the All. The essay on Howells is once again useful as an example. One of Trilling's reasons for reconsidering the case of Howells is to offer an example of a writer who was innocent of "our contemporary impulse to enlarge all experience, to involve it as soon as possible in history, myth, and the oneness of spirit."[26] For Howells a fact is a fact, not a manifestation of the All. As Trilling observes, who but Howells could have devoted no fewer than six chapters in one of his novels to his hero's search for an apartment!

But Trilling's own writing about Howells reflects the loss of the literal and the denotative that he laments. Trilling himself mythicizes middle-class life. After objecting to the modern impulse to enlarge all experience, he says that our neglect of Howells "must be understood in a very large context." That neglect, he says, is "but one aspect of our attitude to *the conditioned,* of the material circumstances in which spirit exists."[27] Trilling makes his own Kierkegaardian leap from middle-class routine in the 1880s to the spiritual malaise of the 1950s. He praises Howells as "the only nineteenth-century American writer of large reputation who deals directly and immediately with the family." But then he has less to say about Howells's representation of family life than about the disappearance of the family from more recent fiction. For Trilling that disappearance is evidence of the modern will to get beyond culture into the purely ideal realm of "unconditioned spirit." As Trilling puts it in a famous sentence: "Somewhere in our mental constitution is the demand for life as pure spirit."[28]

Just what Trilling means by "the demand for life as pure spirit" he never makes wholly clear. One example he does offer is the eschatological politics of Stalinist intellectuals. To these fellow travelers Trilling says, "Communist society is likely to seem a close approximation to the unconditioned, to spirit making its own terms."[29] There is no need in such a society to take account of conflicting wills and pressures, as in parliamentary democracies. Thus the intellectual can fantasize about creating instant utopia, without hindrance. The problem is that Trilling reveals a similar yearning to escape from the world of time, of contingency and responsibility, into a timeless idyll. In the essay on Dickens, as we saw, he sympathizes with the religious impulse to sacrifice one's particular will to "the Will that shall be our peace." In the essay on Wordsworth he writes sympathetically of the Wordsworthian quietism that involves "the contemplative accord with unitary reality." And in his introduction to *Emma*, in 1957, Trilling comments warmly on the "idyllic stillness" that characterizes the world of Highbury. He reveals at every point a craving for "life as pure spirit" even as he warns against it.

This ambivalence makes for a crisis of form in Trilling's criticism. At one moment he gives us the unredeemed facts of middle-class routine in Howells, at the next moment portentous, all-encompassing explanations. This ambivalence in form corresponds to the split in Trilling's identity as a cultural critic in the fifties. In the book club essays he writes in the tradition of the nineteenth-century familiar essayist, of Lamb and De Quincey, Arnold and Henry James. That style carries over to the major essays, but in those major essays Trilling also writes as a man of large if unsystematic views, who seems always about to pronounce on the spiritual condition of modern man. The latter Trilling calls to mind modern philosophers of culture like Ortega y Gasset on the right and, on the left, Lukács and Adorno. Trilling in the fifties is excessively portentous, hinting in the major essays at a large philosophical critique that he never carries out. In the same years, in his book club essays, he is too self-limiting in his role as cultural middleman.

The loss of society as the middle ground in criticism was the inevitable consequence of the discrediting in the fifties of all oppositional forms of politics. Revulsion against Marxism and the amnesia of the liberal intellectuals about their radical past intensified the remoteness and abstraction that had always been a part of Trilling's outlook. In the forties that tendency to abstractness had been checked by the need to struggle against Stalinism. In those years there had been a war to be won, at home and abroad, and Trilling was always at his best in reacting to a clearly delineated political-cultural situation. In the fifties life became better but criticism grew confused. With the vindication of American capitalism, the endemic split in the national culture once more became apparent.

Although Trilling stood apart from the new myth-symbol criticism of the fifties, his own writing reflects the general turning away from society and history. He makes major concessions to the tendency represented by myth criticism even in opposing it, and his opposition is of the mildest kind. It is understandable that Trilling should have pulled his punches. As Philip Rahv said in an essay of 1953, "The mythic is the polar opposite of what we mean by the historical, which stands for process, inexorable change, incessant permutation and innovation." The problem, as Rahv said, is that "in our time the movement of history has been so rapid that the mind longs for nothing so much as something permanent to steady it."[30] Trilling was at one with the myth critics in having had enough of history as inexorable change. But in giving in too easily to the desire for stability, he encouraged the spirit of passivity and privatism that dominated the fifties.

Trilling with sister Harriet.
Photograph courtesy of
Dr. Roland Schwartz.

Trilling with sister Harriet and his mother.
Photograph courtesy of Dr. Roland Schwartz.

WILLIAM Y. TINDALL   New York City
Insignia: King's Crown, Gold

Spectator (2) (3), Assistant Managing Editor (4), Philo Show (4), Varsity (4),
Philolexian.

An engaging fellow! Years of ecstatically voluminous reading have
sweetened him, until his entire personality, his speech and writing are
tinct with the peculiar antic beauty of old masters like Browne and Burton.
To use the words of one of the most accomplished of campus humorists,
he has "an appalling amount of 'eryudition'"; but that has not dimmed
the delightfulness of his variegated medieval mind.

ANDREW B. TOOMEY   New York City   Delta Chi
Insignia: 1925

Junior Varsity Football (3) (4), Sophomore Crew, 150 lb. Crew (3) (4).

This is one-half of the firm of Toomey and Webb, Lawyers. Like his
partner he is an enthusiastic exponent of his Alma Mater. Both have given
freely to her cause on the gridiron and on the Harlem. To see Andy is also
to see Ed, for the two are the twinniest pair of twins of whom there is
none whomer. (For further information see Ed Webb.)

LIONEL M. TRILLING   New York City
Soph Show (2), Morningside (4), Boar's Head (4).

Behold the last of the Hartley Corporation—that famous group of intellectuals that tried to monopolize "Sweetness and Light" a few years
ago. Li hid his genius under a bushel-basket (as the Scriptures say) for
two years, until the editors of Morningside caught him wasting his talent
in English classes. Psst! Here's a secret! This master mind used to play
marbles—in the dirt!

Trilling at nineteen, yearbook photograph, Columbia College 1925.
At far left is William York Tindall, who also became a professor of
English at Columbia. Tindall wrote books on literary symbolism and
on James Joyce. Courtesy of Columbia University Library.

Trilling at graduation from Columbia College, 1925. Photograph courtesy of Columbia University Library.

this chair
is for people
who love books
more than
automobiles

Advertisement for the Mid-Century Book Society, *New York Times Sunday Book Review*, May 10, 1959. Trilling, Jacques Barzun (c.), and W. H. Auden were coeditors of this book club, which dissolved in

1962. From 1952 to 1959 they had served in the same capacity at another book club, the Readers' Subscription. Photograph by Wingate Paine.

Trilling, Jacques Barzun (r.), and moderator Lyman Bryson at CBS radio program Invitation to Learning, May 16, 1944. Photograph courtesy of Jacques Barzun.

Trilling in 1947. The photograph was taken by Sylvia Salmi, wife of Trilling's *Menorah Journal* friend Herbert Solow.

Chapter Seven

The Uses of Freud

A crisis in criticism is always a crisis in conceptions of the self. In the American 1950s widespread repudiation of Marxism led to a new search for answers in the self. Intellectuals who had for years rejected all forms of individualism now proclaimed that "the root is man"—and not society. Some found support for that view in Kierkegaard and other religious thinkers, but most of the old New York intellectuals remained overwhelmingly secular-minded. For them the antidote to Marx was typically Freud.

To say that these liberal intellectuals resisted the religious revival of the fifties is not to say that they had given up on the search for a totalizing theory. The turn of once-Marxist intellectuals to Freudianism often betrayed a longing, endemic in American culture, for a one-shot cure for the multiple ailments of the spirit. In *Freud: The Mind of the Moralist,* which appeared in 1959, Philip Rieff says, "In America today, Freud's intellectual influence is greater than that of any other modern thinker."[1] But that Freudianism often appeared in a watered-down, revisionist version. America was on its way to becoming a therapeutic culture, more concerned with emotional well-being than with critical intelligence.

An orthodox Freudian in an age of psychoanalytic revisionism, Trilling defended Freud's own ideas, as he understood them, against the American dilution of those ideas. For Trilling the most important aspect of Freud's thought was its moral dimension. He agreed with Philip Rieff that Freud "has no message; he accepts contradiction and builds his psychology on it."[2] He also accepted Rieff's qualification: "But if [Freud] has no message, in the old sense of something positive and constructive to offer, nevertheless his doctrine contains intellectual and moral implications that, when drawn, constitute a message." In Rieff's view the chief implication was Freud's "ethic of honesty": he "taught us in a unique and subtle way how to grow unsentimental about our-

117

selves."[3] Trilling's Freud, the exemplary moral realist, can be equally unsentimental. At other times, however, the chief implication that Trilling finds in Freud is not so much the ethic of honesty as the ethic of passivity. In the fifties Trilling used Freud's thought, especially the doctrine of the death instinct, to legitimize his own yearning for a great good place, "beyond culture," in which a weary New York intellectual might find peace and rest.

KEATS, KAFKA, AND THE SELF

In the fifties it became commonplace for New York writers to be dabbling in one or another school of psychoanalysis. Trilling was ahead of the crowd. Just as in the forties he had prepared the way for the conservative turn of the next decade by arguing for the continuing legitimacy of middle-class values, so had he also laid the groundwork for the turn to psychoanalysis. Although Freud makes only one brief appearance in the 1939 book on Matthew Arnold, Trilling had been reading Freud since the mid-thirties. In 1940 he published an important essay, "Freud and Literature," offering a synoptic critique of the psychoanalytic approach to literature; in 1941 he used Freudian ideas as the framework of his essay on Wordsworth's "Immortality Ode"; and in 1945, in "Art and Neurosis," he criticized popular notions of artistic creativity as a compensation for psychological handicaps.

Trilling understood psychoanalysis more fully than his contemporaries William Empson, Edmund Wilson, and Kenneth Burke, who also made use of it in their criticism. Still, Trilling's Freud was to some degree his own invention. He invented the Freud he needed and reinvented him from decade to decade as the cultural situation changed. In the forties, in his essay on Wordsworth's "Immortality Ode," Trilling adapted psychoanalysis to an ideologically charged celebration of "moral realism." He says that Wordsworth's ode is about a change in the poet's perception of the natural world. It speaks of the loss of the poet's "visionary gleam," which dies away, fading "into the light of common day." Earlier criticism had interpreted the ode as Wordsworth's farewell to poetry. But for Trilling "it is not about poetry, it is about life," about growing up and the losses and gains it brings. It is a "hard paradox," Trilling says, that "we develop by moving toward death."[4] In this essay of 1941 Trilling weaves together Freud's theories of ego development and of the death instinct with Milton's conception of the Fortunate Fall.

One of Trilling's critics wondered why, given his Freudian orientation, he spoke of "the moral imagination" instead of "psychological insight." Trilling's response was that "in literature as well as in life, the psychological is subsumed in the moral, and to try to make the smaller concept do the work of the larger is only to mask actuality."[5] But in stressing the moral rather than the clinical dimension of Freud's work, Trilling was masking the *political* implications of his particular use of Freud. For in the Wordsworth essay, as always in *The Liberal Imagination,* he was addressing a political-cultural situation, the corruption of America's liberal intellectuals by Stalinism.

Trilling's discussion of the "Immortality Ode" can be read in this light as a disillusioned radical's farewell to (socialist) innocence and an appeal to other liberals to grow up and accept the world as it is. The Freudian moralism that urges the necessity of renouncing the pleasure principle for the sake of reality is also a political appeal to liberals to put away the childish dreams of the radical thirties. A decade later, in the essays collected in *An End to Innocence,* Leslie Fiedler made explicit the political implication of Trilling's moralizing appeal to maturity. Fiedler's essays of the early fifties, like the one on Julius and Ethel Rosenberg, expose retrospectively the direction of Trilling's essays in the forties. They also amount to an unintentional parody of Trilling. Fiedler's cartoon-strip simplifications reveal how much Trilling's essays always depended for their effect on the subtlety and caution of his style.

In Trilling's first psychoanalytically oriented study of a literary text, then, Freud makes his appearance not as a diagnostician of the dynamic unconscious but as a great moralist, "in the line of the classic tragic realism." By the fifties, however, when younger critics like Fiedler were popularizing his ideas, Trilling had moved on to new uses for Freud. Certainly the tragic theme persisted in Trilling's writing, but the moralizing emphasis on maturity was less central to his criticism than his emphasis on a radical instability in the modern self. Trilling's concern was no longer with becoming—growing up older, wiser, chastened by experience—but with *being.* In the fifties Trilling was looking for an elemental quality of the self that could withstand the postwar moral chaos and enable the self to conserve itself. He found this principle of coherence in biology.

Trilling followed Freud in positing that the most primordial quality of being is biological. In the Freud Anniversary Lecture that he presented at the New York Psychoanalytic Institute in 1955, he speaks of "a hard, irreducible, stubborn core of biological urgency, and biological necessity,"[6] which gives the self a kind of immutability. This concern with the biological had appeared only fleetingly before the fifties, as in Trilling's 1946 review of *The Psychology of Sex Relations*, by Theodore Reik. In that essay Trilling objects to Reik's revision of classical psychoanalysis, by which an "egoistic or emotional etiology" of love is offered in place of Freud's own "biological or sexual" explanation. Trilling makes clear that his argument is intended to address a political situation: "Dr. Reik shares with Dr. [Karen] Horney a high disdain for biology, and biology is just now in disrepute with progressive intellectuals."[7] In the fifties Trilling's affirmation of the biological was still involved in his polemic against the liberals, but he was addressing the crisis of selfhood more directly, rather than only as part of a larger political debate.

The impact of the postwar crisis of the self is evident if we compare Trilling's essay "Wordsworth and the Rabbis," which was first published in 1950, with his essay on the "Intimations Ode" nine years before. The later essay introduces what would become one of Trilling's major themes, "the sentiment of being." The source of the phrase is Wordsworth's *The Prelude*, where it appears in connection with the poet's quasireligious conception of the Imagination. But for Trilling "the sentiment of being" is not supernatural but naturalistic, founded in biology. It is involved in the question whether there may be something in the elemental constitution of the self that may serve as a source of strength in bad times. "The sentiment of being" is by no means a sentimental idea. It is involved with the question of emotional strength, as in Wordsworth's conviction that "feeling comes in aid / Of feeling, and diversity of strength / Attends us, if but once we have been strong." Trilling does not use Freudian language, but the quality of being he has in mind is what psychoanalysts call "ego-strength," a fundamental certainty about the continuity and substantiality of the self and about the efficacy of the ego as the executive agency within the psyche.

There would be no need to celebrate Wordsworth's ego-strength if the sense of selfhood had not become attenuated in our own time. For Trilling a basic confidence about the self is a nineteenth-century quality that unites Wordsworth and Keats and distinguishes them from representative figures of the modern period such as Kafka and Beckett. Keats is Trilling's type of "the opposing self" by virtue of the moral and psychological strength with which he faces his death. For Trilling, Keats's self-certitude and his strong attachment to reality—"stronger and more complex than ours usually is"—make a contrast with the diminished self of Kafka. Death for Kafka's characters has a very different meaning than for Keats because they live without ever having had a sense of being existentially alive. As Trilling puts it, "Kafka's knowledge of evil exists without the contradictory knowledge of the self in its health and validity."[8] Kafka's characters embody no principle of opposition because they lack at the core of their being something solid and perdurable, a basic conviction that amounts to a guarantee of indestructibility.

"The sentiment of being" became important in a specific historical situation. *The Prelude*, Wordsworth's great crisis-autobiography, is about the poet's struggle to recover his imaginative vitality, which had been damaged by his infatuation with the radical doctrines of the French Revolution. Book 11 of *The Prelude*, "Imagination, How Impaired and Restored," is the clue to Trilling's similar project of recovery in the fifties. Just as Wordsworth, Edmund Burke, and others in the early nineteenth century were reacting against the utopian rationalism of the Revolution, Trilling was recovering from the excesses of the radical movement of the American 1930s.

Trilling's own situation, of course, was not exactly the same as that of the English Romantic conservatives whom he took as models. For in America the Communist Revolution had never gotten beyond the stage of fantasy. Moreover, as a revolutionary Trilling had never been as exultant as Wordsworth had been prior to the Terror in France. The postrevolutionary despair of Wordsworth is a measure of his earlier hope, whereas Trilling, even in his most radical period, seems not to have been so thoroughly committed. Still, there can be little doubt of the visceral force of Trilling's revulsion against the spirit of the radical thirties, even as that spirit continued to pervade intellectual life

121

through the next decade. And, as with the first-generation British Romantics, Trilling's solution to the violation of his own imagination was custom, nature, the organic, all of which he summed up under the heading of "the biological."

The moral conservatism of this biologism is clear in Trilling's appreciation of Wordsworth's rocklike solitaries, like the Leech Gatherer of "Resolution and Independence." Trilling says that such Wordsworthian figures in the landscape "survive out of a kind of biological faith, which is not the less human because it is nearly an animal or vegetable faith."[9] They exhibit the Wordsworthian wise passivity and natural piety which Trilling describes as "a certain insouciant acquiescence in the anomalies of the moral order of the universe."[10] This acquiescence was implicitly social as well as spiritual. We need only compare Trilling's idea of "the sentiment of being" with the dialectic of authenticity and bad faith in Sartre, who was probably the major intellectual influence on Trilling's preoccupation with ontological issues. In the postwar years Sartre was marrying his existentialism to Marxism. In the same years Trilling was using Freud's biologism to forge a worldview that would displace Marxism. Trilling's "sentiment of being" was a sentiment not of action and commitment but of disengagement and detachment from motion and struggle.

THE PRINCIPLE OF INERTIA

The appeal to a conservatively tinged biologism also marks Trilling's essay of 1953 on Henry James's *The Bostonians*. This essay is not one of Trilling's best, but it has the virtue for my purposes of making explicit the Freudian schema that is the organizing principle of so many of his essays in the fifties. According to Trilling, James's fiction has at its center "the conflict of two principles, of which one is radical, the other conservative." This conflict, Trilling says, may be thought of in terms of "energy and inertia . . . or force and form . . . or Libido and Thanatos."[11] He goes on to argue that in *The Bostonians* James leans toward the conservative pole of his characteristic dialectic.

Most readers of *The Bostonians* will be surprised by Trilling's emphasis on Henry James's mother, Mary James. He speculates that Mrs. James's death in the early 1880s may have been the germ of her son's satire on Boston's feminist reformers. James had called his mother "the keystone of the arch" in the James family, and Trilling suggests that Mary James's death may have plunged Henry into an emotional crisis experienced in terms of a threat to his manhood. Trilling interprets James's satire on feminism as an expression of intense sexual anxiety.

According to Trilling's schema, the feminists are led into perversity by their radical impulse to rearrange life according to an abstract theory. Mary James, on the other hand, stands for "the strength of conservation, the unseen, unregarded, seemingly unexerted force that holds things to their center." Trilling says that James's mother "had lived the ancient elemental course of life, which is without theory or formulation, too certain of itself and too much at one with itself even to aspire."[12] If Olive Chancellor, the most militant of the novel's feminists, symbolizes the ideological mind, Mary James is an emblem of the biological. Biology, then, is associated with the habitual, the immemorial, all that protects us from the ravages of abstract reason and violent change. Altogether, what Trilling gives us here is a Freudianized version of Edmund Burke's Romantic conservatism.

The source of the psychoanalytic elements in Trilling's reading of *The Bostonians* is the late Freud of *Beyond the Pleasure Principle* (1920). In that extraordinary text, Freud revises his dualistic theory of the drives, opposing sexual libido to a newly defined instinct, the biological drive toward death. Freud defines the death instinct as a drive to *"restore an earlier state of things."*[13] It is independent of, "beyond," the pleasure principle; not even Eros can withstand it. The earlier state of things to which the death instinct impels humanity is "the final goal of all organic striving," inorganic stasis. For Freud the goal of life is, simply, death. Far from justifying any hope of historical progress, his theory proposes that life itself is nothing but a detour, a circuitous path imposed on living substance by external influences: "The elementary living entity would from its very beginning have had no wish to change; if conditions remained the same, it would do no more than constantly repeat the same course of life."[14] The cry of much American literature in the fifties was the "I want, I want" of Saul Bellow's Henderson the Rain King. But in *Beyond the Pleasure Principle* we have a very different view of the instinctual life. All that the organism wants is to be beyond wanting. As Freud says, "We

123

have become used to see in [the instincts] a factor impelling towards change and development, whereas we are now asked to recognize in them the precise contrary—an expression of the *conservative* nature of living substance."[15]

Trilling adapts Freud's biologically grounded metapsychological speculation to a moral-cultural argument. He makes Freud's theory of "the conservative nature of living substance" the basis of a moral and aesthetic recommendation. To the degree that a text exemplifies the principle of inertia, it is for Trilling a useful corrective to a culture sick from the hypertrophy of the radical will. Freud writes that "it would be in contradiction to the conservative nature of the instincts if the goal of life were a state of things which had never yet been attained."[16] This idea is echoed many times in Trilling's polemics against the spiritual overreaching of modernism.

Biology is morally neutral, and there certainly were different cultural positions in the fifties no less indebted to biological conceptions. Here I want only to note, by way of contrast with Trilling's conservative biologism, some radical alternatives. One example is the Wilhelm Reichianism of Norman Mailer in *The Deer Park* and such stories of his as "The Time of Her Time." Another is the Nietzschean revision of Freud in Norman O. Brown's *Life Against Death*. Brown's ideal is very different from Mailer's, but it too is dedicated to a substantially liberated sexuality. It's not at all clear what forms of society are implied by Brown's endorsement of the "polymorphous perverse" and Mailer's celebration of "the White Negro," but such notions represent the Dionysiac underside of the fifties, which only became a dominant force with the renewed cultural radicalism of the next decade.

As a spokesman for the Apollonian* official culture of the

---

*After this book was in press I came upon William V. Spanos's ambitious essay "The Apollonian Investment of Modern Humanistic Education: The Examples of Matthew Arnold, Irving Babbitt, and I. A. Richards (Part One)," in a new journal, *Cultural Critique* 1 (Fall 1985), 7–72. Spanos includes Trilling, M. H. Abrams, and Denis Donoghue as continuators of that "Apollonian" tradition in modern criticism. He attempts to deconstruct that tradition by way of a kind of left-wing Heideggerianism and the later Foucault of *Discipline and Punish*. The positive implications of Spanos's critique for a new pedagogy are not clear; negatively, he contends that Anglo-American humanism since Matthew Arnold has acted to "secure and legitimate the authority of the bourgeois capitalist version of civilized society" (57).

fifties, Trilling seemed to be turning against his own earlier self. It's not that he had ever been a great partisan of the *élan vital*, but in the forties, as we have seen, he had been very sympathetic toward the ambitions of Sorel and Rastignac and their American progeny in Henry James and Fitzgerald. The appetitiveness and ardor of these Young Men from the Provinces had seemed to Trilling the evidence of healthy energy and spirit. In the fifties he turned from the spectacle of his ardent young men to bestow his blessings on the "moveless" and sexless: aged mothers, Wordsworthian solitaries, and assorted instances of being-without-will in Lawrence, Faulkner, and Hemingway. We have only to compare the complementary essays on Henry James. The 1948 essay on *The Princess Casamassima* celebrates youth, beauty, and a young man's initiation into the glories of high civilization; the essay, only five years later, on *The Bostonians* allies itself with inertia and Thanatos at the expense of energy and Eros.

THE FATE OF PLEASURE

Up to now I have emphasized the way in which Trilling favored the "conservative principle" in his essays of the fifties. But other texts and other passages from the same years might be cited to suggest a contradictory trend. From the early fifties on, every "yes" in Trilling's writing is followed soon after by a "no," in a rhythm nearly as regular as breathing or the systole and diastole of the heart. It is the rhythm of man thinking—and usually thinking against himself. In essays of the forties like that on *The Princess Casamassima* Trilling had tried to achieve a perilous balance of contradictory aims; in the fifties he was more likely to argue one side and then the other in alternation.

The critic of Trilling has to guard against making too much of any particular expression of opinion. Each essay is likely to present only a part of Trilling's mind, a reaction not only to the dominant cultural mood but also to a previous mood of his own. We need to speak not of fixed ideological positions but of alternations and fluctuations of mood. Trilling refines and corrects the culture by performing these operations first on himself.

The antiheroic, antierotic strain does seem to me the dominant one in his writing of the fifties. Yet in Trilling's essay on Keats in 1951 he locates the origin of the poet's strong selfhood in his early erotic bond with his mother. As an adult, Trilling says,

125

Keats "did not repress the infantile wish; he confronted it, recognized it, and delighted in it."[17] Trilling's essay delights in that delight and makes Keats's sensuousness the key to his seriousness. Trilling's speculations anticipate by a decade Erik Erikson's on the parallel development of the capacity for psychosexual love and ethical responsibility.[18] But Trilling's tone is not at all that of the psychoanalytic clinician. His essay moves with the meditative rhythms of poems like Coleridge's "Frost at Midnight" and Yeats's "A Prayer for My Daughter." Trilling's only child, a son, had been born only three years before, when the father was already 43. He is eloquent in praise of Keats's ideal manliness and at the same time wistful in recalling a possibility of happiness that has been lost in the modern age.

A similar wistfulness suffuses Trilling's essay of 1955 on the Russian-Jewish writer Isaac Babel. That essay, too, reveals Trilling's knack for investing a literary-critical appreciation with his own wished-for way of being. The Babel essay mourns the loss of "the truth of the body, the truth of full sexuality, the truth of open aggressiveness,"[19] which Jewish intellectuals like Babel (and, by implication, Trilling himself) have often had to sacrifice as the price of culture. Babel complained about being an intellectual, "with spectacles on his nose and autumn in his heart," and he rebelled against that condition by joining a company of Cossack cavalrymen who were fighting on the side of the Red Army in the Bolshevik Revolution. With the great social upheaval that overtook Russia, old oppositions like that between peaceable Jew and untamed Cossack had been temporarily unsettled, and a young Jew was able for a while to live out his fantasy of being as untamed as the warriors who had been the traditional persecutors of his own people.

A peaceable Jewish intellectual himself, Trilling had argued for an ethos of moderation in the fifties. In the Howells essay he had even argued for the virtues of middle-class routine. But Trilling's imagination of felicity had always implied a protest against the sacrifice of instinctual gratification for the sake of middle-class respectability. In the forties, ridiculing the scientism of the Kinsey Report on male sexuality, he had appealed to "the mystery and wildness of spirit which it is still our grace to believe is the mark of full humanness."[20] But it was only in the fifties that the protest of biology against culture became a central theme of his criticism. It was then, in the preface to *The Opposing Self*, that Trilling wrote of "the despair of those who, having committed themselves to culture, have surrendered the life of surprise and elevation, of impulse, pleasure, and imagination."[21]

I have emphasized the antivitalist idea of the biological that distinguishes most of Trilling's essays of the fifties from the writing of more extreme figures like Norman O. Brown and Norman Mailer. But it's more complicated than that, as Trilling used to say. We need to take account also of his sympathetic book club essays on Brown's *Life Against Death* and Leslie Fiedler's *Love and Death in the American Novel*. Moreover, there is the biographical fact of his friendship with Norman Mailer. Mailer's *Advertisements for Myself* is obviously more extreme than anything Trilling wrote, but its critique of a dessicated, rationalistic American culture draws heavily on Trilling's polemic in the forties against "the liberal imagination." And Trilling's essay "The Fate of Pleasure," in 1963, reveals a strong, even fierce, imagination of instinctual happiness. That imagination remained submerged during most of his career, but it peeps out sufficiently often to refute any simplistic reading of his work as merely genteel or elegiac.

There is a clue to that mainly buried life of feeling in his vivid response to Isaac Babel's short story "Di Grasso: A Tale of Odessa." In that story the lead performer in a traveling repertory company enacts on stage the vengeful passion of a wronged suitor. The actor Di Grasso, playing the wronged lover, "gave a smile, soared into the air, sailed across the stage, plunged down on [the villain's] shoulders, and having bitten through the latter's throat, began growling and squinting, to suck blood from the wound." To which Babel adds this gloss: "There is more justice in outbursts of noble passion than in all the joyless rules that run the world."[22]

Trilling comments, in connection with moments like this, on Babel's "lyric joy in the midst of violence," and he reveals something like lyric joy himself in his response to Di Grasso's great leap. By way of analogy he adduces the great leaps of the dancer Nijinsky, whose seeming ability to fly across the stage gave his audience a precious "intimation of the possibility of freedom from the bondage of our human condition."[23] Trilling risks inconsistency here. Usually in the fifties he had opposed the impulse in modernist literature to leap free of "the conditions." Only a year before the Babel essay, in an essay on Jane Austen's *Mansfield Park*, he had specifically argued for a morality of Christian

127

self-abnegation in opposition to the Nietzschean imagination of self-transcendence. Di Grasso's leap is hardly a case of the will seeking its own negation or of its consent to being bound to diurnal routine. But Trilling obviously felt it was possible to be bound too tightly. And so the great contraries—energy and inertia, lion and lamb—had to coexist because Trilling had no way of reconciling them.

THE CRITIQUE OF BIOLOGISM

The commentary on "Di Grasso" goes on to specify the liberation that Trilling had in mind. It was a liberation "not from the general human condition but from the constraints of society, from the dullness, the passivity, the acquiescence in which we live most of our lives." The weight of the Eisenhower years lay heavily on Trilling, and the appeal to biology, whether as a radical or conservative principle, was increasingly directed against a normalcy that had gone too far. In stressing adjustment, "togetherness," and consensus, American culture threatened to weaken countervailing impulses to resistance and opposition.

American social science participated in the general mood. David Riesman's work on "the lonely crowd" was an exception, and Trilling wrote appreciatively of Riesman's implicit detestation of the new, "other-directed" character type of the fifties.[24] But Riesman was in the minority in speaking up for the humanist idea of the autonomous self. The dream of social science as a whole was a perfect fit between individual and social order in which the self was conceived to be infinitely malleable. Trilling's biologism was a protest against what he regarded as an oversocialized conception of human nature in psychoanalytic writing as well as in the new sociology.

In his Freud Anniversary Lecture of 1955, "Freud: Within and Beyond Culture," Trilling points out the denial of individual autonomy implicit in the exaggerated emphasis on social adjustment in the writing of various Freudian revisionists. Without once mentioning Erich Fromm, Karen Horney, or Harry Stack Sullivan by name, he criticizes the tendency they represented for exaggerating culture's influence on the self and for minimizing Freud's own biological orientation. Against their sociologically grounded optimism about the end to the conflict between the self and culture, Trilling reaffirms Freud's own pessimism, grounded in a biological conception of the unavoidability of intrapsychic conflict. For Trilling happiness through social change had to remain chimerical as long as human nature was divided against itself. Instead of the revisionists' view of the individual totally defined by culture, Trilling insists on what he says was Freud's view of the self, "within" but also "beyond" culture. According to Trilling, Freud "needed to believe that there was some point at which it was possible to stand beyond the reach of culture,"[25] a "beyond" Trilling defines as "biological." Biology provided a way to argue that the self contained an inherent principle of resistance to absorption and dissolution in culture.

That Freud was a great hero of culture few would deny, but few will be able to assent to Trilling's formulation of the relation between the biologically grounded "opposing self" and the culture that self opposes. As Joseph Frank argued in 1956, "the problem still remains of understanding . . . how purely biological attributes can 'criticize' culture and exhibit 'human quality' without the intervention of some more positively human spiritual force."* Freud's moral courage was a triumph of spirit and will, after all. It was not an epiphenomenon of his biological endow-

---

*Frank is alert to the social-political implications of Trilling's quietist biologism in "Lionel Trilling and the Conservative Imagination," which originally appeared in *Sewanee Review* and is reprinted in *Salmagundi* 41 (Spring 1978). Many younger critics were defining their own positions in relation to Trilling's in those years. Their struggle to affirm themselves was difficult because in many cases they had themselves been deeply influenced by Trilling's work. But sharp criticism was not lacking. See, in particular, Delmore Schwartz, "The Duchess' Red Shoes," *Partisan Review* 20 (Jan.-Feb. 1953); Irving Howe, "This Age of Conformity," *Partisan Review* 21 (Jan.-Feb. 1954); and Richard Chase, *The Democratic Vista* (1958). The relation of these younger critics to Trilling was very complicated. Irving Howe, for example, who is fifteen years younger than Trilling, started out in the late forties defending him against "calcified" critics on the left like James T. Farrell. But in the mid-fifties, Howe himself was criticizing Trilling from the left. Then in the late sixties, under pressure from "the adversary culture," Howe swung back to become Trilling's most ardent and articulate champion. Richard Chase was a younger colleague and protegé of Trilling in the English department at Columbia in the late forties. Ten years later, in books like *The American Novel and Its Tradition* (1957) and *The Democratic Vista*, Chase was struggling to establish an independent position, as exponent of a new cultural radicalism. Chase's early death cut short his interesting development. The story of Trilling and his critics would also take account of other New York contemporaries, colleagues, and former students, like Alfred Kazin, Quentin Anderson, and Norman Podhoretz.

ment, which is the same in everyone.

This skepticism is surely the right response to Trilling's celebration, in the Freud Anniversary Lecture, of Socrates and Giordano Bruno as "opposing selves" who became martyrs, in Trilling's view, out of the "hard, irreducible, stubborn core of biological urgency" that led them to conceive of their egos and
superegos "as not being culturally conditioned and dependent but
as being virtually biological facts, and immutable."[26] Trilling's
"virtually" begs the question. His saving biologism turns out to be
culture by another name, for the moral principle in the name of
which Socrates died was, preeminently, a cultural ideal. We may
grant that this cultural ideal transcended the limited moral perspective of ancient Greek society, but what moved Socrates was not
biological in any sense a biologist would recognize.

THE BURDEN OF SELF-MAKING

The question remains as to *why* Trilling should have adopted so
seemingly uncongenial a position. What possible use is "biology"
to a critic so concerned to affirm human freedom, "gratuitously
chosen images of personal being"? Looking back over Trilling's
career in criticism, Joseph Frank describes his central project as an
"attempt to construct a defense of classical humanism in terms of
Freudian insights and by an appeal to Freudian ideas."[27] And
Frank wonders how a stress on instinct-life can be reconciled with
Trilling's appeal to consciousness and culture. It does not really
matter whether the implications of biologism are radical or conservative. Freudian biologism and classical humanism are difficult to
reconcile.

One might see Trilling's dialectic of biology and culture as a
new expression of his old conflict between downtown, radicalism,
and Jewishness as against uptown, academia, and gentile refinement. But that conflict is complicated by the fluctuating connotations of the key terms. "Biology" was a complex word. In Trilling's writing it became humanized such that it no longer represented a principle antithetical to that of culture. The instinct-life
was identified with the conservative principle and thereby neut-
ralized; id and superego were conflated.

"Biology," then, became a way of affirming ultimate values.
It served Trilling as a foundational principle, a solid rock in rela-

130

tion to which contemporary threats to the self, like totalitarian ideologies and mass culture, might seem less threatening. The war had brought into being a new society that placed new, more difficult burdens on the self. The self needed a principle of permanence to fend off the increasing threats to its autonomy. It was not enough to urge the importance of vivacity and variousness, wit and style, as Trilling had in *The Liberal Imagination*. These positives might only contribute to the self's volatility. Trilling was looking for something more fundamental, more "archaic," to use his own word. The self needed ballast, and "biology" became the conservative principle that would help to hold things to their center.

The crisis of the postpolitical fifties was a crisis of the self. In retrospect this decade appears to have been a transitional time for Trilling, in which he moved from his earlier Hellenizing positives to the Hebraism of his last period. Variousness and complexity now seemed less to the point than self-survival. Inevitably the dialectical imagination, insofar as it implied cultural relativism, began to give way to a vestigial feeling for absolute values. Gravity, stability, permanence began to emerge as Trilling's chief positives.

We need to keep coming back to the crucial passage of 1961 in which Trilling describes his concern with "moral issues as having something to do with gratuitously chosen images of personal being." It is just as well that Trilling is vague about the relation between moral-cultural debates and different ideals of the self. For he seems never finally to have made up his mind about whether selves really do get made on the basis of "gratuitously chosen images of personal being." His criticism raises again and again the question to what degree we are the products of the culture, and his anxiety focuses on whether there is anything in the self that can withstand cultural determination. Are we merely playthings of history, as Trilling's early historical relativism might suggest? Are we only functions of every new cultural situation, re-creating ourselves every five or ten years?

Trilling's great theme is freedom, but he is never really clear about how much freedom he thinks we have in defining ourselves. From the early fifties on he argued against the modernist dream of "unconditioned" freedom. But if he was suspicious of eschatological thinking, so was he also increasingly cool to the idea of the self as an active, history-making agent. He emphasized, instead of

131

active freedom, a primordial, static, essentially conservative principle within the self that allows it to cohere and resist the disintegrative process of modernity. That is to say, Trilling's way of thinking about the self draws less on the tradition of Enlightenment liberalism than on the countertradition of Romantic conservatism. But what has the permanent, perdurable, immutable, "biological" core of selfhood to do with gratuitous choice among various images of selfhood?

These issues are familiar to readers who have followed recent theoretical debates about "the problem of the subject": the death of the centered self, the death of the author, indeed the death of man. The debate between the last generation of critics and our own comes to a focus over this question of the self and the metaphysics that underwrites, or fails to, the dream of stable selfhood. The rejection by Lacan and Derrida of an origin for the self might usefully be read alongside Trilling's attempt to find in "biology" just such an origin. I want here to take up two brief passages from Trilling's essays of the fifties to illustrate his way of thinking about the self in relation to an older metaphysics that we have lately come to distrust.

The first of these passages is from Trilling's 1956 essay on the philosopher George Santayana. Trilling marvels in that essay on the "stern and graceful self-possession" that the young Santayana reveals in his letters, and he explains "the firmness of [Santayana's] self-definition" in terms of his idea of reality. For Santayana, Trilling says, the world was really there, permanent and material and alien from us. That objectivity makes a contrast with the sentimentality of New England culture in Santayana's early years. The various strands in Santayana's writings—his metaphysics, his views of American character and culture, and so on—come together in his novel *The Last Puritan*. The hero of that novel is a gifted New Englander, a belated heir of Emerson, who, despite advantages of social background and high intelligence, "peters out." Trilling comments on the reasons for that failure:

> Petering out was, it seems, the fate of most of [Santayana's] Harvard friends—it was not that they were worn out by American life, nor that they were hampered by economic circumstances, or perverted by bad ideals; it was that they did not know how to define themselves, that they did not know how to grasp and possess; we might say that they did not know how

to break their hearts on the idea of the hardness of the world, to admit the defeat which is requisite for any victory, to begin their effective life in the world by taking the point of view of the grave.[28]

In an essay on the Boston social critic John Jay Chapman, Edmund Wilson had argued that high-minded Harvard Brahmins were pushed aside during the Gilded Age because their virtues put them at a disadvantage in the economic struggle for survival. Trilling takes a very different tack. He is much more concerned with the failure of Santayana's friends "to define themselves" than he is with social and economic circumstance. He says that the best and finest of the young Brahmins came to nothing because of bad ideas, because of an inadequate conception of reality. Their watered-down Emersonianism betrayed them by giving them no sense of the world's materiality, life's "hardness," the abyss that separates human desire from the intractable conditions that hedge us in. That abyss requires—if we are to survive spiritually—that we set about defining ourselves.

William James overcame the genteel tradition into which he was born. But Trilling seems never to have been deeply influenced by James. Santayana was more to the point because his Latin-Catholic culture gave him a European sense of the tragic. Santayana's naturalism helps bind us to this earth, counteracting the centrifugal and volatilizing tendencies of modern American culture. Self-definition, as Trilling conceived it, requires a foundational principle, a permanent bedrock. Hence the appeal of biology, as a ground for the self.

The second passage, from Trilling's 1957 essay on Jane Austen, is concerned with the new social circumstances that put a premium on conscious self-invention:

Jane Austen, conservative and conventional as she was, perceived the nature of the deep psychological change which accompanied the establishment of democratic society—she was aware of the increase of the psychological burden of the individual, she understood the necessity of conscious self-definition and self-criticism, the need to make private judgments of reality.[29]

The Santayana passage relates the need for "conscious self-definition" to a tragic metaphysics; the Austen passage relates it to the expansion of democracy.

The economic boom of the American 1950s had made for a vastly expanded mass culture. At first Trilling had welcomed the democratization of culture as an opportunity for the intellectuals to shape opinion. But as the decade wore on he was increasingly disillusioned by the general relaxation of standards, and perhaps above all by the vulgarization of the modernist movement in art and culture. Several of Trilling's seemingly eccentric gestures in the fifties—his praise of biology, his self-conscious appeal to "the archaic," his revulsion against the worldly world—can be seen as a protest against the effects of postwar prosperity and the expansion of mass society. High-culture attitudes were accessible now to a much larger group than ever before, and one consequence was trivialization. Trilling found himself withdrawing from the present, very consciously defining himself as an old-fashioned man making "private judgments" about the sleaziness of modernity. Trilling's distaste in the fifties for the culture industry and the crass knowingness that it fostered ushered in his critique of "the adversary culture" in the sixties.

Chapter Eight

The Fate of Modernism

In the preface to *The Opposing Self* Trilling writes that since the time of the French Revolution the modern self has had "one distinguishing characteristic, . . . its intense and adverse imagination of the culture in which it has its being."[1] In the forties and fifties Trilling looked upon that adversary attitude with favor. In the sixties, threatened by the aggressive irrationalism of a new, more widely diffused counterculture, he became much more skeptical about the adversary impulse of modernism. The adversary imagination had turned out to be as subject to corruption as the liberal imagination had been in the 1940s.

Trilling's major essays of the 1960s are confusing because "the adversary culture" refers sometimes to a large tendency of literature since 1800 and sometimes to the specific literary-cultural movement of the sixties. Trilling very clearly regretted the latter, but his regret about what he took to be the betrayal of the modernist heritage did not quite become a correspondingly total disillusionment with modernism itself. As with liberalism, the "primal imagination" of modernism had to be distinguished from its "present particular manifestations." Since Trilling's response to the adversary manifestations of the sixties only makes sense against the background of his more general conception of a century and a half of modernism, it is with that conception that I begin.

WHAT WAS MODERNISM?

In his well-known essay of 1961, "On the Teaching of Modern Literature," which is reprinted in *Beyond Culture* (1965), Trilling defines modernism in terms of "the disenchantment of our culture with culture itself." He says, "It seems to me that the characteristic element of modern literature, or at least of the most highly developed modern literature, is the bitter line of hostility to civilization which runs through it."[2] Trilling goes on to describe the syllabus and rationale for his undergraduate course on modern literature at Columbia, which had been organized to illustrate that theme. The focus is on modernism as a middle-class revolt against its own mode of existence. In Trilling's view that revolt has been the most important concern of literature since the time of the French Revolution.

Trilling begins with Frazer's *The Golden Bough* and its chapters about dying and reborn gods (Attis, Osiris, Adonis). He then turns to Nietzsche's *The Birth of Tragedy*. Comparing Nietzsche and Blake on the theme of art and energy, Trilling remarks on "the discovery and canonization of the primal, non-ethical energies" in modern literature. His next selection is Conrad's *Heart of Darkness*, which he praises for "its strange and terrible message of ambivalence toward the life of civilization." Then Trilling takes up Mann's *Death in Venice*, as another illustration of the Apollonian-Dionysian opposition in *The Birth of Tragedy*. The next work in his course is Nietzsche's *The Genealogy of Morals* because its view of society "is consonant with . . . the validation and ratification of the primitive energies."[3]

Nietzsche is central to Trilling's idea of the modern, but, because Nietzsche has been so pervasive an influence on contemporary French philosophy, it should be noted that Trilling's Nietzsche represents much less of a break with bourgeois humanism than does the Nietzsche of Derrida and Foucault. In Trilling's course *The Genealogy of Morals* is linked with Freud's *Civilization and Its Discontents*, and Trilling's Nietzsche, like Trilling's Freud, turns out to be in many respects a cultural conservative. Trilling says that Nietzsche raises the question of the origins of society but only, in the end, "in the interests of culture." Like Freud, Nietzsche sees culture as a cause of human suffering but believes that we have no choice but to accept it. Trilling understands Nietzsche's reply to the question of whether to accept civilization as "essentially in the line of traditional humanism."

The texts for the second half of Trilling's course include Diderot's *Rameau's Nephew*, Dostoevsky's *Notes from Underground*, Tolstoy's "The Death of Ivan Ilych," and two of Pirandello's plays. The chief theme continues to be the "dreadful force" of these modern works in destroying "the citadel of the commonplace life in which we all believe we can take refuge from ourselves and our fate."[4] Trilling insists on the "radicalism" of these works in exposing the hollowness of Western civilization. But it is not a

136

political radicalism he has in mind. Trilling understands modernism as a "spiritual" project—"more than with anything else, our literature is concerned with salvation."[5] This spiritual critique implicitly rules out an interpretation of modernism in social terms.

What, then, are the political implications of Trilling's view of modern literature? Raymond Williams seems to me right in describing Trilling's arrangement of modernist texts as "post-liberal" rather than truly adversary. In Williams's view, Trilling's interpretation of the modern represents "the desperate adherence to a liberal idea of the self at the point where the liberal idea of society had broken down."[6] We have already seen Trilling dramatizing that liberal idea of the self in the fiction which he wrote in the 1940s. In his short stories and in *The Middle of the Journey* the refined middle-class individual distances himself from the hated social process so as to safeguard his sensibility and autonomy. The isolated self stands apart from and in opposition to a crushing, largely undifferentiated social order.

But in the forties Trilling still emphasized the importance of social class. By the sixties "the self" had largely displaced the social categories of his earlier writing. In his 1972 book *Sincerity and Authenticity* Trilling attacks the "existential" idiom of self-hood that had grown up in the preceding decade. But the following passage, from an essay on Tolstoy's "The Death of Ivan Ilych" that Trilling published in 1967, shows that he had himself contributed to the popularity of that idiom:

> [Ivan Ilych] had never admired anyone or anything; he had never been interested in anything or anyone, not even, really, in himself. He had never questioned or doubted anything, not even himself.
>   Indeed he had lived without any sense that he had a self or was a self. He had assumed all the roles that respectable society had assigned to him: he had been a public official, a husband, a father. But a self he had never been. . . . Only at the point of his extinction is selfhood revealed to him.[7]

But what is this "self" that would exist abstracted from all social roles and determination? One notes how little Trilling makes of Ivan Ilych's social position as a middle-level bureaucrat or of the place in the story of Gerasim, the peasant who represents for Tolstoy an alternative to the soulless existence of his master.

Trotsky and Lenin found in Tolstoy the germ of a socialist critique of czarist society. After the thirties Trilling was opposed to the search for left-wing political implications in the great texts of literature. He was, on the other hand, surprisingly sympathetic to the notorious flirtation with fascism of several early modernists. That sympathy was not political. Rather, Trilling understood the incipiently fascist politics of Yeats, Pound, and Eliot as a cultural fact, part of bourgeois culture's quarrel with itself. The politics of these poets was "an act of critical energy on the part of society . . . to identify in itself that which is but speciously good,"[8] so that it might be rooted out.

The "specious good"—the phrase is discussed in Trilling's important essay of 1963, "The Fate of Pleasure"—refers to the Benthamite-utilitarian vision of human happiness as it had been advanced during Trilling's youth by Shaw and Wells. But it goes beyond liberalism to stand for the good of traditional humanism. And, as Trilling liked to remind his readers, humanism's idea of the good—truth, beauty, order, pleasure, peace—remains the good of most of us, except in our lives as readers and acolytes of modernist literature.

What, then, was the greater good for which the specious good must be sacrificed? The adversary imagination of the great modernists is directed, Trilling says, not to pleasure but to the recovery of contact with the deep, primitive sources of life. The boast of Dostoevsky's Underground Man sums up the new self-ideal: "I have more life in me than you have." This cry replaces an older, traditional form of self-affirmation in which men and women derive their sense of self-worth through duty and obedience. Trilling would later develop this opposition of self-ideals in terms of a contrast between the traditional, sociable ideal of "sincerity" and the antinomian ideal of "authenticity."

This new mode of self-affirmation and self-realization attracts Trilling but at the same time frightens him. For Trilling does not understand the revulsion against the specious good as an attack on a particular kind of society. The modernists are not antagonistic to bourgeois society alone, as Marxist critics argue. Rather, Trilling says, modernism's protest is global; it is a protest against the very idea of social existence. Modernism's revolt against the specious good implies a thoroughgoing rejection of human limitation, of the conditions which make society necessary in the first place. Trilling argues that no reorganization of society could satisfy the modernists' demand, for it is a demand for nothing less than absolute freedom, freedom from limitation and the human condition itself.

Trilling himself often seems sympathetic to that dream of absolute freedom. An example is when he writes of Jay Gatsby, who "sprang," as Fitzgerald says, "from his Platonic conception of himself." Unlike Gatsby, however, Trilling accepts "the conditions." He even seems at times to be grateful for them, however much his idea of "gratuitous" choice of selfhood would seem to imply a denial of limitations imposed by the past. Trilling's ideal conception of the self remains social. For the heroes of modernist irrationalism, on the other hand, freedom is asocial, limitless. For them, as Trilling says,

> the end is not merely freedom from the middle class but freedom from society itself. I venture to say that the idea of losing oneself up to the point of self-destruction, of surrendering oneself to experience without regard to self-interest or conventional morality, of escaping wholly from the societal bonds, is an "element" somewhere in the mind of every modern person who dares to think of what Arnold in his unaffected Victorian way called "the fullness of spiritual perfection."[9]

ENCOUNTERS WITH INDIVIDUAL MODERNISTS

This passage, from "On the Teaching of Modern Literature," is typical of Trilling's generalizing mode in dealing with modernism in *Beyond Culture*. Only in his essay on Isaac Babel does Trilling offer a sustained interpretation of any single twentieth-century writer. The other essays are about large cultural issues ("Freud: Within and Beyond Culture," "The Leavis-Snow Controversy," and "The Fate of Pleasure"); or the question of the literary curriculum ("On the Teaching of Modern Literature" and "The Two Environments: Reflections on the Study of English"); or major nineteenth-century figures ("*Emma* and the Legend of Jane Austen" and "Hawthorne in Our Time").

Although Trilling frequently invoked the moderns en masse, he rarely wrestled with them one-on-one. He had very little to say about poetry altogether, and what little he did say about the few modern poets he mentioned was more concerned with their cultural attitude than with their verse as such. In the case of prose fiction, he wrote at greater length about Austen, Dickens, and James than about any twentieth-century novelist except perhaps Forster.* And the Forster he admired was the author of the relatively conventional *Howards End* rather than the more modern Forster of *A Passage to India*. Trilling had very little to say about Conrad and Lawrence, whom he admired, and even less about Virginia Woolf, whom he disliked. He was halfhearted about modern American literature, according only to Henry James the kind of respect he gave to the great Europeans. Of the American modernists, he wrote only short pieces about Dos Passos, Fitzgerald, Hemingway, and Faulkner, and then only in the thirties and forties.

There is, however, one volume in which Trilling does write about specific works of the great modernists: *The Experience of Literature* (1967), a 1300-page anthology edited by Trilling with fifty-two "commentaries," of about 1000–2000 words each, on individual selections. *The Experience of Literature* was ten years in the making, which makes it a parallel volume to *Beyond Culture*, the collection of Trilling's major critical essays between 1955 and 1965. In many respects the textbook is a more satisfying work than the collection. Having to be brief and pointed saved Trilling from the abstractness and digressiveness that often mar his later work.

About half of the anthology is given over to classics of modernism. In addition to the specifically modernist texts, there are many nineteenth-century English and American works, like "Bartleby the Scrivener," that Trilling reads in the light of modern issues. Among the texts for which he provides a commentary are: in drama, Yeats's *Purgatory* and Pirandello's *Six Characters in Search of an Author;* in short fiction, Hawthorne's "My Kinsman, Major Molineux," Tolstoy's "The Death of Ivan Ilych," Conrad's "The Secret Sharer," Joyce's "The Dead," Kafka's "The Hunter Gracchus," and Lawrence's "Tickets, Please"; and in poetry, Wordsworth's "Resolution and Independence," Whitman's "Out of the Cradle Endlessly Rocking," Yeats's "Sailing to Byzantium," Eliot's "The Waste Land," Cummings's "My Father Moved

*Trilling also wrote a long essay on James Joyce, which I take up at the end of this chapter.

140

Through Dooms of Love," and Auden's "In Memory of Sigmund Freud."

Denis Donoghue seems to me right in praising *The Experience of Literature* as "a significant document in contemporary American culture."[10] It is a massive summation of the literary taste of an entire generation of New York critics, and only the conventional disdain of academics for textbooks accounts for its neglect. The original textbook is hard to find, but Harcourt Brace Jovanovich has performed a service in reprinting the commentaries in a convenient volume in its Uniform Edition of Trilling's works. When the anthology first appeared in 1967, Donoghue invoked Yeats in describing it as an "attempt to assemble . . . a Sacred Book of the Arts." But in praising Trilling's taste it is useful to keep in mind Raymond Williams's warning about the tendentiousness of Trilling's selection, his "particular North Atlantic definition and structure of 'the modern,' . . . with its built-in connections and its built-in implacable conclusions."[11]

I have already had occasion to quote from the commentaries on Tolstoy, Babel, and Mann. Now I want to suggest the overall tendency of *The Experience of Literature*. The anthology is unified by a number of recurrent motifs, of which the most important is that of initiation, which links such selections as "My Kinsman, Major Molineux," "The Secret Sharer," "Di Grasso," and Isak Dinesen's "The Sailor-Boy's Tale." But even in discussing such stories about Young Men from the Provinces setting forth to make their way in the great world, Trilling is not at all satisfied with a prosaically social understanding of their progress. Coming into one's own suggests to him fairy tale and fable. For Trilling, even more than the nineteenth-century European novelists he liked to cite, the drama of youthful ambition was a romance.

In his commentary on Isak Dinesen, Trilling observes that initiation tales seem always to involve "happenings of a marvelous kind."[12] Not realism but romance, not history but myth: that is the tendency of Trilling's commentaries on modern literature in the sixties. I don't wish to overstate the point, for Trilling remains a historically minded critic of culture. But it's curious to see how he pulls away from history to timeless mythic themes even when he is discussing texts that are drenched in history.

Consider his commentary on D. H. Lawrence's story "Tickets, Please." Trilling begins by stating the story's social theme: the emergence of the new liberated woman of the World War I period and the battle of the sexes that ensued. But as Trilling discusses that battle, it loses its historical specificity and takes on a mythic resonance. He seems less interested in the new feminist consciousness as a social fact than in the mythic theme, which Lawrence no doubt took from *The Bacchae*, of the maenads' revenge.

Lawrence's handsome tram inspector is aptly nicknamed "Coddy" Raynor. The cocksure Coddy has been sexually exploiting the young women who work as conductors on the trams. Transfigured by their righteous anger into "fearless young hussies," the women determine to revenge themselves on their arrogant exploiter. But in the event—this is Trilling's main point—they have little pleasure in their victory. As Trilling says:

> No sooner have the girls succeeded in redressing the balance against him . . . than they are appalled by what they have done. They undertook to destroy this arrogant male, to humiliate him and make him ridiculous; their success makes them feel lost and miserable. For it is exactly what they resent in Coddy Raynor—his masculine pride and arrogance, his lordly independence—that constitutes his attraction as a man and draws them to him.[13]

This is no misreading of Lawrence's story. Still, in conjunction with other readings in *The Experience of Literature*, it makes for a certain tendency. If in 1930 Lawrence had been important to Trilling as a passionate critic of capitalism, now it is Lawrence's conservatism that appeals to Trilling. Unchanging female biology and emotional needs—the myth of feminine Nature—are now more to Trilling's purpose than any historically derived critique of society.

At first it seems perfectly appropriate that an anthology intended for a mainly adolescent undergraduate audience should focus on stories of initiation. But it becomes apparent, as we move through this book, that the particular texts and interpretations are chiefly concerned with one special kind of initiation: dying to nature and history and being reborn to a higher, timeless order of being. Take Forster's "The Road from Colonus." That story might have been interpreted in the light of Forster's grand theme of the panic and emptiness of the Edwardian upper middle class. Instead, Trilling stresses the Sophoclean mythic theme. Forster's Mr. Lucas has his moment of self-transcendence at Colonus, in his realization and acceptance of death. Joyce's "The Dead" receives a similar gloss, as does John O'Hara's "Summer's Day."

The Experience of Literature is likely to have been a dispiriting experience for the young. For its larger theme, achieved by way of the particular selections and their juxtaposition, is the futility of the personal and social will. Death can be the mother of beauty, but in Trilling's commentaries it has the effect of making ordinary existence valueless. In 1951 Trilling had praised Howells for his attachment to the routine details of everyday middle-class life. But now Trilling wants to get "beyond culture." That phrase has more than one sense in Trilling's writing of the sixties, but often it seems to imply not resistance to culture but remoteness and detachment, an attitude that appeared in Trilling's teaching as well as in his writing.*

That same tendency to disenchantment and detachment also appears in Trilling's commentaries on the poems he has selected. Given his mood, Yeats's "Sailing to Byzantium" is an obvious choice. It becomes yet another expression of the artist's wish to escape from history to a condition of "fixity and timelessness." The theme, which Trilling takes up repeatedly in his last years, is "the imagination of beautiful permanence": art as an alternative to history and as the transcendence of the human condition of struggle and suffering.

THE ADVERSARY CULTURE

One of Trilling's major objections to literary culture in the sixties concerns the loss of the high seriousness of the early modernists. The spirit of the sixties adversary culture was the spirit of parody.

---

*Phillip Lopate was a student of Trilling at Columbia in the early sixties. In a memoir of those years Lopate evokes a teacher puzzled by his students ("But what is it you young people want?") and compelled by the "symbolic role" he had created for himself to surrender "a part of his contact with life, and a certain levity and flexibility of movement." See Lopate, "Remembering Lionel Trilling," *American Review* (October 1976): 176.

Trilling complained of the "devaluation of clear moralizing intention" in writers like Philip Roth and Donald Barthelme. But they did in fact have a moralizing intention: they were throwing off the burden of high seriousness that they had inherited from high modernism and from such moralizing critics of the fifties as Trilling himself.

However different in tone, Trilling's analysis of cultural change was not altogether dissimilar from that of the rebellious new generation of writers and critics. He was very conscious, in teaching the modernist texts that had shaped his own generation, that a decisive change had occurred in the reception of these texts. In "On the Teaching of Modern Literature," he describes his dismay over his students' easy adaptation to a body of work that he himself professed still to fear on account of its energy of subversion. Trilling despaired of his students, not because they "fail to respond to ideas, [but] because they respond to ideas . . . with a delighted glibness, a joyous sense of power in the use of received or receivable generalizations."[14]

Of course, Trilling had himself had a role in the transformation of modernism into "received generalizations." By the early sixties modern literature had become institutionalized in the college classroom. During that decade there was a great expansion of university education, bringing with it a vast army of English majors, many more than today. These students formed a ready market for the proliferating "casebooks," "critical editions," and "reader's guides," many of them devoted to unlocking the difficulties of works by writers like Yeats, Joyce, and Eliot. In addition, there were a variety of textbooks and anthologies, including *The Experience of Literature*, to make the assimilation of modernism easier than ever.* Inevitably assimilation meant domestica-

*Irving Howe recalls that by the mid-sixties "the tradition of the New . . . had acquired wrinkles and a paunch" (*A Margin of Hope* [New York: Harcourt Brace Jovanovich, 1982], 289). But that did not keep critics, including Howe himself, from trying to synthesize modernism anew. See, for example, Howe's essay "The Culture of Modernism," *Commentary* 40 (November 1967), which is reprinted as the introduction to his anthology *Literary Modernism* (New York: Fawcett, 1967). See also the huge anthology compiled by Richard Ellmann and Charles Feidelson, Jr., *The Modern Tradition: Backgrounds of Modern Literature* (New York: Oxford Univ. Press, 1965). Frank Kermode discusses various recent theories of the modern in the opening section of his book *Continuities* (New York: Random House, 1968).

tion, the taming of modernism. Trilling's undergraduate course at Columbia had hardly been a pioneering effort. Rather, it had sought to fix and make permanent a once-radical view of life that goes back to 1921–25, the *anni mirabiles* that coincided with Trilling's own years as an undergraduate at Columbia.

The modernism of the early twenties had been a minority culture. Intransigently adversary in temper, it had also been profoundly elitist. By the sixties, Trilling argued, a "new class" had arisen, forming a "second environment" that was solidly entrenched. The adversary spirit of the generation of 1914 had become "the adversary culture" of the 1960s. That new adversary culture appeared as a parody of the older minority culture. It was the latest "orthodoxy of dissent," as rock-solid in its philistinism as the old-style philistinism it prided itself on defying. Trilling wrote of a new "ecology" of culture. The adversary culture had consolidated itself in the universities and the media, not in textbooks alone but in movies and rock music and advertising. Hardly anyone was untouched by the rebellious mood of the sixties. But it was the students in the humanities who led the way in what Trilling called, not without irony, "the socialization of the anti-social, . . . the acculturation of the anti-cultural, . . . the legitimation of the subversive."[15]

Trilling's remark appears in his 1961 essay, "On the Teaching of Modern Literature." His intuition of radical cultural change was confirmed by the bohemian radicalism of the last part of the decade. Trilling may or may not have coined the phrase "modernism in the streets," but as much as any commentator he spelled out its cultural implications. College students were taking to the streets to protest the Vietnam War and the bureaucratic impersonality of their academic institutions and a range of other, less easily articulated complaints. As Trilling saw it, this was modernism at the end of its tether. What had been theory or fantasy in the writings of the great modernists was being turned into street theater in the conduct of the students and young drop-outs. As Trilling said to a newspaper interviewer in 1969, "everything that was speculatively implied in literature is being actualized in politics, in social action":

> In our time it seems quite natural to act out what were once thought of as moral fantasies. Take, for example, the idea of violence as we got it in Yeats or D. H. Lawrence or Gide. . . . It was represented as something

145

that intellectuals might want to take into account as offering a challenge to their characteristically peaceable ethos. No one ever thought that when these writers represented violence as interesting or beneficent they were really urging their readers to bloody actions. But now violence is proposed and justified on moral and psychological grounds.*

The key phrase in Trilling's formulation is "acting out," a term used by psychoanalysts to describe activity in which patients externalize their conflicts instead of remembering and analyzing them. "The essence of the concept," as the British psychoanalyst Charles Rycroft says, "is the replacement of thought by action."[16] Trilling had always followed Matthew Arnold, and then Freud, in arguing for reflection as against the satisfactions of unconsidered action.

Trilling was not alone in warning against the rage to action. But whereas for an American critic the language of psychoanalysis came quickly to mind, for European intellectuals the Marxist idiom of "theory" and "praxis" was more typical. The message, however, was essentially the same. Thus, just about the time that Trilling was lamenting student violence at Columbia in an interview with a reporter from the *New York Times*, Theodor Adorno was being quoted in a German newspaper complaining about the uses to which his own earlier political ideas were being put by radical students at Frankfurt: "When I made my theoretical model, I could not have guessed that people would try to realize it with Molotov cocktails."[17]

The difference in idiom is important to the degree that Central European liberals and radicals had seen a similarly polarized politics in the Weimar years eventuate in the triumph of Nazism. They took very seriously the violence of some elements of the student left. Trilling does not seem to have been nearly as

*I am grateful to Morris Dickstein for sending me a copy of the article in which this quotation appears. See Israel Shenker, "The Crucial Years: We Survived Them," *New York Times*, December 30, 1969. Dickstein attributes the phrase "modernism in the streets" to Trilling in his book *Gates of Eden: American Culture in the Sixties* (New York: Basic Books, 1977), 266. But, as he notes in a letter to me, the idea appears at the end of the sixties in a number of places, including "On the Steps of Low Library," Diana Trilling's essay on the Columbia student uprising. That essay, originally published in *Commentary* in 1968, is reprinted in *We Must March, My Darlings* (New York: Harcourt Brace Jovanovich, 1977). See also Harold Rosenberg's essay "Surrealism in the Streets," which first appeared in the *New Yorker* and is reprinted in *The Dedefinition of Art* (New York: Horizon Press, 1972); and Saul Bellow's novel *Mr. Sammler's Planet* (New York: Viking Press, 1970).

alarmed. Indeed, as we shall see, his remoteness infuriated some who thought that he should have been far more active in opposing the new orthodoxy of dissent. It is typical of the later Trilling that he should have translated the social crisis of the sixties into psychological terms. He wholly rejected the political terms of debate proposed by the student radicals. "The explicit issues," he told an interviewer, "were largely factitious." What was at stake was not Columbia University's complicity in an immoral war but the wish of the students to be different kinds of persons than "the system" seemed to allow. Without knowing what they were doing, the students were acting out fantasies of identity: "For young people now, being political serves much the same purpose as being literary has long done—it expresses and validates the personality."[18] For the later Trilling social-political issues always came back to the single question of "the self."

THE NEOCONSERVATIVES

Trilling's critique of the adversary culture was adapted for their own purposes and popularized by a number of New York intellectuals who had previously been associated with the political left but who, from the late sixties on, formed the nucleus of a new neoconservativism. These writers—above all Daniel Bell, Irving Kristol, Hilton Kramer, and Norman Podhoretz[19]—have been zealous in trying to liquidate the residues of the sixties. But, indifferent to "the imagination of complication" that was Trilling's ideal, they have often simplified his antiradicalism nearly as much as the student radicals of the sixties had simplified his earlier advocacy of the adversary impulse of modernism.

Right-wing simplification has usually taken the form of politicizing concepts originally intended to be more specifically cultural in their reference. Thus, for example, Kristol and Podhoretz expanded Trilling's idea of "the new class" far beyond anything that Trilling himself had intended. There is nothing in fact in Trilling's own writing to indicate that he shared the neoconservative belief in the existence of a newly dominant class that functions as a kind of radical fifth column within the government, media, and academe to mold society according to its own "anti-American," anticapitalist views.

Although Trilling's major themes, like that of the adversary

147

culture, were easily appropriated for neoconservative ends, he never assented to the political program of the neoconservatives. On cultural issues he was clearly conservative, but politically he remained an old-fashioned liberal, closer in sensibility, say, to nineteenth-century English liberals like Arnold than to contemporaries like Irving Howe. It is true that Trilling's 1972 Jefferson Lecture, "Mind in the Modern World," argues, as do the neoconservatives, against affirmative action quotas in the universities.[20] But liberals have traditionally supported the principle of meritocracy, and such a commitment by itself does not place Trilling on the political right.

Some neoconservatives have oscillated between claiming Trilling as a distinguished forerunner and being irritated that he never conferred his blessing on their movement. Podhoretz in particular has made explicit the group's frustration with Trilling. In his "political memoir" *Breaking Ranks* (1979), Podhoretz says that Trilling "retreated in the face of the radicalism of the late sixties."[21] Podhoretz says that, far from having joined the neoconservative campaign against the adversary culture, Trilling displayed a "failure of nerve." In a roundtable discussion of contemporary culture sponsored by *Commentary* in 1974, Podhoretz nearly confronted Trilling directly in proposing to the conferees that the aversion of some New York intellectuals from fighting more aggressively against the new radicalism of the late sixties had been owing to "an epidemic of cowardice." Trilling gave this response:

> There is a reason to say cowardice in individual cases, but as a general explanation of the situation Norman Podhoretz refers to I think the word *cowardice* might lead us astray. One has to conceive of it in terms of fatigue. . . . Subjects and problems got presented in a way that made one's spirits fail. It wasn't that one was afraid to go into it, or afraid of being in opposition—I suppose I am speaking personally—but rather that in looking at the matter one's reaction was likely to be a despairing shrug.[22]

Trilling's repeated "one," instead of "I," suggests the awkwardness, the "despairing shrug," to which he alludes. But embarassed as this statement may be, it has the ring of sincerity. There is no evidence that this was not the way Trilling actually experienced the sixties, or at least the way he remembered that experience in 1974. But in his memoir Podhoretz does not accept Trilling's testimony at face value. He argues that Trilling avoided polemic in the sixties not because he was uncertain but because of a "venerability" complex. According to Podhoretz, Trilling wanted to end his days as "Professor Sir Lionel Trilling," an American equivalent of England's Isaiah Berlin. And to protect his reputation as a cultural elder he had to remain above the battle.

Certainly it is reasonable to have been disappointed with Trilling in the late sixties. But the disappointment might just as well have focused on his failure to oppose the Vietnam War rather than his failure to oppose that war's opponents. Writers on both the left and the right had reason to feel let down by Trilling. His remoteness saved him from the polemical excesses of intellectuals more deeply involved in the cultural debates of those years. But Trilling's coolness was purchased at too high a price. It now appears that Trilling's disengagement may have had less to do with a cowardly concern to protect his reputation than with a sense of bafflement.

I missed Trilling's leadership at the time and wrote about him with some bitterness in 1971.* I am not disposed to judge him as harshly now as I did fifteen years ago. Given the uncertainties Trilling had about nearly everything, it was right for him to turn to history for understanding rather than to trumpet opinions about which he was unsure simply because, in his intellectual milieu, everyone was supposed to have a ready opinion about everything. He may have intuited something wrong in the tone and the spirit of the neoconservatives, who would have liked his blessing. Certainly he distanced himself from their simplifications, like the notion that the new radicalism was a simple repetition of the old, corrupted leftism of the forties. It was better to be uncertain than to equate, for polemical purposes, the new adversary culture with the old Stalinism.**

---

*See Mark Krupnick, "Lionel Trilling: Criticism and Illusion," in *Modern Occasions* 1 (Winter 1971): 282–87.

**Most reviewers were irritated by Trilling's uncertainty. Graham Hough, who had praised Trilling's earlier books, spoke for many readers of *Beyond Culture* when he complained, in a review, that "to indulge so consistently in these hesitations, dissociations, and withdrawals is not, it seems to me, to stand beyond one's culture, but simply to occupy a very indeterminate position within it." See Hough, " 'We' and Lionel Trilling," *Listener* (May 26, 1966): 93. But this negative appraisal should be balanced against Hough's very positive estimate of Trilling's career as a whole, in "Culture and Sincerity," *London Review of Books* (May 6-19, 1982): 6–7.

In the late sixties Trilling was no longer the same kind of critic that he had been in the forties. If the younger Trilling had imitated the manner of Victorian men of letters like Arnold, the older man was moving toward a Central European mode of cultural criticism, a philosophical history of consciousness in the Hegelian mode. It is possible to appreciate the effort of re-creating the self implied in this groping for a new kind of writing while at the same time regretting the detachment and remoteness from immediate issues and events that made it necessary.

"A LOVELY NOTHING"

Trilling's remarks at the *Commentary* forum call to mind the alienation he remembered himself as having suffered at the start of his career. The language he uses in 1974 to describe his situation in the late sixties is similar to the language he had used in 1966 to describe his situation in the late twenties.[23] In both periods "subjects and problems got presented in such a way that made one's spirits fail." The writing that resulted from this bafflement lacks the punch of Trilling's best criticism, which mainly belongs to the period between 1937 and 1955. But it has an authority of its own, the authority of disillusion. As in the sixties Trilling faced the collapse of an intellectual-cultural synthesis he had helped bring into being, he inevitably sought out a writer who faced life with something like his own "despairing shrug." And so he came to James Joyce, the one indisputably modern twentieth-century writer to whom he devoted a major essay. The Joyce essay, originally published in 1968, is reprinted in Trilling's posthumously published collection *The Last Decade: Essays and Reviews, 1965–75.*

In 1957 Trilling had written a short notice to introduce an edition of Joyce's letters to the members of the Readers' Subscription. That essay is mainly a tribute to Joyce's normalcy as a middle-aged family man. In the fifties Trilling had been looking for instances of devotion to ordinary life. The usual view of Joyce had stressed his intransigent commitment to art and his defiance of the binding principles of family, church, and nation. But Trilling was concerned in the mid-fifties with a different Joyce. Trilling says that after *Ulysses* Joyce was trying to reintegrate himself into quotidian existence; he was taking a more positive view of the binding principles. Trilling describes that Joyce as "the simplest of men, the most (save the mark!) 'human,' the most conventional."[24]

But as the culture changes so does Trilling, and the Joyce whom he admires in the sixties stands for a very different attitude toward life. That Joyce has left the domesticity of the fifties far behind. As Trilling's earlier essay had concerned Joyce in early middle age, so his 1968 essay is mainly about Joyce's last years. As Trilling evokes him, this older Joyce has passed wholly beyond the earthly desires of his younger self and attained a condition of sublime detachment, godlike not only in his creative self-confidence but also in having died to all normal human wishes.

Trilling's long essay is cast as a reflection on a passage in a letter Joyce wrote his son George in 1935: "Here I conclude. My eyes are tired. For over half a century they have gazed into nullity, where they have found a lovely nothing."[25] This older Joyce is beyond culture, beyond desire, beyond everything. If Joyce's humanness had impressed Trilling in 1957, it is his inhumanness that most impresses him in 1968. As Trilling says,

> Nothing in the way of "humanness" contradicts our sense that the letters of [Joyce's] years of fame were written by a being who had departed this life as it is generally known and had become such a ghost as Henry James and Yeats imagined, a sentient soul that has passed from temporal existence into nullity yet still has a burden of energy to discharge, a destiny still to be worked out.[26]

Trilling's 1968 essay on Joyce takes on new meaning when set alongside his essay of twenty years before on *The Princess Casamassima*. The earlier essay is notable for Trilling's rapt identification with James's Napoleonic fantasy of earthly power and glory. The later essay, written from the other side of fame, is nearly as remarkable for its ghostly detachment from earthly things. Together these two essays sum up Trilling's personal myth early and late. They mark a transition that Trilling calls, in reference to Joyce, a "devolution . . . from [an] early egotism of the world to a later egotism of nullity."[27]

This appreciation of disengagement, indeed of a quiet nihilism, is not totally new in Trilling's writing. Even in *The Middle of the Journey*, his most overtly political piece of writing, there is a preoccupation with nullity. John Bayley has commented on that novel's "judicious and meticulous coolness with something

151

else—is it emptiness and despair?—just behind it."²⁸ But it took the special circumstances of the late sixties to draw out that emptiness and despair, which had previously appeared only sporadically in Trilling's writing, most conspicuously in the fiction he wrote in the twenties and forties.

But it is not the sense of nullity that links Trilling's days each to each. As with Joyce, what connects the early world-hunger and the later cosmic detachment is "egotism." In Trilling's essay on Joyce that word has only positive connotations. It has nothing to do with mere selfishness. Rather, it is much closer in sense to Emerson's "self-reliance" and Whitman's "thought of identity." That thought, Whitman had said, is the "miracle of miracles, beyond statement, most spiritual and vaguest of earth's dreams, yet hardest basic fact, and only entrance to all facts."²⁹ In his last years Trilling wrote much about the fate in the modern world of that healthy, confident egotism of the nineteenth century.

He believed that with Joyce's death in 1941 some older idea of human possibility had gone out of the world:

> Never in our time will a young man focus this much power of love and hate into so sustained a rage of effectual intention as Joyce was capable of, so ferocious an ambition, so nearly absolute a commitment of himself to himself.³⁰

That rapt preoccupation with self-commitment is the thread connecting Trilling's different phases. Nearly twenty-five years earlier, in his essay on Scott Fitzgerald, Trilling had sounded the same note:

> Fitzgerald was perhaps the last notable writer to affirm the Romantic fantasy, descended from the Renaissance, of personal ambition and heroism, of life committed to, or thrown away for, some ideal of self.³¹

Fitzgerald and Joyce had in common that they both died on the eve of World War II. So did Freud and Yeats. When Trilling wrote about these heroes of modernism, he almost always stressed their links to the nineteenth century and the nineteenth-century humanistic ideal of self-making. These writers became "figures" not only because of gifts granted them at birth but because the culture in which they grew up made available to them better ideas of how the self is made than does contemporary culture. In Trilling's last few years alienation from American society drove him back to "the self" as his single, all-purpose principle of cultural explanation. In his next book, *Sincerity and Authenticity* (1972), he discusses rival modes of selfhood without much reference to specific social tendencies of the modern age. His revulsion against politics led him to create a much thinner background for the play of individual personality than in *Matthew Arnold*. We may regret the abstractness of Trilling's late conception of the self. But ideas and ideologies of the self had been the inner theme of his criticism from the beginning, although that theme is usually muffled. Even at the end Trilling's own self remains hooded and somewhat equivocal, but it is good to see him dealing with his preoccupation more directly.

Chapter Nine

The Struggle with Weightlessness

In the *Commentary* forum on "Culture at the Present Time" Norman Podhoretz proposed that the function of the critic at present was "to stand in an adversary relation to the adversary culture itself." He cited Trilling's own writing as a precedent for that stance. But Trilling, in his remarks on that occasion, was leery of the uses to which Podhoretz was proposing to put his ideas. To begin with he rejected the idea that the function of criticism ought to be "oppositional." This may sound inconsistent coming from the critic of Stalinism and the author of *The Opposing Self*. But Trilling wanted to distinguish his own project in criticism from that of neoconservatives who thought of themselves as carrying on his tradition in their crusade against the spirit of the radical sixties. Trilling pointed out that the great critical movement inspired by modernist literature had been mainly positive in its program of elucidation and diffusion.

Podhoretz denied that he conceived the critic's role as "necessarily negative." The problem, in his view, was that there is no great new literature to explicate. Later in the discussion Podhoretz offered this definition of the present situation:

> The counterrevolution of the 60's, with its repudiation of the modernist canon, and indeed of rationality itself, posed as a further development of the modernist revolution but was in actuality a resurgence of philistinism, very often of simple cultural barbarism. [1]

What, Podhoretz asked, ought a critic to be doing in such a cultural situation? His own answer, clearly indicated, is that he ought to come out fighting.

Trilling's answer to the question as to what the critic does in a bad time is very different: "You become historical-minded." [2] He thereby summed up the program that he had set himself in the last decade of his life. The critic ought not to take to the streets, but neither should he fulminate against "barbarism." Rather, the critic's task is to find out how we got to where we are. It may be, as Podhoretz later wrote, that Trilling turned away from immediate issues to history because he was carving his bust for posterity and wished not to offend powerful critics on the left. But Trilling's remarks at the 1974 forum suggest an alternative explanation: he was feeling too much a stranger to this new culture to experience the righteous indignation that a cultural crusade requires.

More in sorrow than in anger, he registered a general sense that his own values and assumptions were now at the lowest possible discount. He speculated that the sixties may have marked a fundamental "disjunction . . . between the tradition and what is happening now." His evidence was his students at Columbia. They did not read Joyce, Eliot, Lawrence, Mann as he had. Trilling also noted a *Columbia Forum* article he had read "about W. H. Auden's giving a class at Columbia, and the students' simply not understanding what he was saying about poetry."[3] Trilling's melancholy feeling of disconnection is the main note of his observations at the *Commentary* meeting. That sense, of having outlived himself, underlies the historical-mindedness of *Sincerity and Authenticity*.

HEGELIAN THEMES

Sincerity and Authenticity is a large historical overview of changing ideals of moral consciousness. Four hundred years ago, in response to the pervasive Machiavellianism of public life, "sincerity" emerges as a dominant self-ideal. In a famous formulation of the new ideal Polonius enjoins Laertes to be true to himself so that he may "not then be false to any man." Thus sincerity begins as a sociable ideal, founded on the individual's voluntary acceptance of a public morality to which all civilized (i.e., sincere) men subscribe.

Trilling offers no single, concise definition of his key terms. But we may say, in general, that sincerity, the older ideal, involves being true to oneself within the context of a shared morality. It assumes the existence of positive values outside the individual. Authenticity, on the other hand, tends to be antisocial or at least antinomian. It is private and subjective, emphasizing individual experience as the sole source of value. Moreover, the only experience that matters is the experience of oneself, the more intense the better. What is good is what enhances the individual's sentiment of his own being. Sincerity had been the antidote to the duplicity and dissembling we find in the Renaissance court and in such fictional characters as Shakespeare's Iago and Edmund. Authenticity arises as a response to a later culture in which the sense of self has become fragmented and attenuated. It is the answer to the death of the spirit depicted by modern writers like Joyce and Lawrence.

It appears that sincerity was problematic from the start. Trilling points to Alceste in Molière's *Le Misanthrope* (1666) as an early instance of the self-deception inherent in sincerity assumed as a self-conscious posture. Alceste, we feel, uses sincerity as the vehicle of his vanity, to establish his moral superiority to his contemporaries. Like them he exists only to the degree that he is acknowledged by the worldly world. Molière is only one of many figures invoked in Trilling's first chapter. *Sincerity and Authenticity* is rich in examples, and for many readers its chief virtue will have less to do with its overall historical argument than with Trilling's local observations on particular authors and texts.

The opening chapter—with its remarks on dissembling in Jacobean drama, the manufacture of mirrors by Venetian craftsmen, and seventeenth-century English Puritan autobiographies—is mainly background. Trilling is chiefly concerned not with the early modern period but with the history of consciousness from the era of the French Revolution to the present. He is concerned above all with how sincerity came to be challenged by authenticity. Sincerity appears in Trilling's historical schema as an "archaic," humanistic self-ideal; authenticity is more specifically modernist, in a line that includes Diderot, Hegel (Kierkegaard, however, is not mentioned), Conrad, Sartre, and others. The relation between the two ideals is presented as a debate rather than as a linear unfolding in which one ideal is superseded by a later, historically more progressive ideal. The result is a book that reflects the oscillations of Trilling's own thinking. As history *Sincerity and Authenticity* is sketchy, deliberately tentative. Where it succeeds best is in dramatizing the quarrel of Trilling's mind with itself, and the exemplary critical temper—flexible, persistent, patient—that a writer can achieve when he remains true to his own fluctuations of belief.

It is only with the Enlightenment that the paradoxes of sincerity appear more fully. The key text for Trilling is *Rameau's Nephew*, a fictional dialogue by Diderot written around 1760 but not published until after Diderot's death, in Goethe's 1805 translation. *Rameau's Nephew* is the occasion for Trilling's difficult account of how sincerity gave way to authenticity as the dominant European moral ideal. He offers that account by way of a reading of Hegel's interpretation of the Nephew in the section on "self-estranged Spirit" in *The Phenomenology of Mind*.

Trilling had earlier drawn on Hegel for his discussion of "unconditioned spirit" in his 1951 essay on William Dean Howells, and for his remarks on art and morality in the preface to *The Opposing Self*. Hegel's influence is pervasive in Trilling's essays of the fifties and sixties, but preoccupation with Trilling's more obvious debt to Arnold and the lack of attention to Hegel in American literary studies have kept readers from appreciating just how much Trilling's understanding of the dynamic of modernism derives from the *Phenomenology*. Hegel's concepts provide the scaffolding for *Sincerity and Authenticity*. Chapter 2 of that book shows how the distinction between sincerity and authenticity grows out of Hegel's contrast of the "honest soul" of traditional humanistic culture with the "disintegrated consciousness" of modernity.

Trilling says that the honesty, or sincerity, of the character designated *Moi* in Diderot's dialogue consists in "his wholeness of self, in the directness and consistency of his relation to things, and in his submission to a traditional morality." But it is not the reasonableness and singleness of purpose of Diderot-*Moi* that Hegel praises. Rather, Hegel celebrates the Nephew, the speaker designated in the dialogue as *Lui*. As Trilling says, Hegel admires in the Nephew "the urge of Spirit to escape from the conditions which circumscribe it and to enter into an existence which will be determined by itself alone."[4] The Nephew, shameless buffoon that he is, nevertheless represents for Hegel a decisive turning-point in the history of consciousness. In defying the abstract morality of Enlightenment reason, represented by Diderot-*Moi*, he becomes the first authentic man.

In Hegel's view it is possible to achieve self-realization only through self-alienation. Trilling stresses the incompatibility of this "exigent spiritual enterprise" with the traditional humanistic ideals of order, peace, honor, and beauty. Trilling himself is not as willing as Hegel to consign the old humanistic virtues and aims to the ash heap of history. Developing a theme from his essay "The Fate of Pleasure," he recalls the now-lost imagination of happiness that animates such classic texts of English literature as

Shakespeare's late romances and the country-house poems of Jonson, Marvell, and Yeats. The ardor with which Trilling comments on the older ambition to enter "the fair courts of life" recalls his earlier tenderness for the drive to success and pleasure of the Young Man from the Provinces in the novels of Balzac, Stendhal, and Henry James.

From the point of view of developing Spirit, however, that old dream is regressive because it involves a dubious acquiescence in the "specious good." The self-defeating perversities of the Nephew (*Lui*) place him outside respectable society. But, as Hegel says in praising him, the proper business of Spirit is not the pursuit of happiness but its own self-realization. As Trilling states Hegel's view:

> It is the nature of Spirit . . . to seek "existence on its own account"—that is, to free itself from limiting conditions, to press towards autonomy. . . . If it is to fulfill its natural destiny of self-realization, it must bring to an end its accord with the external power of society.[5]

The rest of *Sincerity and Authenticity* grows out of Trilling's exposition of Hegel's notion of Spirit seeking its perfect self-realization. Trilling stresses the price of such self-insistence, as in the shame and envy of Rameau's Nephew and the spite and malice of Dostoevsky's Underground Man. A moderate man himself, Trilling recoils from the self-estrangement and even madness that are part of the drive to absolute freedom. But his repudiation of the Hegelian will to freedom is not total. It is a measure of Trilling's continuing commitment to this conception of modernism that only the debasement of it in the adversary culture of the sixties caused him to withdraw his credence to the extent that he did.

THE AUTHENTICITY OF MADNESS

Trilling's second chapter, on Diderot and Hegel, is the high point of *Sincerity and Authenticity*. But his sympathy with Hegel's ideal of spirit on its own is countered by his attraction to traditional conceptions of the self in the four remaining chapters of the book. Oscillating between traditional and modernist styles of selfhood, Trilling never arrives at an unambivalent affirmation of one against the other. But his heart seems to be with the old order. It often appears that it is only a piety of the avant-garde that keeps him from surrendering to a temperamental preference for what he calls the "archaic" mode of being. Trilling clung to a piety of literary modernism as others of his generation clung to a piety of political radicalism. But the fact is that when he does praise a modernist writer or thinker, it is usually for his most old-fashioned qualities. He admired the classical strain in the great Romantics and the Victorian residues in the great modernists.

Trilling's resistance to the modernist ideal of authenticity is manifest in the texts of Rousseau, Austen, and Wordsworth that he singles out for discussion. Thus he discusses at considerable length the Rousseau of the *Letter to d'Alembert,* a Rousseau who is self-consciously antimodernist in his objections to the frivolousness of the arts and their bad effect on individual character and the polity. It is a short step from Rousseau's attack on the theater to Jane Austen's *Mansfield Park*, with its fears about role-playing and the loss of personal integrity. Austen's novel, which Trilling had earlier discussed in *The Opposing Self*, allows him to sum up his critique of the artistic ethos of modernity, which he now sees as committed to style, sensibility, and personality at the expense of principle, rational argument, and character.

In chapter 4, on "The Heroic, the Beautiful, the Authentic," Trilling presents Wordsworth as a great exponent of integral, authentic being. But Wordsworth is a mixed case, sincere and authentic at the same time. Rural solitaries like Michael and the Leech Gatherer of "Resolution and Independence" are models for Trilling of the perdurable, unified self, but clearly they do not exemplify the progress of Spirit through self-estrangement. The whole point about Wordsworth's rocklike figures is that they do not change at all. They simply *are*. Trilling argues that, though they are forlorn, Wordsworth's solitaries provide the reader some measure of comfort in a culture that conceives of all things, and especially the self, in the light of process and development. Wordsworth's figures, with their strong "sentiment of being," remind us that we are not only what we are becoming but what, in the present moment, we are. This is a very different kind of authenticity than that promised by Hegel under the aspect of futurity.

Freud is for Trilling the most important source of a conception of stable authenticity that serves as an alternative to the Hegelian-Nietzschean model, and Trilling's last chapter, "The Authentic Unconscious," is in part a defense of Freud against Sartre's

160

charge that psychoanalysis is invalidated by inauthenticity ("bad faith"). The response to Sartre leads on to Trilling's concluding polemic, his attack on three Freudian revisionists who achieved celebrity in the sixties as prophets of authenticity and the adversary culture: Norman O. Brown, Herbert Marcuse, and R. D. Laing.

Laing in particular is marked out for Trilling's most passionate denunciation since his polemics of the forties against Stalinism. Elaine Showalter has remarked the irony in that fact.[6] Laing had been deeply devoted to Trilling in the fifties. Indeed, the whole argument of Laing's influential early book, *The Divided Self*, is an elaboration in psychological terms of Trilling's brilliant contrast, in his 1951 essay on Keats, of the strong self of Keats with the debilitated modern selfhood of Kafka. On the basis of a long passage from the Keats essay, which is quoted near the beginning of *The Divided Self*, Laing develops his famous conception of "ontological insecurity." But Laing shifted course in the mid-sixties, arguing in *The Politics of Experience* that madness is not a debility but a kind of liberation.

Not surprisingly, in view of the unillusioned view of madness in his own story "Of This Time, Of That Place," Trilling was horrified by this mystification. But his attack on Laing is most interesting for its genealogical approach. In denouncing Laing, Trilling is denouncing what the sixties adversary culture had made of its modernist sources, including Hegel's celebration of unconditioned spirit, Nietzsche's hymn to the overcoming of the individuated ego, and Sartre's affirmation of authenticity as a repudiation of bourgeois bad faith. Laing had shown how far it was possible to go in playing out the implications of the older adversary culture, with its dream of unconditioned freedom.

Laing's theory of madness made sanity itself an obstacle to the achievement of authenticity. Trilling could only despair of this modern way to apotheosis. In the last paragraph of *Sincerity and Authenticity* he attacks Laing's parody of earlier conceptions of self-transcendence. But his anger is directed as much against Laing's audience as against Laing himself. Trilling comments dryly on the disposition of comfortable middle-class intellectuals to "entertain the thought that alienation is to be overcome only by the completeness of alienation," in the form of madness. Since those who praise Laing "don't have it in mind to go mad," what does their praise signify? Trilling's reply to this question opens onto a more general denunciation: "It is characteristic of the intellectual life of our culture that it fosters a form of assent which does not involve actual credence."[7]

Trilling is describing the inauthenticity, or bad faith, of Laing's audience. But he does not resort to the fashionable vocabulary of existentialism. Rather, he turns the existential tradition against itself, exposing the inauthenticity of authenticity. By the 1960s authenticity had become a "jargon," as Theodor Adorno argued in a book of 1964.[8] Adorno, responding to the influence of German-style existentialism, which was mainly hopeful and affirmative, argued for keeping open "the wound of the negative." The phrase comes from Kierkegaard, whose influence coexists with that of Marx and the socialist tradition in Adorno's "critical theory." Trilling might praise "the opposing self," but he had little of Adorno's commitment to negativity as such. He was more and more drawn to positive belief as a counter to the institutionalized negativism of the American adversary culture. And so he appeals to a Christian thinker very different from Kierkegaard, finding an idiom that suits his purposes in Cardinal Newman's *Essay in Aid of a Grammar of Assent* (1870), an examination of the grounds of religious belief. Instead of the Sartrian opposition of authenticity and bad faith, Trilling invokes Newman's distinction between "real" and "notional" assent.

The modern existential tradition is primarily concerned not with belief but with intensities of being, as when the Underground Man of Dostoevsky preens himself on having "more life" in him than his more successful, happier contemporaries. At times, as in his essay on Isaac Babel, Trilling had sympathized with this modernist hunger for "more life," the yearning to recover contact with the deep, irrational springs of being. But at the end of his career Trilling turned against modernist irrationalism and defended the older humanist tradition of reasonableness and its acceptance of "the conditions." Newman, though a Christian, belonged to that older tradition. For him, as for Trilling, self-perfection required correct ideas and holding them in the correct (i.e., "sincere") way.

Trilling's long-standing concern with the intellectuals' relation to their ideas is summed up in a statement he made at the *Salmagundi* conference on *Sincerity and Authenticity* in 1974, just a year before his death:

> I think this is the great sin of the intellectual: that he never really tests his ideas by what it would mean to him if he were to undergo the experience that he is recommending.*

This statement was relevant to the cult of madness, to which many intellectuals had assented in a facile, "notional" way in the sixties, just as many had assented in a notional way to the idea of social revolution in the thirties.

But Trilling's appeal to Newman inevitably raises a question. Real assent for Newman implied Christian faith, with God as guarantor of the authenticity of His creatures. Trilling was not prepared to go this far, but in his last years he did move much closer to an affirmation of absolutes than ever before. His concern for the strong, autonomous self almost seems to require a supernatural principle. As Trilling grew older he became ever more concerned that the basis of the self be solid and secure, proof against the shifting fashions of culture. But to go beyond culture must ultimately imply getting outside of history altogether. In his last decade it seemed increasingly to Trilling that the absolutes of the great Victorians made for a stronger "sentiment of being" than did the "weightless" culture of modernity.

VICTORIAN VESTIGES

A useful clue to where Trilling came out in his last decade appears in the 1974 *Commentary* forum from which I quoted at the beginning of this chapter. Noting the impulse to parody in postmodern fiction, Trilling speaks of the repudiation in contemporary literature of the "vestigial religious intention of art." This vestigial religious intention does not require actual religious conviction, as it obviously did not in the case of three lapsed believers Trilling cites: Joyce, Lawrence, and Gide. The important thing is not belief as such but the continuing link of these writers to their religious backgrounds. Trilling says that "this is largely what is being mocked or parodied today, all notions that consort with religion—the notions of salvation, of the shaping of a life which can be approved, and so on." The natural supernaturalism of the

---

*"*Sincerity and Authenticity:* A Symposium," *Salmagundi* 41 (Spring 1978): 109. Though it may sound like it, Trilling is not urging intellectuals to "act out." He is only saying what he had been saying for years, that ideas ought to be tested by their practical implications, and specifically by their likely political consequences.

High Romantics had led on to modernist notions of the priestly function of the artist. But with the adversary culture of the sixties there was a break, as a new facetiousness replaced the high seriousness of early modernism. The new writing seemed finally and inexorably to have broken, as the early modernists had not, with the vestigially religious "Victorian ideals of 'nobility,' of 'making a good life,' of 'fulfilling an ideal.' "[9]

The result is the great modern "weightlessness." Trilling found the word in Karl Jaspers's book *Nietzsche and Christianity*. The word is Nietzsche's own and refers to the giddiness and loss of direction that follow our realization of the death of God. It suggests a diminished sense of the reality of the world, of other persons, and—most fundamentally—of oneself. *Sincerity and Authenticity* offers many examples of weightlessness. Most of these examples come from older writers who had intuited the epochal importance of a new character type liberated from the moral sanctions of the old religious culture.

Weightlessness is exemplified, for example, by a flirtatious, histrionic brother and sister in Austen's *Mansfield Park*. For Trilling, Henry and Mary Crawford exemplify "a consciousness characterized by its departure from singleness and simplicity, by the negation of self through role-playing, by commitment to an artistic culture and what this entails of alienation from the traditional ethos."[10] They are both consummate actors, not only in amateur theatricals but in their everyday life. But in *Mansfield Park* the Crawfords' protean shape-shifting tells against them. Austen shows none of Hegel's admiration for the "great pandemic impersonation" of Rameau's Nephew. On the contrary, Austen shows the departure from singleness and simplicity leading not to the self's realization but to its enslavement. Trilling says of Henry Crawford that his dalliance with Maria Bertram "is not only loveless but lustless; so far from being forgivable as passion, a free expression of selfhood, it is merely a role undertaken, a part played as the plot requires." And Trilling says of Mary Crawford that "we are led to expect that her vivaciousness and audacity will constitute the beneficent counter-principle to the stodginess . . . of Mansfield Park." But the effect of her charm "is regressive—its depreciation of Mansfield Park is not an effort of liberation but an acquiescence in bondage, a cynical commitment to the way of the world."[11]

Trilling does not refer to French theoreticians like Lacan, Derrida, and Foucault, who were still little known in America in 1970. But his critique of the protean self of modernity bears more germanely on their ideas than on the figures Trilling does cite: Brown, Marcuse, and Laing. Nietzsche's idea of weightlessness gives Trilling his key for understanding the adversary culture of the sixties, but it was Nietzsche's own thinking, absorbed into the postmodern French theory, that provided the inspiration for the new ideas of self and culture that were displacing Trilling's own. The new avant-garde spoke in the name of difference, heterogeneity, disunity, and marginality. In contrast, "the sentiment of being" that Trilling recommends is a sentiment of wholeness. As a corrective to the modern will to disunity and discontinuity, Trilling invokes older writers with a more "organic," centered ideal of the self. Thus in *Sincerity and Authenticity* he appeals to the antimodernist impulse in Rousseau, Wordsworth, and Schiller, and he shares their concern to shore up a selfhood that is unified and possesses "such energy as contrives that the center shall hold, that the circumference of the self keep unbroken, that the person be an integer, impenetrable, perdurable, and autonomous in being."[12]

These positives point to a real change of emphasis from *The Liberal Imagination* to *Sincerity and Authenticity*. In the earlier book Trilling had argued for "Hellenism" as Matthew Arnold had expounded it in *Culture and Anarchy*. Hellenism, Arnold says, stands for the free play of mind as against the narrowness and bigotry of English-style "Hebraism," which was always more concerned with piety and conduct than with the disinterested play of critical intelligence. We have seen how Trilling used Arnold's Hellenizing critique of British middle-class philistinism in the 1860s to attack the corruption of the liberal mind in the American 1940s. But if his purpose in that decade was to remind liberals of the importance of complexity and variousness, in *Sincerity and Authenticity* he is urging the importance of all that does not vary, all that is immune to the volatility of an aestheticized culture. His positive terms now are hardness, weight, solidity, and his piety is

165

directed toward the permanent background of existence that gives actuality and meaning to human existence. The notion of "an efficacious but largely unfathomed 'background' of human experience," which Trilling borrows from Santayana,[13] would seem to be an atheist's way of talking about God.

For Matthew Arnold "Hebraism" was a metaphor; Trilling's Hebraism was more directly involved with his actual relationship to his own Jewishness. Certainly Wordsworth was an exemplary instance of the primordial integrity of being that Trilling admired. But his chief instance, as always after 1940, was a non-Jewish Jew like himself, a "Jew of culture," to use Philip Rieff's phrase.[14] It is to Freud that Trilling comes at the end. The last chapter of *Sincerity and Authenticity* shows that Trilling's commitment to orthodox Freudianism had not diminished since the fifties. More than any other single individual, Freud provided Trilling with a fixed point for surveying American culture and defining his own self.

The question Trilling puts to Freud in *Sincerity and Authenticity* is this: "What was his motive in pressing upon us the ineluctability of the pain and frustration of human existence?" The answer Trilling gives is that Freud's view of the mind as incurably divided against itself is more than a psychology. It has the larger purpose of "sustaining the authenticity of human existence that formerly had been ratified by God. It was [Freud's] purpose to keep all things from becoming 'weightless.' "[15] Freud, then, has replaced God. Maintaining the orderliness of the universe and the self-sameness of every thing in it is the deep intention underlying his explicitly formulated theory of mind.

Freud, according to this view, meant to keep alive a vestigially religious view of life despite his explicit attack on religion in *Future of an Illusion* and elsewhere. Trilling's Freud, then, is less modern than he is "archaic." He has none of Hegel's or Nietzsche's imagination of the self freed of its tragic "conditions":

> The fabric of contradictions that Freud conceives human existence to be is recalcitrant to preference, to will, to reason; it is not to be lightly manipulated. His imagination of the human condition preserves something— much—of the hardness that runs through the Jewish and Christian traditions as they respond to the hardness of human destiny.[16]

Hardness of destiny, and a corresponding hardness, a kind of immutability, at the core of the self.

AN AESTHETIC OF PERSONALITY

Trilling's main concern in *Sincerity and Authenticity* is with styles of personality. What is at stake are aesthetic preferences in self-hood, "gratuitous" choices of one or another way of being that seems to be more attractive or more dignified. Sometimes Trilling's own idea of self-making suggests weightlessness, as if we could put on one or another kind of selfhood as we adopt one or another image or look. But how can we "gratuitously" choose a kind of selfhood in a world presided over by the principle of permanence and inevitability? That hard, perdurable something is not in the external world alone, according to Trilling; it is the basis of the self. No doubt he would have denied any contradiction here. In Trilling's view self-definition is possible only if there is an objective, impersonal "background" to human experience, something larger than the self—a father-principle? God?—against which the individual can define himself. But the abstractness to which we are led in formulating the issue points to a major change in Trilling's way of thinking about the self. From an emphasis on the social-political context of the self in the thirties and forties he had moved to the aesthetic-metaphysical emphasis of the sixties and seventies.

We can begin to unravel the knots in Trilling's later idea of the self if we go back to the early fifties, when he first sharply withdrew from politics. In those years he evolved the conception of an "opposing self" that existed not so much to oppose specific social arrangements as to oppose "the culture" in some general sense and to oppose death and lesser evils of the human condition. The noblest version of this nonpolitical version of the opposing self is summed up in a passage from one of Keats's letters. That passage, which served Trilling as a kind of touchstone, appears in a letter Keats wrote his brother George in 1819:

> The common cognomen of this world among the misguided and superstitious is "a vale of tears" from which we are to be redeemed by a certain arbitrary interposition of God and taken to Heaven—What a little circumscribed straightened notion! Call the World if you Please "The vale of Soul-making." Then you will see the use of the world.

Keats asks his brother, "Do you not see how necessary a World of Pains and troubles is to school an Intelligence and make it a Soul?"[17]

167

By the sixties Trilling had subjected that essentially purgatorial view of the self to considerable aestheticizing, as when in 1961 he expressed his view of literature "as having something to do with gratuitously chosen images of personal being, and images of personal being as having something to do with literary style."[18] No doubt we do try to define ourselves on the basis of one or another ego-ideal. But these ego-ideals are themselves conditioned by historical circumstances. It is hard not to think, for example, of Trilling's youthful admiration of the English gentleman type as having something to do with his family background and social aspirations. In what sense can we speak of choosing such an ideal as "gratuitous"?

Trilling's preoccupation with styles of personality is present in his writing from the beginning. In *The Liberal Imagination* he goes to great trouble to abstract the conceptions of personality of certain conservative thinkers from their larger views of society. This process of abstracting a thinker from his social context is visible in the use Trilling makes of figures like Burke and Wordsworth. But it is only later, in the fifties and sixties, that manners and tone and style outweigh all other considerations. An instance in *Sincerity and Authenticity* is Trilling's treatment of the most influential theoretician of radical politics in the sixties: Herbert Marcuse.

Marcuse was one of the Freudian revisionists who had argued in the sixties for a utopian program of instinctual liberation, as against Freud's own doctrine of the necessity of repression and the impossibility of significantly mitigating the discontents of civilization. He prophesied that a new socialist society would be founded on the abolition of instinctual repression. Marcuse reasoned that the internalized prohibitions enforced by the superego would be dissolved, because unnecessary, in a newly affluent, technologically advanced society. For the first time in history, thanks to the conquest of scarcity, men and women would achieve full sensual expression and be free of the guilt and other discontents of civilized life.

Trilling notes a contradiction in Marcuse's thought. Marcuse, he says, has "an aesthetic of personality" that is at odds with his wish for the abolition of repression. Trilling points out that political radicals of Marcuse's type need to have a strict superego; their activism requires a large capacity for renunciation and sacrifice of instinctual pleasure. But the desublimation that Marcuse urges would make an end to that personality type, replacing it with a more malleable ego structure less capable of resisting the blandishments of mass culture and totalitarian politics. Marcuse's sociosexual radicalism, then, is an aberration. At bottom, Trilling says, Marcuse shares his own aesthetic of personality: "He *likes* people to have 'character,' cost what it may in frustration. He holds fast to the belief that the right quality of human life, its intensity, its creativity, its felt actuality, its weightiness, requires the stimulus of exigence."[19]

The strategy of Trilling's criticism of Marcuse is the same as in his aesthetic-cultural appreciation of Trotsky in an essay of 1960. In that essay Trilling has nothing to say about Trotsky as ideologist of the Russian Revolution or leader of the Red Army. Instead, he focuses on Trotsky's personality, above all the aristocratic pride that, according to Trilling, "manifested itself in his style of conduct which was large-minded and graced by the sense of *noblesse oblige,* in his grave dignity, in the high valuation he put upon personal manners."[20] What Trilling gives us here is an idealization of the revolutionary as modern-day instance of Aristotle's "magnanimous man." It is an image that corresponds very imperfectly with the historical Trotsky, who could be fierce and ill-mannered in debate. And how odd, this rapt attention to manners and style in the case of a figure so important for his acts and ideas.

The strategy, however, is familiar in Trilling's writing. It involves emphasizing the traditional, "archaic" taste of a writer whose political or cultural radicalism might otherwise seem to make him irredeemably alien to Trilling's own moderation. Trilling uses it to good effect in recuperating such heroes of high modernism as Joyce and Lawrence. The effect of the strategy is to abolish difference, the difference between traditional and modern and the difference between Trilling and his subject.

But sometimes the differences are very real and shouldn't be blurred. Marcuse's taste in styles of selfhood might resemble Trilling's, but his sense of the crisis in culture is very different. For Marcuse, as for other intellectuals of the Frankfurt School, that crisis was a consequence of hierarchical systems of domination within the capitalist system and within the psyche. For Trilling, on the other hand, the problem was the *absence* of hierarchy, discipline, authority. Trilling worried about the absence of a context of resistance and about social theories that called for the abolition of such contexts. He held it against American culture that it lacked the institutions and ideas that might contribute to making strong selves and shoring up the sentiment of being.

WEIGHTLESS IN AMERICA

I have suggested that Trilling's critical procedure, whereby he abstracts a writer's ideal conception of the self from everything else in that writer's work, may itself suggest a certain weightlessness about Trilling as a critic. That is not to say that Trilling lacks heft and solidity in his writing. It seems to me, on the contrary, that his cultural criticism gives us more to think about than that of any other American of his generation. By associating him with the weightlessness he depreciated I mean, rather, to point to a certain *Luftmensch* quality about him. That quality is suggested by the extreme abstractness, a very American abstractness, of his later writing.

Trilling created his ideal of self and society out of bits and pieces of the European humanist literary and intellectual tradition. His ideal had no existing social embodiment, nor had it ever existed in any specific time and place. We need only compare Trilling's later writing with that of Saul Bellow and Irving Howe, who have shared Trilling's admiration for the old ethos but who have been able to attach their nostalgia to a specific chapter of Jewish social history. Trilling, for his part, had only a vague, general ideal of high-bourgeois Europe. His nostalgia, I would say, was founded on a Platonic idea of the humanist past, an American's dream of "Europe."

In Trilling's last period "the conditions" have become very vague indeed. His way of dealing with Marcuse raises the question of what it may mean for a critic to praise a specific style of being while distancing himself from the whole context, the way of life and thought, which produced that style. How are we to understand, culturally, Trilling's view of culture as a great struggle about "gratuitously" chosen images of personal being?

As we have seen, he does not distinguish between aesthetic of personality and social-political direction in the work only of political radicals. In Trilling's 1956 essay on Santayana, which I quoted in chapter 7, he praises that philosopher's precise and firm self-definition, contrasting it with the failure of his Harvard contemporaries. Trilling says that at the root of the difference between Santayana's character and that of his Harvard friends is a difference between the exhausted Unitarianism and watered-down Emersonianism of "the last Puritans," and Santayana's classical, conservative, Latin-Catholic outlook. Trilling wants to praise Santayana's selfhood, but he himself remains an American liberal humanist, at least as distant in his own convictions from Santayana's Catholic intellectual tradition as from the genteel tradition of of New England during the Gilded Age. Can it be anything more than playacting at "Europe" for an American liberal intellectual to praise Santayana's style of being without affirming the philosophy which gives point to that style?

As an American Trilling is deeply implicated in the weightlessness he wishes to criticize. It is clear from what he says at different points in his career that his most fundamental belief was that people could, to a considerable extent, create themselves according to some ideal conception, often some image of the heroic formed in childhood. It is no wonder that Trilling wrote tenderly of his various Young Men from the Provinces in nineteenth-century fiction. There is something peculiarly American in Trilling's preoccupation with the solitary self inventing itself and going forth to meet its destiny. It is American even though Trilling's favorite examples, like Julien Sorel, were European.

That turn to Europe, with the resulting conflict between an American aesthetic of personality and an Old World metaphysics, calls to mind Henry James even more than Fitzgerald. Like a character in James, or like James himself, Trilling was divided between a dream of freedom and the experience of limitation, between the romantic and the real, between America and Europe. But the conflict within a mid-twentieth-century cultural critic inevitably took a different form than in the careers of fictional characters like Isabel Archer and Lambert Strether.

James's innocent Americans conceive of the self as an essence independent of circumstance. They find themselves betrayed by Europeanized characters skeptical of the self's inviolate separateness. In Trilling's career the problem of the self took another form. The cultural relativism enunciated in his preface to *Matthew Arnold* had the purpose of freeing the self to achieve a greater flexibility and variousness than were encouraged by the left-wing culture of the thirties. But in practice Trilling found that what should have been a happy plasticity of spirit had the unexpected effect of condemning the conscientious cultural critic to a program of nearly continual self-renovation. His quest from the fifties on for a principle of permanence in the self seems to me an oblique admission of the unhappy implications, for Trilling himself, of that earlier relativism.

The problem of cultural criticism in America is essentially the problem of American culture. For what happens when cultural situations evanesce nearly as soon as they can be named, when intellectual "periods" last hardly a full decade? The critic, even the critic steadied by an unchanging social commitment and ideology, is bound to experience the most extreme discontinuity and wonder if the self is anything more than a mere effect of culture. Trilling's quest for a principle of permanence can be conceived as a protest against the genre of cultural criticism itself. It is a protest against a role that condemns the critic to live wholly in culture, as a plaything of history, shaping and reshaping his self and his writing for every new occasion. This is hardly the way to shape the strong self Trilling admired.

American culture in Trilling's later years had become weightless, changing rapidly and offering little in the way of memory or background against which the self could define itself. The impressive thing is that Trilling, who was not held firm by any social ideology, was able nevertheless to stand for something over the course of his long career: not a single set of opinions, but a single problem. In the last few years of Trilling's life, after *Sincerity and Authenticity*, his mood was mainly historical and retrospective. Gloomily, perhaps, but without perceptible rancor, he accepted the passing of the older culture in which he had formed himself and been formed. More remote than ever from immediate social issues, but uncomfortably aware of the pressure of new ideas and ideals of selfhood, he tried to sum up the principles on which he had shaped his own self.

Chapter Ten

Last Essays

To the end of his life Trilling continued to proliferate dualistic oppositions while resisting any resolution. We have considered a number of antithetical categories about which in successive decades Trilling organized his cultural criticism: gentleman/Jew, capitalism/socialism, literary imagination/ liberal imagination, biology/culture, sincerity/authenticity, and so on. For Trilling the larger the oppositions the better the art and thought. But he did not limit himself to any one framework or dialectic. His quarrel with Stalinism provided a unifying perspective through the forties, but after that decade he found no similarly comprehensive organizing principle. The result is that his later career is difficult to summarize.

Trilling was a reactive critic who characteristically defined himself against what he took to be the dominant cultural tendencies of his time. And because American culture has been changing at an accelerating pace since 1945, he found himself redefining his position ever more frequently, often opposing in a later essay the position he had taken in an earlier essay. At the same time the vestigially religious elements in his attitude made him long for a resting place, and he became increasingly attracted to the idea of absolute values as an alternative to the "weightlessness" of contemporary culture. In social terms this desire for stability often translated into nostalgia for the decorum of the nineteenth-century high bourgeoisie. But Trilling seldom wrote explicitly about social arrangements as such; he was more disposed to write about commonly shared feelings and sentiments and especially about wished-for ways of being.

Increasingly, Trilling was drawn to quietude and seemed always about to strike a separate peace, far from the mental strife of New York political-cultural debate. Thus in the fifties he was drawn to the nineteenth-century imagination of idyll, and in the sixties he envisioned an ideal unity of being, "beyond culture." Trilling never ceased to present himself as a public mind, but in-

173

creasingly in his last years he seemed more like Edmund Spenser's Sir Calidore, tempted like Spenser's knight to truancy. The chief contradiction in his last phase was his continuing fidelity to his duty as sentry monitoring the bloody crossroads of literature and politics, opposed by an equally strong impulse to give up the vigil, to walk away from his post.

It is curious to find this impulse to the pastoral in a modern urban critic who never ceased to urge awareness of complexities and a commitment to history. But it is only an impulse, the expression of part of Trilling's mind. It is a mood rather than a fully formulated conviction. Trilling remained, as ever, divided. Certainly he grew more conservative over the years, moving from radicalism in the thirties to his latter-day role as exponent of traditional humanism. But his shifts of position seem only the present particular manifestations of a prior dualism of mind that remained essentially unchanged. Trilling's irresolution is especially marked in contrast with the last essays of Matthew Arnold, who mounted an unambivalent defense of orthodox Victorian cultural values against the encroachments of the new French naturalism. Trilling, on the other hand, was having trouble, even at the end, in making up his mind.

BEYOND HISTORY

The duty about which Trilling registered the greatest ambivalence is the duty that modernity imposes of continually defining and redefining oneself. From the time of Hegel, self-formation (*Bildung*) has been conceived as an ordeal of permanent psychic renovation; modern dialecticians have allowed no rest for self-estranged humanity on its way to ever-higher forms of self-awareness and self-realization. Trilling was uneasy about this modern straining after an impossible apotheosis. He was more sympathetic to another, more traditional ideal, of the modulated—we might say "socialized"—will. That ideal is dramatized in the classic novels of the European nineteenth century. The ambition for preeminence of Stendhal's Julien Sorel remained Trilling's norm of the "shaped" self.

The essays of *The Last Decade* are a defense of that older ideal of the self. Yet even here, near the end, Trilling imagines how beautiful it would be not to have to shape a self at all. He continues to admire Keats's idea of the soul chastened by "a world of pains and troubles." But he is also moved by another poetic idea, which he finds in Yeats, of an integrity of being that would not require submitting to "the ordeal of man's life in history."

In the 1970s Trilling is still writing mainly about alternative cultural ideals of the self, and his essays derive from the same impulse that had issued in *Sincerity and Authenticity*. But once again the categories have changed. We hear no more about sincerity and authenticity or about honest soul and disintegrated consciousness. Instead, the last essays are organized about a dialectic of "will" and "idea." That dialectic is summed up in an idea that Trilling calls "definitive of the high culture of humanism" which holds that "a chief value of life lies in its ability to make itself, and especially its various forms of aggressivity, the object of its own admiring contemplation."[1] This notion of the will had appeared earlier, in Trilling's 1950 essay "Wordsworth and the Rabbis." And these new categories, will and idea, are not wholly unrelated to previous sets of categories in Trilling's criticism, particularly the dialectic of energy and inertia, of life and death, that he had borrowed from Freud in the fifties.

But twenty years later, in the early seventies, Trilling was recoiling even more strongly against the intense political activism of a period just completed. His key terms come from Schopenhauer, who had influenced the great modernists who had earlier influenced Trilling himself: Nietzsche, Freud, and Mann. Schopenhauer believed that the will is purified when it becomes idea; life is best realized not in will but in idea (or representation). "Representation" replaces "idea" in the title of the most recent translation of Schopenhauer's great work. It serves better than "idea" because it points to the aestheticism that is one implication, nirvana being another, of Schopenhauer's detestation of the will.

The trouble for a humanist critic who means to speak for the possibilities of life is that representation inevitably involves arresting the will and stopping the processes of life itself. Art, as Trilling says, has about it a strong tincture of death. A consciousness of this paradox leads Trilling to irresolution. One part of him remains committed to the disciplined will, shaping the self within history. Another part of him envisions a very different fate for the self, in a great good place outside of history, the world not as will but as idea.

Trilling is not much concerned about strict accuracy in his adaptation of Schopenhauer's terms; he is working out his destiny, not worrying technical problems in philosophy. And so he rummages about in Schopenhauer, as he had in Hegel, in search of hints, metaphors, and catchphrases that might enable him to name his fluctuating sentiments and better define himself. Thus he uses "will" in a variety of ways.* In Schopenhauer, as in Nietzsche, that term refers to the impersonal, amoral, anarchical nature of things. When Trilling uses the word, he is just as likely to charge it with the familiar moral and psychological associations it has, say, in George Eliot or William James. But Trilling is not being merely arbitrary in appealing to Schopenhauer. He shares that philosopher's sense of the pain of temporal existence. Trilling admires the energy and self-commitment of Balzac and Dickens, but he also has a good deal of Arnold's melancholy and Joyce's sense of the nullity of things. If Trilling in his last essays is not a full-blown pessimist like Schopenhauer, it is because he remains a man of two minds, suspended in uncertainty, as committed to the personal will as to its overcoming in aesthetic representation.

THE POLITICS OF THE SELF

The Last Decade appeared four years after Trilling's death. As a collection it is far more miscellaneous and casual than *The Liberal Imagination, The Opposing Self,* and *Beyond Culture.* The most interesting pieces are the 1968 essay on James Joyce, which I dis-

---

*Trilling refers to Schopenhauer in "Why We Read Jane Austen," in *The Last Decade: Essays and Reviews, 1965–75* (New York: Harcourt Brace Jovanovich, 1979). Schopenhauer's influence is discernible throughout that collection, in which the idea of "will" looms so importantly. Trilling usually kept his philosophical borrowings implicit, thereby avoiding challenge when he did cite specific passages and ideas. Still, his use of the great philosophers did not go unchallenged during his lifetime. See, for example, Joseph Frank's objection, in "Lionel Trilling and the Conservative Imagination" (*Salmagundi* 41 [Spring 1978]), to Trilling's statement that Hegel makes "the aesthetic the criterion of the moral" (*The Opposing Self,* xiii). Trilling also misconstrues John Dewey when he gives a similarly aestheticizing turn to a key passage from Dewey's *Ethics.* Trilling cites that passage in his 1938 essay "The America of John Dos Passos," from which I quote in chapter 1. Similar objections might be made to Trilling's use of passages from Rousseau and Nietzsche.

cussed in chapter 8, and the essay "Why We Read Jane Austen," which was left unfinished at Trilling's death but still has a claim to being considered his last word.

Before coming to the Austen essay I want to fill in the biographical and cultural context of these last essays. Only three of the book's eleven pieces were written before 1970. The remainder belong to the five years between Trilling's Norton Lectures and his death in 1975. In these last five years Trilling seems more removed than ever from contemporary social issues, but his Olympian detachment goes along with much greater informality. It is as if, after the great public success of *Sincerity and Authenticity*, Trilling feels able to relax in his role as a senior statesman of culture. Earlier in his career he had not taken much advantage of the opportunity for visiting professorships and trips to conferences that are the conventional rewards of academic success. For the most part he stayed close to home, as if on sentry duty. But in his last years Trilling seems to be nearly everywhere: at Harvard for the Norton Lectures in 1969–70 and then at Oxford in 1972–73; at meetings of the American Psychoanalytic Association and the Aspen Institute for Humanistic Studies; at conferences organized around him by *Commentary* and *Salmagundi*; and at various universities in England and America to deliver lectures. This was a season of honors, including the distinction in 1972 of delivering the first Thomas Jefferson Lecture in the Humanities of the National Endowment for the Humanities.

These biographical details help explain the impression these essays give of a writer allowing himself more pleasure in himself than in his earlier writing. In his praise of the "shaped" self Trilling is summing up his own career and defending his own style of selfhood against a new generation formed by a very different experience of history. That Trilling had entered a period of self-review is suggested also by the explicitly autobiographical cast of his last essays. Instances are his 1966 afterword to Tess Slesinger's *The Unpossessed*; his account of his early acquaintance with Whittaker Chambers in the preface he wrote for the 1975 reissue of *The Middle of the Journey*; a posthumously published memoir of his early association with Jacques Barzun;[2] and "Notes for an Autobiographical Lecture," which he used in addressing a seminar at Purdue in 1971. The intrinsic interest of these pieces is such that one regrets Trilling did not live to write a full-length memoir.

177

When in his last essays Trilling is not writing directly about himself, he is continuing the work of *Sincerity and Authenticity* in writing about ideas of the self. He particularly mourns what seemed to him the passing of the older dream of personal ambition and heroism that had motivated him as a young man. That older conception of self-formation had always emphasized struggle against the resistance of the intractable conditions of existence, and Trilling had usually emphasized the sacrifice of instinctual life implicit in such a model of self-making. The younger generation of the late sixties was less sympathetic to Trilling's self-ideal, emphasizing the competitiveness and aggressiveness inseparable from the drive to individual preeminence. In Trilling's view the new generation unjustifiably identified the positive kind of aggression that goes into artistic and intellectual achievement with the hostile forms of aggression imputed to America, during the Vietnam War, as an allegedly militarist and racist society.

A statement by Susan Sontag in 1966 ("What's Happening in America") conveys the mood that Trilling sought to counter. For Sontag the Vietnam War revealed the ultimately destructive tendency of Western civilization itself. She blamed the war on the ravening egoism of "Western 'Faustian' man, with his idealism, his magnificent art, his sense of intellectual adventure, his world-devouring energies for conquest."[3] Sontag looked for help to a saving remnant among the young who had found in Eastern philosophy a self-ideal founded on gentleness. That ideal, in Sontag's view, would serve as the antidote to the Faustian dynamism of the West.* Trilling, no Faustian type himself, was nevertheless defending our civilization's emphasis on the active, shaping will.

Since Trilling's late essays often appear far removed from immediate issues, we ought to be clear about the ways in which they do respond to his cultural situation. His essay "Aggression and Utopia" takes up the question of the relation between capitalism and character that had engaged Sontag in her statement of 1966. The subject of Trilling's essay is William Morris's uto-

*Sontag's praise of Eastern passivity seems to have been a once-only response to the specific cultural crisis of the Vietnam War years. It does not appear in her earlier essays. Nor does it appear in such later books as *On Photography* or *Under the Sign of Saturn*, in the latter of which she celebrates the sense of intellectual adventure of such heirs of the Western tradition as Walter Benjamin and Elias Canetti.

pian romance *News from Nowhere* (1890), the portrait of an idyllic society from which the high ambition and fierce assertiveness of the modern artistic and intellectual will have been banished. In Morris's socialist utopia the emphasis is all on the possible goodness of life, not on the dignity and largeness that seem to require a world of pains and troubles. Trilling summarizes Morris's position in these terms:

> To the cruel demands that the superego makes in the economy of genius, Morris offered a principled opposition. He believed that these demands went along with the externally directed aggression of genius, with its impulse to be pre-eminent and dominant which, in his view, put the nature of genius all too much in accord with the ruthless ethos of capitalist competition.[4]

Trilling is attracted by Morris's socialist dream of perfect felicity, but he ultimately rejects it in the name of freedom, dignity, and the possibility of a finer individuality. Trilling's preference for the self-shaping will of Western individualism, at whatever cost in suffering to the individual who shapes himself, is ultimately a political choice, an affirmation of the postradical message of *The Liberal Imagination*. "Aggression and Utopia" is an argument for Trilling's ideal of the active but modulated will; at the same time it is also implicitly an argument for the liberal capitalist society in which that ideal of selfhood has had the best chance of being realized.

But Trilling stays away from the political implication of his preference in styles of personhood. Certainly if he opposes Morris's ideal vision of the socialist society, it is not in order to justify the "ruthless ethos of capitalist competition." If we speak of Trilling as a conservative, it is not as an economic or political conservative. He nowhere writes admiringly of capitalism. He accepts that the shaped self that he admires is historically specific in having arisen along with industrial capitalism in the nineteenth century. But he goes on to resist the analogy, argued by the sixties counterculture, between the drive to intellectual preeminence of a Balzac or Goethe and capitalist entrepreneurialism.

Trilling's aesthetic of personality is linked to the nineteenth-century middle class, but he consistently distinguishes between the cultural attitudes of that class and the economic basis of those attitudes. The personality type Trilling admires is as much a product of the aristocratic ethos of the old regime as it is of the new age of industrialism and political democracy. He placed himself in the line of nineteenth-century middle-class intellectuals like Stendhal and Arnold who tried to rescue something of the old aristocratic largeness of spirit amidst the newly democratic society. The sixties counterculture preferred an affectionate, peaceable style of person-hood ("make love not war") to the fierce self-insistence of per-sonalities formed on the basis of military-aristocratic models of heroism. Trilling's taste in personality was closer to Stendhal's Sorel, who wanted to be like Napoleon, and to the young Freud, who revered Hannibal and Cromwell. Shaping the self, as Trilling conceived that activity, required something like the discipline and fortitude of the soldier.

He attacks the sentimental populism of the counterculture in his 1973 essay "Art, Will, and Necessity." That essay is a rejoin-der to an earlier essay, "The Illiberal Imagination," by the American structuralist critic Robert Scholes. In *The Liberal Imagi-nation* Trilling had stressed the nineteenth century's overriding concern with individual personality and destiny. In his critique Scholes opposes Trilling's liberal individualism in the name of structuralism's emphasis on the universal and systematic. He praises certain modern "fabulists"—he mentions Iris Murdoch, John Barth, Thomas Pynchon, John Fowles, and Robert Coover—as having "strong affinities with structuralism" to the degree that they share structuralism's concern with system and pat-tern at the expense of the uniquely individual. Scholes values these postmodern fabulists, Trilling says, because they "are no longer interested in individual fates" and because "they represent human existence not as a series of contingencies but as a *structure*, a dis-cernible pattern of reiterated destinies in which personal intention is but one of several formal elements."[5]

Scholes understands that devaluation of "personal intention" to be politically progressive. What he does, in effect, is to arrange a shotgun wedding of an austere French critical method with the humanitarian sentimentality of the American counterculture. He says that by playing down the individual will, structuralism has "worked against nationalism and against egotism in general." Scholes makes his millennial impulse clear in concluding with an appeal that we turn to structuralism in order to be "born again": "The literary imagination has moved from liberalism through exis-tentialism and into structuralism in our time. The question re-mains whether the political imagination can follow. We desperately need a politics of structure (and a politics of love)."[6] The point for Trilling is that the "politics of love" as Scholes presents it portends a politics that leaps beyond the conflict of particular individual wills. As presented by Scholes, American-style structuralism appears as a recrudescence of a familiar kind of "liberalism" that Trilling had spent his best years attacking. Scholes's passion for system and type becomes yet another manifestation of "the animus against individual will" that was the distinctive mark of Stalinism.

One only wishes that Trilling had lived long enough to attempt a fuller critique of the new French thought. Structuralist and poststructuralist theorists like Lacan, Foucault, and Derrida were still little known in America in the early seventies, but their arguments are a far more substantial challenge to Trilling's humanist ideal of the shaped, unified self than those of the comparatively ephemeral spokesmen for the American counterculture. "Art, Will, and Necessity" is not a major critique of structuralism, but it does indicate the form Trilling's more fully developed argument might have taken. It has its interest also in showing Trilling trying to make sense of a new intellectual situation in terms of the situation that had prevailed in the late thirties and early forties, when he was carving out his characteristic position.

THE SELF AS WORK OF ART

In *Sincerity and Authenticity* Trilling was arguing against the excessive willfulness revealed in the modernist rage for an ultimate freedom transcending the conditions of human existence. In his last essays he paid more attention to the fuzzy, self-consciously antiheroic stance revealed in the countercultural depreciation of aggression, ambition, and the defined self. If Trilling's patrician rationality was offended by the sentimental irrationalism of the adversary culture, so was his patrician sense of discipline offended by its formlessness. In the lecture he presented at Aspen, "The Uncertain Future of the Humanistic Educational Ideal," Trilling explains that uncertain future in terms of the passing of the older mode of self-formation. That older mode involved living out one's life according to a self-ideal that is consciously chosen and adhered to despite all vicissitudes.

The traditional humanities may be declining, Trilling says,

because young people increasingly resist the notion that a person ought to be limited to one job, one self, one destiny. In the emergent culture the notion of what Trilling calls "a conceived and executed life" seems to suggest a lack of imagination. As he puts it:

> If you set yourself to shaping a self, a life, you limit yourself to that self and that life. You preclude any other kind of selfhood remaining available to you. . . . Such limitation, once acceptable, now goes against the cultural grain. . . . Any doctrine, that of the family, religion, the school, that does not sustain this increasingly felt need for a multiplicity of options and instead offers an ideal of a shaped self, a formed life, has the sign on it of a retrograde and depriving authority, which, it is felt, must be resisted.[7]

Stated so nakedly, Trilling's positive conception of the "shaped self" is vulnerable to various kinds of criticism. First, despite Trilling's idealization of Freud the man, he takes very little account of Freud the theorist. Trilling's idea of how the self is formed bears very little resemblance to Freud's view of identity as the sedimentation of a series of unconscious identifications. Moreover, Freud was far more interested in the negative aspects of the superego, above all guilt, than in positive ego-ideals, Trilling's major preoccupation.

Even if we allow for Trilling's emphasis on the *conscious* shaping of personality, his formulation is inadequate in allowing no room for growth. The will as he describes it is frozen, like a statue in the public square. In the passage I have quoted Trilling displays the either/or thinking that had once seemed to him a central weakness of the liberal mind. The will is predetermined and fixed, or we are handed over to weightlessness and chaos. What of Trilling's old positives, variousness and complexity? What of the undulating and diverse temperament that he had once thought appropriate to the work of criticism?

These positives belong to a time when Trilling did not fear change as much as he came to fear it in his last years. To have a shaped self should not mean never changing. A person should be able to shape himself *and* change, shaping the change—as Trilling himself did in his own life. His late conception of self-formation is at odds with his own development, the inconsistencies and contradictions of which we have been tracing. Trilling near the end has become an abstract moralist ("shaped self," "formed life"), but his interest as a critic is as a flexible, fluctuating consciousness wholly responsive to changing circumstances.

But why does Trilling argue so strongly in his last essays for the predetermined, planned, and executed self? What led to his skepticism about the historical mode of perception and judgment that he had once favored? What accounts for his zeal not only to oppose a specific culture but, at times, to escape from culture altogether? We have to keep in mind the actual circumstances of American life. The culture was changing so fast, in so random or contradictory a way, that the individual critic had difficulty keeping up. That tendency to discontinuity and incoherence was a difficult test for Trilling's dialectical imagination, in which the critic leaned one way or the other, became one self or another, depending upon what the culture needed.

That situation brought Trilling face to face with his own suggestibility. In an early short story of his the protagonist regrets his chameleon changeableness, his disposition to grant his "fealty" to whatever group he finds himself a part of. And in Trilling's 1938 letter to Sidney Hook, which I cited in chapter 3, he worries that in writing *Matthew Arnold* he may have been too flexible, too understanding in respect of other possible points of view—to the point of blurring his own (politically radical) argument and causing his book to be admired by people who should have been repulsed by its point of view. Trilling's adaptability saved him at Columbia and spared him the fate of more dogmatic radicals who never recovered from the thirties. But he distrusted his adaptability. His writing suggests that he feared the lack in himself of a central core, a primordial quality that allows some selves to stand aloof and apart from their circumstances.

Trilling rejects historical or developmental models of self-formation in *The Last Decade* in favor of an aesthetic model. He writes in 1974 that our culture tends to "regard the mere energy of impulse as being in every mental and moral way equivalent and even superior to defined intention." To that contemporary way of conceiving the self, in terms of wayward impulse, Trilling opposes an older way: "the idea of 'making a life,' by which was meant conceiving human existence, one's own or another's, as if it were a work of art upon which one might pass judgment, assessing it by established criteria." The latter formulation is Victorian, but it is also modernist. The emphasis is equally on the nineteenth-century idea of duty and the twentieth-century idea of the self as a work of art. The example Trilling offers is from the early Yeats, who "spoke of women dealing with their outward selves as works of art, laboring to be beautiful."[8]

His model, then, is art. A good self lives a shapely life, "a nicely proportioned life, with a beginning, a middle, and an end." Trilling's classical sense of measure hardly accords with the later Yeats of the Crazy Jane poems or the Yeats who wrote of beauty's origin in "the foul rag-and-bone shop of the heart." As a view of art, no less than as a view of self-formation, Trilling's ideal suggests a retreat from his earlier writing. Unlike Yeats, Trilling offers a marmoreal view, again that bust in the public square, as against a conception of art- and self-making as process and performance. Instead of remarking the multiple acts that go into the making, Trilling stresses the dignity and order of the made work. Altogether, in his style as much as his argument, Trilling the public man presents us in his last essays with a completed, ideal self, beyond the uncertainty and improvisations that we have been tracing and which make for the interest of his own earlier work.

Trilling's late view of art, as of the self, reminds us of his will to get beyond willing, beyond culture, beyond history. It is a paradox of his work that he makes the will stand for its opposite, representation, just as earlier, in the fifties, he had redefined biology so as to make it indistinguishable from its seeming opposite, culture. If in "Art, Will, and Necessity" Trilling appears to have finally arrived at his rock-bottom faith, in the shaping will and its place in "the ordeal of man's life in history," in other essays of *The Last Decade* his argument leads yet again to his dream of the transcendence of history, Trilling's ideal of the self as "the experience of art projected into the actuality and totality of life."[9]

ELLIPSIS

Trilling comes back to the dialectic of history and art, will and representation, one last time in "Why We Read Jane Austen." That essay is poignant both in its statements and in its place in Trilling's work. He was to have read the paper at a conference on Austen in Canada in October 1975. Before then, however, he was diagnosed as suffering from cancer. The progress of his disease was very rapid, and he died in November 1975, without having been able to revise the essay. It was published, as Trilling left it, in the *Times Literary Supplement* of March 5, 1976, and is reprinted in *The Last Decade*. The essay is important in that it moves in the opposite direction from the acquiescence in the ordeal of history with which *Sincerity and Authenticity* closes and which continues to be the main tendency of later essays like "Art, Will, and Necessity." "Why We Read Jane Austen" shows how unresolved Trilling's thought remained to the very end.

The most important part of "Why We Read Jane Austen" is not about Jane Austen at all. Her novels only provide the occasion for a reflection on the fate of the humanist intellectual tradition, and especially on two opposing modes of perception, the aesthetic and the historical. This reflection is influenced less directly by Austen's novels than by an important recent essay by Clifford Geertz, "From the Native's Point of View: On the Nature of Anthropological Understanding."[10] Late in that essay Geertz mentions Leo Spitzer's interpretation of Keats's "Ode on a Grecian Urn" as an assertion of "the aesthetic mode of perception over the historical."[11] Trilling revises that formulation. He says that in Keats's poem the aesthetic and historical modes are not opposed but assimilated to each other. Trilling draws on a favorite story of his, Mann's "Disorder and Early Sorrow," to make the point that history itself involves the aestheticizing of experience, which is to say, stopping it, seeing it as idea, or representation, rather than as will.

The dramatic action represented on Keats's urn—the lover pursuing his beloved—is frozen. Movelessness, or death, is an element in our appreciation not only of Keats's poem, Trilling says, but of all art and thought:

> It is not alone the art and thought of Yeats's Byzantium that has in it the element of fixity, of movelessness, or what I am calling death—all thought and art, all conceptual possession of the processes of life, even that form which we call love, has inherent in its celebration and sanctification of life some element of this negation of life.[12]

If elsewhere in *The Last Decade* Trilling celebrates the shaping power of will, in the Austen essay he asks the reader to consider the value to be gained by suspending the will:

> We seek to lay hold of the fluidity of time and to make perdurable the cherished moments of existence. Committed to will as we of the West are, we yet on occasions seek to qualify and even to negate its authority and to

assert the life-affirming power of idea, or . . . to say that life is best affirmed by *representation*, by will realized and negated.[13]

"Perdurable," a favorite word of Trilling, is attributed here not to the strong self defined in its struggle against necessity but to "cherished moments," moments in time that also transcend time, when the self is experienced as a work of art. Trilling's idea of the "shaping" of the self has a different resonance in this passage than in "Art, Will, and Necessity." In Trilling's writing the shaping principle can be associated with the ordeal of man's life in history *or* with the aesthetic representation of that ordeal. The difference is important. It is the difference between conceiving of life as active struggle in history and conceiving of life in Schopenhauer's terms, which allow only passive suffering with the possibility of aesthetic transcendence.

Trilling proceeds to Geertz's discussion of the ideal of selfhood in Java and Bali. He interprets these non-Western ideals differently from Geertz, as attempts to bring "life under the dominion of some form of conceptual or aesthetic 'death.' " Trilling says that far from valuing the particularities of individuals, or encouraging the active will, "Javanese culture has as one of its definitive functions to induce its members to become as much as possible like works of art: the human individual is to have the shapedness, the coherence, the changelessness of an object."[14] The self-ideal of the Balinese is similar. As Geertz puts it, the Balinese perceive life as a "never changing pageant" in which everyone carries out an assigned, impersonal role. Whatever is idiosyncratic to the individual is muted. What matters is the pattern or the pageant, not the person. There is neither the Faustian will to individual achievement nor the purgatorial ordeal of self-definition.

Why, in his last attempt to essay the problem of the self, is Trilling so drawn to Geertz's example of the negation of the Western paradigm of personhood? There is, first of all, the factor of sheer exhaustion. Trilling's writing, as we have seen, is a record of unending struggle, of inner conflict and ambivalence. The aesthetic ideal of self as representation, as death triumphant over will-in-action, offers the promise, finally, of peace and rest. Trilling's revulsion against the idea of individual selfhood can be seen as an inevitable recoil against his earlier burdening of the self with excessive cultural demands. Self as representation is personality's protest against the public, civic responsibilities heaped upon it once Trilling had turned away from politics. "The self," as Trilling elaborated it, cannot by itself be a repository of all human hope; neither is it adequate as a single, all-encompassing category in the criticism of culture.

There is another possible explanation of Trilling's skepticism about the Western ideal of self-realization. We get a clue to that explanation in his paraphrase of Geertz's account of the Javanese imagination of the self in terms of the binary opposition of "refined" and "vulgar":

> The goal of the Javanese person-system is to order inward feelings and outward actions in such a way that the result may be described as "refined" (or "polished," "exquisite," "ethereal," "subtle," "civilized" . . .) rather than as "vulgar" (or "impolite," "insensitive," "rough," "uncivilized," "coarse" . . .).[15]

The dialectic of vulgarity and refinement was Trilling's as well. In the thirties that dialectic manifested itself in the clash of Trilling's left-wing politics with his humanist-modernist cultural attitudes. By the fifties the dialectic took the form of a debate between biology and culture. "Vulgarity" might imply positive values, as when, in Trilling's essay on Isaac Babel, he defended the instinctual life as against the smothering demands of civilization. But by the seventies Trilling was leaning toward refinement, as is evident in the abstractness of his defense of traditional humanism and his argument for idea, or representation, as against will, for art as against history.

The drift of Trilling's criticism is unmistakable. He moved from a social conception of personality in the thirties and forties to a more abstract moral and aesthetic conception in the sixties and seventies. That altered conception of the self corresponds to a change in critical mode, from the concreteness and polemical energy of Trilling's early essays, which remind us of nineteenth-century Englishmen of letters like Hazlitt and Arnold, to the high generality of his last essays, which move in the direction of Central European philosophical criticism of culture. The early essays are informed by an acute sense of immediate social and political issues; the late essays rely on large general notions of "the self." It has been the fate of cultural criticism to become more refined, less material, as the social context of culture becomes less accessible to rational comprehension. Criticism falls back on "the self" when the culture itself becomes more heterogeneous and resistant to interpretation.

Trilling's early essays, especially those he wrote in the forties, seem to me his best. But his later books, even if they are less successful as wholes, are full of useful insights and suggestions. Even Trilling's defense of the "shaped" self, abstract as it is, has value as a principled rejoinder to contemporary theoretical arguments for the discontinuity and constitutive disunity of the subject. It is disappointing that since Trilling's death no literary critic has defended with anything like Trilling's cogency this older idea of the self against the arguments of Lacan, Barthes, and Derrida.

But the real mystery is not Trilling's development but his continuing irresolution, or what might be called his allergy to closure. The dialectic of will and idea, history and art, life and death, is never resolved in his writing. That dualism—I regard it as the salient quality of Trilling's criticism—calls for a cultural rather than a personal explanation. It will involve us in a brief speculation on the social history of the New York intellectuals of Trilling's generation.

As outsiders to American culture these intellectuals of the thirties and forties were committed to a left-wing politics founded on optimism of the will. Their political aim was a more just society. On a more personal level the intellectual as marginal figure (as Jew, Marxist, Freudian, avant-gardist) had to exert his will on behalf of his own acculturation so that he might enter "the fair courts" of American life. The drive of second-generation Americans like Trilling was inexorably toward acceptance in the mainstream of American life. In the course of their progress the political and cultural radicalism of their early phase was succeeded by a less intransigent posture, even in the case of writers who tried to hold on to their radicalism. These intellectuals are not being cynical when they say, sometimes with an apologetic shrug, that success caught them by surprise, that capitalism did it behind their backs.

It had become clear by the mid-forties that there was a conflict within the first generation of New York intellectuals between their political hope for a socialist society and their commitment to the American ethos of acculturation and success. That conflict—

between old European ideals and American actualities, between tradition and modernity, between politics and art—accounts in part for the extraordinary achievement of figures in Trilling's generation like Meyer Schapiro, Harold Rosenberg, Philip Rahv, Clement Greenberg, and Saul Bellow. That old conflict has ceased to exist in the writing of the present generation of New York critics, the best known of whom are the neoconservatives of *Commentary* and the *New Criterion*. The neoconservatives imitate the polemical gestures of the older New York intellectuals, but their writing lacks the rich, sometimes poignant polarities and contradictions that mark the most interesting work of the older generation.

For Trilling's generation the price of acculturation—as members of the American intellectual class, as inheritors of the Western humanist tradition, as modernists—was always very high, and Trilling in particular never lost sight of what culture had cost in sheer human happiness. It was as if *Civilization and Its Discontents* were an allegory of his own intellectual career. The turn to Schopenhauer at the end represents a protest—such protests appear periodically throughout his career—against the strain of playing the part of culture hero, the "gratuitously chosen image of personal being" that began as a mask and became Trilling's face.

The drama of self-definition was still going on in Trilling's last, uncompleted essay on Jane Austen, in which he once again entertained the old fantasy of truancy to duty, the self as completed, static work of art as an alternative to the purgatorial ordeal of self-making in history. The sentence that ends the essay is mannered in a way that has become unfamiliar in recent criticism, though we have recently grown used to other, no-less-mannered styles. The gravity of the passage also belongs to a lost time. The sentence could only have been written by Trilling, and it has the value, apart from its characteristic style, of summing up his essay and his career as a whole:

> It is, I think, open to us to believe that our alternations of view on this matter of life seeking to approximate art are not a mere display of cultural indecisiveness but, rather, that they constitute a dialectic, with all the dignity that inheres in that word. . . .[16]

The ellipsis at the end of that sentence appears in *The Last Decade*, in which the essay is reprinted. The ellipsis speaks its own message: after the ambivalence, the uncertainty, the long vigil at the crossroads, an end without closure, without resolution. Not a question mark but not a full stop either. The fate of cultural criticism in America remains similarly undecided.

NOTES

Chapter 1

1. References are to Gerald Graff, *Literature Against Itself: Literary Ideas in Modern Society* (Chicago: Univ. of Chicago Press, 1979); Geoffrey H. Hartman, *Criticism in the Wilderness: The Study of Literature Today* (New Haven: Yale Univ. Press, 1980); and Edward W. Said, *The World, the Text, and the Critic* (Cambridge: Harvard Univ. Press, 1983).

2. I discuss the indifference of contemporary left-oriented critics to their American precursors in "The Two Worlds of Cultural Criticism," in *Criticism in the University*, ed. Gerald Graff and Reginald Gibbons (Evanston: Northwestern Univ. Press, 1985).

3. "Reality in America," in *The Liberal Imagination: Essays on Literature and Society* (New York: Viking Press, 1950), 11.

4. Ibid.

5. See W. J. T. Mitchell, ed., *The Politics of Interpretation* (Chicago: Univ. of Chicago Press, 1982).

6. George Elliott, "Who is *We?*" in *A Piece of Lettuce: Personal Essays* (New York: Random House, 1964), 210.

7. See Irving Howe, *A Margin of Hope: An Intellectual Autobiography* (New York: Harcourt Brace Jovanovich, 1982).

8. See R. W. B. Lewis, *The American Adam: Innocence, Tragedy, and Tradition in the Nineteenth Century* (Chicago: Univ. of Chicago Press, 1953).

9. Greenberg was involved, during a large part of the forties and fifties, in Jewish intellectual journalism, as an editor-writer at the *Contemporary Jewish Record* and its successor, *Commentary*. See, for example, his essay "Kafka's Jewishness," in *Art and Culture* (Boston: Beacon Press, 1961).

10. Philip Rahv, "The Native Bias," introduction to *Literature in America: An Anthology of Literary Criticism* (Cleveland: Meridian Books, 1957), 12. Reprinted in Rahv, *Literature and the Sixth Sense* (Boston: Houghton Mifflin, 1969).

11. "On the Teaching of Modern Literature," in *Beyond Culture: Essays on Literature and Learning* (New York: Viking Press, 1965), 13.

12. "The America of John Dos Passos," in *Speaking of Literature and Society*, ed. Diana Trilling (New York: Harcourt Brace Jovanovich, 1980), 109. This essay first appeared in *Partisan Review* 4 (April 1938): 26–32.

13. Ibid., 112.

14. "James Joyce in His Letters," in *The Last Decade: Essays and Reviews, 1965–75* (New York: Harcourt Brace Jovanovich, 1979), 38.

Chapter 2

1. Afterword to Tess Slesinger's novel, *The Unpossessed* (New York: Avon Books, 1966), 322–23. Slesinger's novel, a fictionalized satire of her *Menorah Journal* friends, first appeared in 1934.

2. Mark Van Doren, "Jewish Students I Have Known," *Menorah Journal* 13 (June 1927): 267–68.

3. Maurice Hindus, "The Jew as Radical," *Menorah Journal* 13 (August 1927): 367.

4. "Manners, Morals, and the Novel," in *The Liberal Imagination*, 212.

5. Three of these reviews ("Another Jewish Problem Novel," "Flawed Instruments," and "The Promise of Realism") are reprinted in *Speaking of Literature and Society.*

6. Afterword to *The Unpossessed*, 323.

7. "The Changing Myth of the Jew," in *Speaking of Literature and Society.* The essay was first published in *Commentary* 66 (August 1978): 24–34. It appears to have been written when Trilling was 24 or 25, in connection with his summer-school course, which had been offered under the auspices of the Menorah Society. The essay was accepted for publication in the *Menorah Journal* in 1931 and set in type, but the *Journal* never published it.

8. "Impediments," in *Of This Time, Of That Place and Other Stories* (New York: Harcourt Brace Jovanovich, 1979), 3–4. Hereafter in these notes this volume appears as *Stories.*

9. Ibid., 6.

10. Ibid.

11. "Chapter for a Fashionable Jewish Novel," *Menorah Journal* 12 (June 1926).

12. See John Murray Cuddihy, *The Ordeal of Civility: Freud, Marx, Lévi-Strauss, and the Jewish Struggle with Modernity* (New York: Basic Books, 1974).

13. I am indebted for the details of Lionel Trilling's upbringing to his sister, Harriet Trilling Schwartz. See also Diana Trilling's memoir, "Lionel Trilling: A Jew at Columbia," in *Speaking of Literature and Society*; Mrs. Trilling's essay first appeared in *Commentary* 67 (March 1979).

14. "Notes on a Departure," in *Stories*, 53.

15. "Funeral at the Club, with Lunch," *Menorah Journal* 13 (August 1927): 380–90.

16. On the pariah theme, see Hannah Arendt, "The Jew as Pariah: A Hidden Tradition," *Jewish Social Studies* 6 (1944): 99–122. Reprinted in Arendt, *The Jew as Pariah*, ed. Ron H. Feldman (New York: Grove Press, 1978).

17. William Barrett offers an illuminating view of Trilling's relations with other *Partisan Review* intellectuals during the late forties and early fifties, in *The Truants: Adventures among the Intellectuals* (New York: Doubleday, 1982), 161–86.

18. Richard Poirier, *A World Elsewhere: The Place of Style in American Literature* (New York: Oxford Univ. Press, 1966), ix.

Chapter 3

1. The best full-length account of the American intellectuals' romance with Marxism in the 1930s is still Daniel Aaron's *Writers on the Left* (New York: Oxford Univ. Press, 1961). Another useful account of the period is Richard H. Pells, *Radical Visions and American Dreams: Cultural and Social Thought in the Depression Years* (New York: Harper and Row, 1973). Important recent work on the politics of the literary intellectuals of the thirties has been done by Alan M. Wald. His publications include "Herbert Solow: Portrait of a New York Intellectual," *Prospects* 3 (1977): 260–88; and *James T. Farrell: The*

Revolutionary Socialist Years (New York: New York Univ. Press, 1978). Among Trilling's contemporaries the advice of Sidney Hook, Meyer Schapiro, and George Novack has been most helpful to me. Despite their later political differences, they have mainly confirmed each others' memories of Trilling's politics in the thirties.

2. The quotation from Wilson's diary and the other passage are from Daniel Aaron, "Edmund Wilson's Political Decade," in *Literature at the Barricades: The American Writer in the 1930s*, ed. Ralph Bogardus (University, Alabama: Univ. of Alabama Press, 1982), 180.

3. Diana Trilling, "Lionel Trilling: A Jew at Columbia," in *Speaking of Literature and Society*, 422. Mrs. Trilling's version of her husband's near-firing at Columbia differs from that of Sidney Hook in "Anti-Semitism in the Academy: Some Pages of the Past," *Midstream* 25 (January 1979): 49-54. Trilling's personal notebook entries concerning that episode have recently been published in *Partisan Review* 51 (Winter 1984): 498-503.

4. "Edmund Wilson: A Backward Glance," in *A Gathering of Fugitives* (Boston: Beacon Press, 1956), 49.

5. "The Promise of Realism," in *Speaking of Literature and Society*, 29. This review originally appeared in the *Menorah Journal* 18 (May 1930): 480–84.

6. Ibid., 32.

7. "D. H. Lawrence: A Neglected Aspect," in *Speaking of Literature and Society*, 37. Originally published in the *Symposium* (July 1930). Krutch's essay on Lawrence appeared in the *Nation* 130 (March 19, 1930). Lawrence had died on March 2.

8. Ibid., 41.

9. Not all the members of the American Committee for the Defense of Leon Trotsky were politically aligned with the Trotskyists. They included John Dewey, John Dos Passos, Norman Thomas, and Edmund Wilson.

10. Afterword to *The Unpossessed*, 312.

11. "Politics and the Liberal," *Nation* 139 (July 4, 1934): 25.

12. "The Primal Curse," *New Republic* 96 (October 5, 1938): 247.

13. Letter to Sidney Hook, May 28, 1938. I am grateful to Professor Hook for sending me a photocopy of this letter.

14. "E. M. Forster," *Kenyon Review* 4 (Spring 1942).

15. See Trilling's "A Personal Memoir," in Dora B. Weiner and William R. Keylor, eds., *From Parnassus: Essays in Honor of Jacques Barzun* (New York: Harper and Row, 1976), xv–xxii.

16. On Erskine and his educational innovations at Columbia, see Trilling's "Notes for an Autobiographical Lecture," in *The Last Decade*, 232–34.

17. See John Henry Raleigh, *Matthew Arnold and American Culture* (Berkeley: Univ. of California Press, 1957).

18. Seth Low, "Address," in *Columbia University: Dedication of the New Site, Morningside Heights* (New York: Columbia Univ. Press, 1896), 53.

19. Barzun has published books on literature, music, science, philosophy, and a variety of other subjects. For a sampling of his range, see his most recent book, *Critical Questions: On Music and Letters, Culture and Biography—1940–80* (Chicago: Univ. of Chicago Press, 1984).

20. "Notes for an Autobiographical Lecture," 234.

21. Abram S. Hewitt, "Address," in *Columbia University: Dedication*, 94.

22. The rise and fall of Marxism among American liberal intellectuals can be traced in a series of essays by Sidney Hook between 1928 and 1939 on the Marxist concept of the dialectic. The first of these is "What Is Dialectic?" in the *Journal of Philosophy* 26 (Feb. 14 and 26, 1928): 85–93, 113–23. Five years later, writing on the "Marxist Dialectic" in the *New Republic* 74 (March 22, 1933), Hook affirms that Marx's application of the dialectical method to history and society "leads to a course of action which may free mankind from its major social evils" (150). But five years after that, in "Dialectic in Social and Historical Inquiry," in *Journal of Philosophy* 36 (July 6, 1939), Hook had decided that the orthodox view of the dialectic allowed too small a role for human intelligence and activity in transforming society. Moreover, the word had taken on so many disparate meanings that "it would be best in the interests of clarity to let [it] sink into the desuetude of archaisms" (365).

23. *Matthew Arnold* (New York: W. W. Norton, 1939), x.

24. Compare "Mr. O'Hara's Talent," *Nation* 141 (November 6, 1935): 545, and Trilling's introduction to O'Hara, *Selected Short Stories* (New York: Modern Library, 1956).

25. *Matthew Arnold*, 206.

26. René Wellek situates Trilling's conception of literature in relation to that of the New Critics in a useful summary article, "The Literary Criticism of Lionel Trilling," *New England Review* 2 (March 1979): 26–49.

Chapter 4

1. "Reality in America," in *The Liberal Imagination*, 9.

2. Mark Shechner, "The Elusive Lionel Trilling," *Nation* 222 (September 17 and 22, 1977): 247–50, 278–80.

3. Important questions about the drift of Trilling's thinking surfaced in his own circle even before the publication of the book. See William Barrett, "What Is the Liberal Mind?" *Partisan Review* 16 (March 1949): 331–36. Some important contemporary reviews of *The Liberal Imagination* are: R. P. Blackmur, "The Politics of Human Power," *Kenyon Review* 12 (Autumn 1950): 663–73, reprinted in Blackmur, *The Lion and the Honeycomb* (New York: Harcourt, Brace and World, 1955); R. W. B. Lewis, "Lionel Trilling and the New Stoicism," *Hudson Review* 3 (Summer 1950): 313–17; and Stephen Spender, "Beyond Liberalism," *Commentary* 10 (August 1950): 188–92.

4. Jacques Barzun, "Remembering Lionel Trilling," *Encounter* 47 (September 1976): 85.

5. Delmore Schwartz, "The Duchess' Red Shoes," in *Selected Essays of Delmore Schwartz*, ed. Donald A. Dike and David H. Zucker (Chicago: Univ. of Chicago Press, 1970), 212. Originally published in *Partisan Review* 20 (Jan.-Feb. 1953).

6. *Matthew Arnold*, 178.

7. See Martin Jay, *Marxism and Totality: The Adventures of a Concept from Lukács to Habermas* (Berkeley: Univ. of California Press, 1984).

8. "The Function of the Little Magazine," in *The Liberal Imagination*, 98–99.

9. Preface to *The Liberal Imagination*, xv.

10. Trilling quotes this passage and glosses it in *Matthew Arnold*, 205.

11. Preface to *The Liberal Imagination*, xv.

12. "The Primal Curse," *New Republic* 96 (October 5, 1938): 247.

13. *E. M. Forster*, 2d ed. rev. (New York: New Directions, 1964), 11–12.

14. Ibid., 22.

15. Ibid., 3, 4.

16. "Reality in America," 4, 5.

17. Ibid., 13.

18. Ibid., 9.

19. Preface to *Matthew Arnold*, xiii.

20. "F. Scott Fitzgerald," in *The Liberal Imagination*, 245–46.

21. "The Poet as Hero: Keats in His Letters," in *The Opposing Self: Nine Essays in Criticism* (New York: Viking Press, 1955), 33.

22. Joseph Frank, "Lionel Trilling and the Conservative Imagination," *Salmagundi* 41 (Spring 1978): 37. This essay, originally a review of *The Opposing Self* in *Sewanee Review* (1956), first appeared in book form in Frank's collection *The Widening Gyre* (1963). It is reprinted, with a new appendix by the author, in the *Salmagundi* special issue on Trilling.

23. "The Princess Casamassima," in *The Liberal Imagination*, 85–86.

24. Robert Boyers, *Lionel Trilling: Negative Capability and the Wisdom of Avoidance* (Columbia: Univ. of Missouri Press, 1977), 54.

25. "The Princess Casamassima," 92.

26. "Anna Karenina," in *The Opposing Self*, 60, 61.

27. On James's sense of history, see Charles Swann's unpublished Cambridge University doctoral dissertation, "Fictions of Past and Present: Some Ideas of History and of the Past in Certain Novels of the Nineteenth Century" (1975).

Chapter 5

1. "Notes for an Autobiographical Lecture," in *The Last Decade*, 227.

2. Ibid., 227–28.

3. Ibid., 227.

4. "Of This Time, Of That Place," in *Stories*, 94.

5. Commentary on "Of This Time, Of That Place," in *Prefaces to The Experience of Literature* (New York: Harcourt Brace Jovanovich, 1979), 162. This volume is one of twelve published by Harcourt Brace Jovanovich in 1978–80 in its Uniform Edition of Trilling's works. *Prefaces to The Experience of Literature* is a reprinting of the fifty-two commentaries Trilling wrote for his 1300-page anthology-textbook *The Experience of Literature* (1967). For a discussion of that anthology, see pp. 140–44.

6. Ibid.

7. Ibid., 165.

8. John Bayley, "Middle-Class Futures," *Times Literary Supplement* (April 11, 1975), 399.

9. "The Immortality Ode," in *The Liberal Imagination*, 148.

10. "The Other Margaret," in *Stories*, 12.

11. Ibid., 19.

12. Ibid., 30.

13. Ibid., 33.

14. "A Tragic Situation," rev. of *Black Boy*, by Richard Wright, *Nation* 160 (April 7, 1945): 390.

15. "F. Scott Fitzgerald," in *The Liberal Imagination*, 247. James T. Farrell conceived the problem very differently. He criticizes Elwin for being a "moral spectator" and criticizes "The Other Margaret" for drawing such an "all-encompassing moral conclusion" on the basis of relatively trivial incidents, in "A Comment on Literature and Morality," *New International* 12 (May 1946): 144. That essay is reprinted in Farrell's book *Literature and Morality* (New York: Vanguard, 1947).

16. "Art and Fortune," in *The Liberal Imagination*, 257–58.

17. Ibid., 260.

18. "The Lesson and the Secret," in *Stories*, 60.

19. Preface to *The Middle of the Journey* (New York: Avon Books, 1976), vii.

20. Ibid., xii.

21. "Art and Fortune," 274.

22. Robert Warshow, "The Legacy of the 30's," in *The Immediate Experience* (New York: Atheneum, 1975), 44. Warshow died in 1955 at the age of 37. His essays, mainly on movies and popular culture, were published in 1962.

23. Ibid., 45.

24. Ibid., 47.

25. "Allen Tate as Novelist," *Partisan Review* 6 (Fall 1938): 113.

26. Bayley, "Middle-Class Futures," 399.

Chapter 6

1. Philip Rahv, "Koestler and Homeless Radicalism," in *Literature and the Sixth Sense* (Boston: Houghton Mifflin, 1969), 128.

2. Ibid., 129.

3. *The Liberal Imagination*, 265.

4. Ibid., 266.

5. Quoted in *The Opposing Self*, 99–100.

6. William Phillips, *A Partisan View: Five Decades of the Literary Life* (New York: Stein and Day, 1983), 169.

7. Preface to *The Liberal Imagination*, x.

8. "The Situation of the American Intellectual at the Present Time," in *A Gathering of Fugitives*, 70. Originally published as Trilling's contribution to a symposium on "Our Country and Our Culture," *Partisan Review* 19 (May–June 1952): 318–26.

9. "William Dean Howells and the Roots of Modern Taste," in *The Opposing Self*, 80.

10. "George Orwell and the Politics of Truth," in *The Opposing Self*, 155.

11. Ibid., 157.

12. "Why We Read Jane Austen," in *The Last Decade*, 206–7. The essay was first published, unfinished, as it was left at Trilling's death, in the *Times Literary Supplement* of March 5, 1976.

13. "The Situation of the American Intellectual," 71.

14. Ibid., 70.

15. "A Ramble on Graves," in *A Gathering of Fugitives*, 23.

16. "Adams at Ease," in *A Gathering of Fugitives*, 127.

17. "Angels and Ministers of Grace," *Mid-Century Review* (December 7, 1959).

18. "Wordsworth and the Rabbis," in *The Opposing Self*, 150.

19. "Little Dorrit," in *The Opposing Self*, 6.

20. Ibid., 64.

21. Commentary on "Disorder and Early Sorrow," in *Prefaces to The Experience of Literature*, 135.

22. "William Dean Howells and the Roots of Modern Taste," 102–3.

23. "Wordsworth and the Rabbis," 146.

24. "William Dean Howells and the Roots of Modern Taste," 87.

25. Ibid., 84.

26. Ibid., 93.

27. Ibid., 90.

28. Ibid.

29. Ibid., 91.

30. Philip Rahv, "The Myth and the Powerhouse," in *The Myth and the Powerhouse* (New York: Noonday Press, 1966), 7.

Chapter 7

1. Philip Rieff, *Freud: The Mind of the Moralist*, 3d ed. (Chicago: Univ. of Chicago Press, 1979), xi.

2. Ibid., x.

3. Ibid., xiii.

4. "The Immortality Ode," in *The Liberal Imagination*, 148.

5. "A Rejoinder to Mr. Barrett," *Partisan Review* 16 (June 1949): 657.

6. "Freud: Within and Beyond Culture," in *Beyond Culture*, 115.

7. Review of *The Psychology of Sex Relations*, by Theodore Reik, *Kenyon Review* 8 (Winter 1946): 177.

8. "The Poet as Hero: Keats in His Letters," in *The Opposing Self*, 34.

9. "Wordsworth and the Rabbis," in *The Opposing Self*, 130.

10. Ibid., 128.

11. "The Bostonians," in *The Opposing Self*, 108.

12. Ibid., 116–17.

13. Sigmund Freud, *Beyond the Pleasure Principle*, vol. 18, *Complete Psychological Works*, trans. Alix Strachey (London: Hogarth Press, 1955), 36.

14. Ibid., 38.

15. Ibid., 36.

16. Ibid., 38.

17. "The Poet as Hero: Keats in His Letters," 18.
18. See especially the section "Human Strength and the Cycle of Genera-tions," in Erik H. Erikson, *Insight and Responsibility: Lectures on the Ethical Implications of Psychoanalytic Insight* (New York: W. W. Norton, 1964).
19. "Isaac Babel," in *Beyond Culture*, 128.
20. "The Kinsey Report," in *The Liberal Imagination*, 227.
21. Preface to *The Opposing Self*, xiii.
22. Trilling's remarks on "Di Grasso" in his essay of 1955 on Babel are fleshed out in his commentary on the story in *Prefaces to The Experience of Lit-erature*.
23. *Prefaces to The Experience of Literature*, 139.
24. Trilling wrote separate book club essays on *The Lonely Crowd* and *In-dividualism Reconsidered*. These are reprinted in *A Gathering of Fugitives*.
25. "Freud: Within and Beyond Culture," 108.
26. Ibid., 115–16.
27. Joseph Frank, appendix to "Lionel Trilling and the Conservative Im-agination," *Salmagundi* 41 (Spring 1978): 52.
28. " 'That Smile of Parmenides Made Me Think,' " in *A Gathering of Fugitives*, 176–77. Trilling's essentially mythopoeic interpretation of Freud's *Beyond the Pleasure Principle* had been anticipated by Santayana, in his 1933 essay "The Long Way Round to Nirvana." Santayana's essay is included in Irwin Edman's edition of *The Philosophy of Santayana* (New York: Scribner's, 1936). Trilling had been a student of Edman as an undergraduate at Columbia.
29. "*Emma* and the Legend of Jane Austen," in *Beyond Culture*, 46.

Chapter 8

1. Preface to *The Opposing Self*, x.
2. "On the Teaching of Modern Literature," in *Beyond Culture*, 3.
3. Ibid., 19, 22.
4. Ibid., 25–26.
5. Ibid., 8.
6. Raymond Williams, "Beyond Liberalism," rev. of *Beyond Culture*, *Manchester Guardian* (April 15, 1966).
7. *Prefaces to The Experience of Literature*, 87.
8. "The Leavis-Snow Controversy," in *Beyond Culture*, 169.
9. "On the Teaching of Modern Literature," 30.
10. Denis Donoghue, "A Literary Gathering," rev. of *The Experience of Literature*, *Commentary* 45 (April 1968): 93.
11. Raymond Williams, "Beyond Liberalism."
12. *Prefaces to The Experience of Literature*, 144.
13. Ibid., 126.
14. "On the Teaching of Modern Literature," 4.
15. Ibid., 26.
16. Charles Rycroft, *A Critical Dictionary of Psychoanalysis* (New York: Basic Books, 1968), 1.
17. Adorno's remark is quoted in Martin Jay, *The Dialectical Imagination: A History of the Frankfurt School* . . . , *1923–1950* (Boston: Little, Brown, 1973), 279.

18. Interview with Trilling by Stephen Donadio, "Columbia: Seven Interviews," *Partisan Review* 35 (Summer 1968): 386–87.

19. I have discussed Bell's derivation from Trilling in "Fathers, Sons, and New York Intellectuals," *Salmagundi* 54 (Fall 1981): 106–20; and Podhoretz on Trilling in "The Neoconservative Imagination," *Salmagundi* 47–48 (Winter-Spring 1980): 202–8.

20. "Mind in the Modern World" was the first Thomas Jefferson Lecture of the National Endowment for the Humanities. It appeared as a pamphlet from Viking Press in 1973 and is reprinted in *The Last Decade*.

21. Norman Podhoretz, *Breaking Ranks* (New York: Harper and Row, 1979), 276.

22. Quoted in *Breaking Ranks*, 276.

23. See Trilling's afterword to Tess Slesinger's novel, *The Unpossessed*.

24. "Impersonal Personal," *Griffin* (Readers' Subscription) (June 1957): 11.

25. "James Joyce in His Letters," in *The Last Decade*, 25.

26. Ibid., 36.

27. Ibid., 37.

28. Bayley, "Middle-Class Futures," 399.

29. Walt Whitman, *Democratic Vistas*, in *Complete Poetry and Selected Prose* (Boston: Houghton Mifflin [Riverside], 1959), 478. Trilling quotes this passage in "Sermon on a Text from Whitman," which was originally published in the *Nation* in 1945 and is reprinted in *Speaking of Literature and Society*.

30. "James Joyce in His Letters," 38.

31. "F. Scott Fitzgerald," in *The Liberal Imagination*, 249.

Chapter 9

1. "Culture and the Present Moment: A Round-Table Discussion," *Commentary* 58 (December 1974): 41, 44.

2. Ibid., 41.

3. Ibid., 43.

4. *Sincerity and Authenticity* (Cambridge: Harvard Univ. Press, 1972), 38–39.

5. Ibid., 35.

6. Elaine Showalter, "R. D. Laing and the Sixties," *Raritan* 1 (Fall 1981): 110, 117.

7. *Sincerity and Authenticity*, 171.

8. Theodor W. Adorno, *The Jargon of Authenticity*, tr. Knut Tarnowski and Frederic Will (Evanston: Northwestern Univ. Press, 1973). Originally published in German in 1964.

9. "Culture and the Present Moment: A Round-Table Discussion," 35.

10. *Sincerity and Authenticity*, 76.

11. Ibid., 78.

12. Ibid., 99.

13. The quotation comes from Daniel Cory's *Santayana: The Later Years* (1963). Trilling quotes Cory in "Hawthorne in Our Time," in *Beyond Culture*, 206.

14. See Philip Rieff, *Fellow Teachers* (New York: Harper and Row, 1973).

15. *Sincerity and Authenticity*, 156.

16. Ibid., 157.

17. Trilling glosses this letter in "The Poet as Hero: Keats in His Letters," in *The Opposing Self*, 43–49.

18. "On the Teaching of Modern Literature," in *Beyond Culture*, 13.

19. *Sincerity and Authenticity*, 166. Morris Dickstein comments on this passage in *Gates of Eden* (New York: Basic Books, 1977), 266.

20. "The Mind of an Assassin," *Mid-Century Review* (January 1960).

Chapter 10

1. "Aggression and Utopia," in *The Last Decade*, 157.

2. For citation see chapter 3, n. 15.

3. Susan Sontag, "What's Happening in America," in *Styles of Radical Will* (New York: Dell, 1970), 203. Sontag's statement originally appeared in *Partisan Review* in 1966.

4. "Aggression and Utopia," 158.

5. "Art, Will, and Necessity," in *The Last Decade*, 142.

6. Robert Scholes, "The Illiberal Imagination," *New Literary History* 4 (Spring 1973): 540.

7. "The Uncertain Future of the Humanistic Educational Ideal," in *The Last Decade*, 175.

8. Ibid., 174, 175.

9. Preface to *The Opposing Self*, xiv.

10. Geertz's essay had appeared in *American Academy of Arts and Sciences Bulletin* 28 (1974): 26–45. It is reprinted in Geertz, *Local Knowledge: Further Essays in Interpretive Anthropology* (New York: Basic Books, 1983).

11. See Spitzer, "The 'Ode on a Grecian Urn,' or Content vs. Meta-grammar," in Spitzer, *Essays on English and American Literature*, ed. Anna Hatcher (Princeton: Princeton Univ. Press, 1962).

12. "Why We Read Jane Austen," in *The Last Decade*, 220.

13. Ibid.

14. Ibid., 222.

15. Ibid., 221.

16. Ibid., 225.

Index

Aaron, Daniel, 38, 192n.1, 193n.2
Abrams, M. H., 124n
Adams, Henry, 106, 111
Adorno, Theodor, 110n, 146, 162
Adversary culture, the. *See*
Modernism
Anderson, Quentin, 66n, 129n
Anderson, Sherwood, 63–64, 66
Arendt, Hannah, 16, 192n.16; *The Origins of Totalitarianism*, 93, 98
Arnold, Matthew, 7, 9, 11, 13, 19, 33, 47, 67; *Culture and Anarchy*, 6, 59, 92–93, 165; and the "dialectical" mode of judgment, 51–54; "disinterestedness," 62–63, 165; "intellectual deliverance," 3, 59; last essays, 174; theory of social classes, 88–90, 92–93, 165, 180
Asch, Nathan, 40–41
Auden, W. H., 102, 156
Austen, Jane, 9, 65, 133, 140, 185; *Emma*, 114; *Mansfield Park*, 127–28, 160, 164–65
Authenticity. *See* Modernism; Self

Babel, Isaac, 126; "Di Grasso: A Tale of Odessa," 127–28, 141, 198n.22
Barrett, William, 192n.17
Barthelme, Donald, 144
Barthes, Roland, 188
Barzun, Jacques, 49, 102, 193n.19; friendship with Trilling, 46–47, 58, 177
Bayley, John, 66n, 82, 96, 151–52
Bell, Daniel, 147, 199n.19
Bellow, Saul, 123, 146n, 170, 189
Benjamin, Walter, 2, 178n
Bettelheim, Bruno, 109–10
Blackmur, R. P., 2, 13, 19, 68, 103
Bloom, Harold, 4
Boyers, Robert, 72–73
Brooks, Cleanth, 10
Brooks, Van Wyck, 2, 3, 4
Brown, Norman O., 124, 127, 161
Bruno, Giordano, 130

Burke, Edmund, 54, 62, 121, 123, 168
Burke, Kenneth, 2, 118

Canetti, Elias, 178n
Chace, William M., 16n
Chambers, Whittaker, 85n, 93n, 177
Chase, Richard, 129n
Clark, Eleanor, 55n, 91n
Cohen, Elliot, 22n, 23, 39
Coleridge, Samuel Taylor, 62, 68, 100
Columbia University, 23, 33, 156, 183; English department in 1930s, 36–38, 44–46; tradition of humanistic education, 46–51
Communist Party, 39–40, 41–43, 90–91; Popular Front policy, 60–63. *See also* Stalinism
Conrad, Joseph, 140, 157; *Heart of Darkness*, 136; "The Secret Sharer," 82–83, 141
Contemporary Jewish Record, The, 31–32
Croly, Herbert, 24
Cuddihy, John Murray, 27

Dahlberg, Edward, 40–41
de Man, Paul, 4, 13
Derrida, Jacques, 132, 136, 165
Dewey, John, 35, 38, 176n, 193n.9
Dickens, Charles, 107, 108, 140
Dickstein, Morris, 5, 146n
Diderot, Denis, 157; *Rameau's Nephew*, 136, 157–59
Dinesen, Isak, 141
Donoghue, Denis, 124n, 141
Dos Passos, John, 15, 20, 39, 41, 140, 193n.9
Dostoevsky, Fyodor, 136, 138, 159
Dreiser, Theodore, 39, 63, 65–66, 66–67

Eliot, T. S., 4, 11, 57, 62–63, 87
Emerson, Ralph Waldo, 10, 14, 33, 133, 152
Empson, William, 118

201

Encounter, 102
Epstein, Jason, 102
Erikson, Erik, 126
Erskine, John, 47–50, 193n.16

Fadiman, Clifton, 23
Faulkner, William, 68, 140
Fiedler, Leslie, 119, 127
Fitzgerald, F. Scott, 68, 69, 89, 90, 140, 152; *The Great Gatsby*, 14–15, 139
Flaubert, Gustave, 73
Forster, E. M., 43–46, 64, 81, 86, 140; *Howards End*, 91, 93; *A Passage to India*, 91–92; "The Road from Colonus," 142–43
Foucault, Michel, 124n, 136, 165
Frank, Joseph, 69, 129, 130, 176n
Frazer, James, 136
Freud, Sigmund, 9, 152, 160–61; *Beyond the Pleasure Principle*, 123–25; biological emphasis, 120–25, 128–30; *Civilization and Its Discontents*, 189; Freudianism and classical humanism, 130, 136; prestige of his ideas in 1950s, 117; and tragic sense of life, 118–19; Trilling's defense of psychoanalytic orthodoxy, 128–29; Trilling's differences from on self-formation, 9, 182; against "weightlessness," 166. *See also* Jewish identity; Self
Fromm, Erich, 128
Frost, Robert, 92
Frye, Northrop, 8

Geertz, Clifford, 185–87
Gide, André, 163
Graff, Gerald, 5
Gramsci, Antonio, 2
Greenberg, Clement, 11, 189, 191n.9
Gross, John, 2

Hartman, Geoffrey, 4
Hawthorne, Nathaniel, 57, 67, 83–84, 141

Hegel, G. W. F., 9, 157, 158, 160, 164, 176n; view of tragedy, 72; on self-alienation and self-realization, 158–59, 166, 171, 174
Heidegger, Martin, 124n
Hemingway, Ernest, 61, 64, 89, 140
Hewitt, Abram S., 50
Hicks, Granville, 65, 69
Highet, Gilbert, 49
Hook, Sidney, 33, 35, 44–45, 51, 193n.1, 194n.22
Hopkins, Gerard Manley, 87
Horney, Karen, 120, 128
Hough, Graham, 149n
Howe, Irving, 9, 11, 101, 103, 129n, 144n, 148, 170
Howells, William Dean: as antidote to modernity, 109–11; as "figure in the culture," 103–4; his representation of middle-class family life, 98, 113–14; Trilling's changing opinion of, 53n; *The Vacation of the Kelwyns*, 111
Humanism: aesthetic representation and the will, 175, 185–87; as Apollonian ideal, 124n; at Columbia University, 44–51; Freud and, 119, 130, 136; its model of self-making, 181–85; and sincerity, 157; and "the specious good," 138–39

James, Henry, 65, 66, 67, 107, 125, 140, 171; *The Ambassadors*, 70–71, 74; *The Bostonians*, 122–23, 125; *The Princess Casamassima*, 69–74, 125
James, William, 133, 176
Jameson, Fredric, 5–6
Jarrell, Randall, 103
Jaspers, Karl, 164
Jewish identity: Freud as model, 166; and Isaac Babel, 126; "positive Jewishness," 22–32
Joyce, James, 11, 16–17, 150–52, 163, 169